PERSON-CENTERED
LEADERSHIP

Dedicated to
the truth
in a porcelain doll
and a pack of baseball cards
abandoned in a fort
now long lost
somewhere
in the South

PERSON-CENTERED LEADERSHIP

An American Approach to
Participatory Management

JEANNE M. PLAS

SAGE Publications
International Educational and Professional Publisher
Thousand Oaks London New Delhi

For information address:

SAGE Publications, Inc.
2455 Teller Road
Thousand Oaks, California 91320
E-mail: order@sagepub.com

SAGE Publications Ltd.
6 Bonhill Street
London EC2A 4PU
United Kingdom

SAGE Publications India Pvt. Ltd.
M-32 Market
Greater Kailash I
New Delhi 110 048 India

Printed in the United States of America

Library of Congress Cataloging-in-Publication Data

Plas, Jeanne M.
   Person-centered leadership: An American approach to participatory management / Author, Jeanne M. Plas.
    p. cm.
   Includes bibliographical references and index.
   ISBN 0-8039-5598-7 (cloth: acid-free paper). —
   ISBN 0-8039-5999-0 (pbk.: acid-free paper).
    1. Management—Employee participation—United States.
2. Interpersonal relations—United States. 3. Leadership—United States—Case studies. 4. Work groups—United States. I. Title.
HD5660.U5P53 1996   95-50204
658.3—dc20

This book is printed on acid-free paper.

96 97 98 99 00 10 9 8 7 6 5 4 3 2 1

Sage Production Editor: Tricia K. Bennett
Sage Typesetter: Janelle LeMaster

Contents

PART I: Person-Centered Leadership:
The Fundamentals, the Past, the Future

PART II: Person-Centered Leadership:
The Basics, the Variations, the
Corporate Chiefs Who Make It Work

PART III: Making the Changes
That Make a Difference

Acknowledgments

A variety of people all over the country were instrumental in helping this book become reality. Very special thanks to Joseph Seltzer at LaSalle in Philadelphia for his careful and creative reading of earlier drafts of the manuscript. His comments were invaluable in helping me think about the material in new and more useful ways. Craig Lundberg, Blanchard Professor at Cornell, offered several comments that prompted a rewrite of two key chapters. Peter Lorenzi at Loyola (Maryland) provided some happily received comments about the readability of the book. Bill Shoptaw at Shoptaw-James in Atlanta was a trouper, who reportedly read a draft late into the night on several occasions. Despite the late hour, he was the only one to catch a major redundancy and omission. Michael Fisher, president at Premier, provided useful perspectives. Then, he told a group of corporate presidents with whom I was visiting about his reading of a very first draft of the manuscript. Blessedly, he refrained from sharing his candid opinions of that draft—a fact for which I'll long be grateful.

At Sage, my editor, C. Deborah Laughton, was magnificent. At every stage of the process, she remained creative, understanding, and witty. I suspect that it would be impossible for most authors to report that they always laughed at some point during every conversation with their editors. But with C. Deborah and this project, that was always true. Another person at Sage, Esther Papagaay, has been a treasure. Her strong enthusiasm for the book's ideas has been consistent and gratifying. Special thanks go to Susan Lewis, friend and colleague at Vanderbilt, who provided excellent early help with background information, and to Tova Vaknin for assistance above and beyond what one has a right to expect from a graduate student.

My deepest appreciation goes to Robert Davis, Dean Kamen, and Jim Mullen, presidents of stellar person-centered corporations that are at the cutting edge of their fields in product, service, and leadership. The time I spent with each of these men and with their companies was very special, and it taught me much about what is possible. These are the kind of leaders who are changing the heart of corporate America, making it a place for personal growth as well as financial growth and the achievement of quality. The companies they head are filled with some of this country's most talented and downright "real" people. It was a genuine privilege to meet DEKA, Mullen, and Seaside associates. Listening to their stories gave me an almost certain knowledge that person-centered management is going to be one of the most important leadership developments of the next century.

1

Leadership Person by Person

An Introduction

Not too long ago, a Southeastern Conference team abruptly lost its football coach to a rival school that could guarantee almost double the income package. The team had just lost its last game of the season. Three days later, the coach accepted another job without saying good-bye to his team or announcing his resignation. His student-athletes were confused. Some were hurt, others angry. Several thought his decision had been driven by the bottom line; in the new organization, the coach would get more money and more control. Nonetheless, why wouldn't this coach they'd played so hard for during the past months and years have taken the time to talk to them, to tell them, personally, of his decision? How could he walk away without a good-bye—and maybe a comment or two about how hard it was to leave such a great bunch of guys? A local newspaper article describing the quick departure reported that one player's attitude was, "Just don't let the door hit him on the way out." But in speculating on whether the coach would ever say good-bye to his team, another athlete's response was, "I don't think he's going to talk to us. I don't mean that in a bad way—he's just taking care of business."

That last remark communicates volumes about this century's attitudes toward the role of business in our lives—about the separation
of a business ethic from a life ethic, the separation of feelings from
rationality in the business world. Translation: What you are and do
in your business life aren't expected to be the same as what you are
and do in your personal life. We have had a double set of standards,
and the standards for business conduct often have been much lower.
That young player had uncritically accepted a set of less stringent
attitudes about the proper way of doing business in this country. But
as many corporate leaders and business school professors are beginning to suggest, that set of attitudes is an old set, a way of thinking
about business values, ethics, and actions that will likely undergo a
fast fade from the American cultural landscape. Participatory management has become the catalytic agent in the development of new
attitudes about the role of work in our lives. Person-centered participatory management has begun to distinguish itself as one of the most
effective models.

The plethora of quality improvement and participatory management initiatives that have infiltrated U.S. companies, as well as those
born and developed here, have shown promise for enhancing not
only the quality of our products but also the quality of our work lives
(Katzenbach & Smith, 1993; Manz & Sims, 1993; Walton, 1986). Nonetheless, during the past few years, we have watched a large number
of these management initiatives fail (Levinson, 1994; Nohria &
Berkley, 1994; Rust, Zahorik, & Keiningham, 1994). This book dem-
onstrates that the recent participatory management strategy failures
are the result of a lack of appreciation for the cultural role of rugged
individualism within this country—the same phenomenon that also
has been part of more traditional, linear management failures.

Person-centered leadership is an approach to management that is
uniquely suited to American organizations because it works with—
rather than against—U.S. individualism values. It emphasizes process, creative risk taking, learning, teamwork, and other successful
participatory management strategies but relentlessly shifts the focus
off those strategies and onto the individual. The emphasis on the
individual means that there is an emphasis on psychology tools as

well as management tools. It also means, necessarily, that words like *heart, caring, needs,* and *feelings* are no longer ignored in the workplace —they move to center stage.

With roots, in part, in psychology, person-centered leadership and management encourage the elimination of sharp dividing lines between the personal, so-called real, self and the public self that comes to work each day. They use the best of the quality management teamwork strategies while respecting the need of the U.S. worker to protect and enhance individuality. They emphasize *related individualism* (Arnold & Plas, 1993), a set of culture-based strategies for working productively within a team without sacrificing individuality. This is leadership and management person by person.

Current person-centered leaders—for the most part corporate rather than service organization heads—are growing in number at a fast pace. In addition to a keen understanding of their products, markets, and competition, these new leaders expect themselves to know a fair amount about the psychological facts of human valuing, motivation, and needs. They expect their executives and department heads to encourage self-leadership, creativity, and autonomous decision making. They value individualism as much as they prize good teamwork. They are not only interested in corporate ethics and values, they are willing to develop ethical positions and processes that can meet the challenges of a rapidly changing world. But above all, for them, taking care of business means taking care to respect and value the individual worker.

Summing Up

Person-centered leadership is uniquely suited to the U.S. workplace because it emphasizes individuality as much as teamwork and removes barriers so the "real" self can come to work. The model does not just focus on workers; it focuses on the *individual* worker.

The Need for the
Primacy of the Person

These days, many managers and leaders are coming to realize that when promising new participative management strategies begin to fail, the problem is not that the ingredients of the method were badly handled. The problem is that something critical has been missing. *In this country, the primary reason participatory management programs fail is because the individual has been left out of the equation.*

At first blush, this seems illogical. After all, whether it's TQM, servant leadership, the learning organization, or something else, participative management is supposed to be all about letting the people who actually do the work make the important decisions. Isn't that, necessarily, all about involving the individual?

We are coming to understand that it is not. As practiced by many companies today, participative management, in practice, has not been concentrating on the individual worker. Whether intended or not, most of these strategies have been focused on problem solving and decision making even as they claim to be focused on shared responsibility and individual creativity. They have been problem centered, not person centered. To center a management model on the worker, you have to accomplish three things: (a) Fully understand and include the cultural norms and values of the worker. (b) Appreciate and support what workers want from their jobs and their lives. (c) Concentrate on individuals one at a time.

UNDERSTANDING U.S.
INDIVIDUALISM NORMS
AND VALUES

For most of the 15 years that Denise Kropps has been an administrative assistant, she was in Detroit, working for General Motors. When the Saturn division started up, Denise agreed to move south to become part of the pioneering teamwork adventure that Saturn was to become. As the right arm of the director of purchasing at Saturn, Denise has learned to "love her job and love Saturn." As she tells you why, she consistently contrasts her current functioning with her old ways of functioning back in Detroit. Although clearly a member of an important operational team at Saturn, the thing that inspires all her loyalty is

> the way I can make my job fit me here. In many cases, I get to decide what things I'm good at or want to learn—and then I have the freedom to go do those things. I'm treated like a true individual at Saturn.

Since its inception, this is a country that has prized its stubborn investment in the individual (Hsu, 1983; Tocqueville, 1835/1969). But when the W. Edwards Deming (Walton, 1986, 1990) approach to continuous improvement was introduced to this country from overseas, it arrived with Japanese team-oriented fundamentals (Durlbahji & Marks, 1993; Florida & Kenney, 1991) that made sense to U.S. companies but didn't exactly fit with this culture's philosophy of meritocracy. Independent of athletics, few Americans had ever had experience with working in teams or making teams work. Few individuals could understand the value of getting rewarded only as the group is rewarded.

Historically, the American corporation has had an unfortunate tradition of overlooking the cultural primacy of the individual (Arnold & Plas, 1993; Larson & LaFasto, 1989). This is a country that fell hopelessly in love with Adam Smith's most basic idea: More things can be made much faster if a single individual is not responsible for crafting the entire product. In addition to a variety of good outcomes— more products, more choices, and an improved standard of living—a negative outcome also developed. The emphasis on the value of the individual worker was diminished. As the century turned, we moved individuals to the periphery to make hundredsfold more products. This book illustrates that even though it has appeared otherwise, prior to the emerging popularity of the person-centered paradigm, we had begun to push the individual even further aside as we embraced TQM teamwork approaches prior to effectively confronting the cultural necessity of individualism.

Summing Up

To center a management model on the worker, you have
to accomplish three things: (a) Fully understand and include workers' cultural norms and values. (b) Appreciate
and support what workers want from their jobs and their
lives. (c) Concentrate on one individual at a time.

TQM, Teamwork, and the Individual. It would be very difficult in
business today to find more than a handful of people who haven't
heard of Total Quality Management or been involved in a TQM project in some way. Many credit continuous improvement management
methods with having raised the level of quality in U.S. products
(Juran, 1989; Labovitz & Rosansky, 1993). Most credit these TQM
models with having inspired development of current models of participatory management (Bradford & Cohen, 1984; Dinkmeyer, 1991).
For several years now, the popular press and management research
periodicals have filled thousands of pages with descriptions of quality improvement models and methods and the resulting successes
and failures within U.S. businesses. Lately, the failures have been
receiving by far the greatest amount of attention (Doyle, 1992; Ivey
& Carey, 1991; Steininger, 1993; Wood, 1991). For reasons that are still
unclear to many, continuous improvement models haven't worked
as well here as they have in other countries—notably, of course,
in Japan (Cusamano, 1985; Ouchi, 1982). The now oft-told story of
W. Edwards Deming's failure to convince American management of
the wisdom of continuous improvement cycling—and his subsequent success at convincing the Japanese—has been strongly sugges-
tive to many that the United States ought to provide perfect soil for
the development of continuous improvement management models.
"After all, Deming was an American," many have reasoned; "therefore, continuous improvement strategies must be fundamentally
very compatible with our culture and the way we do things here."

But, not so. One of the main theses of this book is that this assumption is the primary reason we are seeing so many failures of quality management methods in U.S. companies today. Indeed, a competing assumption can prove more useful. That is, American business leaders resisted the original Deming message, in part because they understood—either rationally or intuitively—that the philosophy and strategies were not compatible with the current culture—they didn't "fit." And as the Japanese successes became known here and we began to experiment with imported continuous improvement management models, their incompatibility with some basic cultural differences here began to result in failures.

Japanese continuous quality improvement methods are based on a philosophical assumption that the group is the source of most new knowledge and achievement and that good is created by the group as individuals work toward a common goal, submerging individual talents and needs within the communal spirit (Ouchi, 1982; Pugh & Hickson, 1989). In contrast, one of the most fundamental U.S. cultural assumptions is that individual initiative is critical, the source of most new knowledge and achievement, and that we are wise to habitually reward it (Hsu, 1983; Wilkinson, 1988). These two assumptions create fundamentally very different attitudes toward such issues as teamwork, the role of the department in a corporate organization, skill training, and the fairness, function, and use of praise and blame.

Although the work of some social psychologists (Kerr, 1983; Williams & Karau, 1991) suggests that the solution to the TQM failures in this country might be dependent on making certain modifications in our approach to teamwork, management theoreticians and researchers have suggested changes in such things as attention to the external customer (Griffin & Hauser, 1993; Zeithaml, Parasuraman, & Berry, 1990), finance dynamics (Garvin, 1987; Gyrna, 1988), middle management (Herzberg, 1990; Levinson, 1990), and lack of senior leadership commitment (Block, 1993; Levering & Moskowitz, 1993). In fact, as is pointed out in Chapter 4, no amount of mere tinkering with aspects of the TQM model can be truly successful. The required solution has to involve a fundamental reworking of the mind-set and the methods.

Summing Up

Today's corporate leaders must meet the challenge of edu-
cating the organization in methods of developing strong
teams that place the emphasis on strong individuals.

SUPPORTING WHAT WORKERS WANT
OUT OF LIFE AND OUT OF THE JOB

A middle manager I talked with a year ago in an Ohio-based company told me about his boy who was playing baseball in the minors
with a good chance of making it to the big time. With frustration in
his voice, he also told me about his boss's requirement that he not
wear to work any baseball buttons from his son's successful team.
Furthermore, this manager complained about what he called "the
stupidity" of the organization that required him to file several copies
of a Problem Identification form—color coded—before he was permitted to pick up the phone to talk with anyone directly about the
issue. He also told me that he never disagreed with any of the bosses
above him—even when he knew their decisions were going to cost
the company a great deal of money. "I really don't care about this
company's profits," he said. "This company doesn't really care about
the profits in my life—if you know what I mean."

A second critical reason the individual worker needs to be center
stage if the new management strategies are to realize their potential
is that as the century closes, a wide variety of demographically different people have come to want the same thing. Like that Ohio
manufacturing manager, they want more from their lives and their
jobs—things like recognition, fulfillment, and the sense that they
make a difference in their jobs as well as within their families and
communities. With each passing year, more and more people are
expecting their work institutions to provide many of the same intan-
gible necessities that other institutions have traditionally provided.
Although families, churches, recreation groups, service and interest
groups, and the like have specific functions and goals, each is also in
some fundamental way interested in the growth and development of

the people who join the organization. Meanwhile, through the first parts of this century, U.S. businesses, for the most part, focused almost exclusively on production and revenue. Heretofore, the corporation has seen its primary mission in terms of a single goal—the development of a quality product or service that can bring profit to the company and shareholders.

Now, however, companies are pushing themselves to reconstrue their missions (Handy, 1994; Mullen, 1995; Sabel, 1993). Revenue isn't enough anymore. Many of today's U.S. corporations are genuinely engaged in a redefinition of the basic mission. Instead of a single goal, there are now two goals: (a) the production of revenue through a quality product and (b) the development of the people who work within the company—the people who *are* the company. When we consider that each working person—no matter what the job—spends at least half of his or her waking hours during the week at work, the enormous potential of the organization for personal impact becomes very clear. Stead and Stead (1992) have written:

> What many believe to be the most significant transition from the old to the new management paradigm is the shifting perspective toward the profit motive. Once considered to be the only purpose of business organizations, profits today are more often considered indicators of how well organizations are serving the needs of their stakeholders—their customers, shareholders, employees, and society at large, all of whom have an interest in the practices of the corporation. (p. 110)

Psychological work, especially the motivation literature (Eisenberger, Fasolo, & Davis-LaMastro, 1990; Evans, 1989; Maehr & Braskamp, 1986; Tjosvold & Tjosvold, 1995; Yost, Strube, & Bailey, 1992) has often suggested that when the organization rewards acquiescence rather than authenticity and acknowledges a profit motive but not a human development motive, the system will produce unwanted consequences. People will work from 9 to 5 only for the paycheck—and because the weekend is in sight. They may even take home a few of the company's paper clips, nails, or maintenance supplies because, sadly, that becomes easy to justify. The company itself isn't something they care about. Prior to this decade, we haven't really expected that workers could or would identify with their company or love it enough to deal with it as they do other important organizations in their lives. Our corporate heritage has contained a legacy of separations. Our traditional management models have helped to create unfortunate separations between the public and private selves, the heart and the reason, management and labor, as well as the disconnection of the employee's personal values from corporate goals. In this culture, the reality has been a profound separation between the individual worker and the company.

But things are changing. As we reach the close of the century, it has become clear that a new wave of participatory management models has overcome older, more linear organizational structures. Managers are learning to think of their employees as associates and experts. The typical worker—no matter what the job—wants a lot more from the company than did the worker of a quarter century ago. But that doesn't mean he or she simply wants better pay, more retirement benefits, and more attractive perks. Although those things remain important, U.S. workers in geometrically increasing numbers want the opportunity to develop themselves through their work (Frey, 1993; Huey, 1993; Loeb, 1995). They want to use their creativities to add spice to the workday and value to the product. They want to be part of a winning team that makes a difference—within the company and within the market. It is not just the hungry junior executives who now want these things; it is also the people on the PCs in accounts receivable and the people who clean the toilets.

Summing Up

Corporate organizations no longer have a single mission. Now, for many companies, there is a dual focus on (a) the creation of profit through the development of quality products and (b) the development of each individual who is part of the company.

CONCENTRATING ON
INDIVIDUALS ONE AT A TIME

Bill Arnold (Arnold & Plas, 1993), a person-centered leader, talks about the discomfort he felt when first embarking on a person-centered organizational transformation. As president of one of the country's largest medical centers, he took his office door off the hinges to make it clear that he believed his number one job was to listen to the associates. At first, it made him feel a little foolish to spend a large amount of his precious executive time listening to complaints about the quality of the soap in the rest rooms and the inadequate number of eggs ordered for the kitchens. Shouldn't he be spending his time on more important issues? Wasn't this just another form of micromanagement? But as he and his associates came to learn, quality improvement initiatives can only be instantiated one person at a time. It is individuals who make or break an organization, so it is individuals who need executive attention.

The spirit behind the idea of an open-door policy rests on person-centered management theory. Open doors are to be an invitation to the individual—an invitation to feel free to come to a boss to share a good idea, a frustrating complaint, or maybe just a little old-fashioned camaraderie. In more potent variations on the open-door theme, executives leave their offices to walk the talk, approaching individuals in their work areas, bringing the boss's office into the company—where the workers are. As I watched Bill Arnold do this and worked with him on developing strategies for reaching individuals in an efficient and effective way, I calculated (Arnold & Plas, 1993, p. 255) that he was able to get to 1,000 individuals in his organization about every 2 months. The scheduling of these contacts and their content can be a very important and relatively easy thing for a leader to make part of a routine schedule. Although the task may seem formidable, it actually is not. (See Part III of this book for effective strategies for accomplishing this goal.) The pressure and stress of modern business, quite understandably, find many executives locked into dealing with their daily schedules on a problem-by-problem basis. But it is individual workers who ultimately have to create, implement, and sustain solutions within their areas of responsibility.

Summing Up

Many executives are coming to understand that managing person by person rather than problem by problem is a far more efficient way of not only putting out fires but also developing the forward momentum necessary to bring the company into a strategic position as the century comes to a close.

Influences From Psychology

A person-centered concentration on the individual worker necessarily means that leaders and managers must recognize the need to use relevant theory, research, and perspectives from the field of psychology. Psychology has been the discipline most interested in trying to understand the individual. Now that leaders in our corporate cultures are realizing the need to focus on the individual as the center of the management program, information from the field of psychology can be particularly useful. But despite the press to soak up all kinds of information as we enter this Information Age, many managers are reluctant to think seriously about using what psychology has to offer.

Not too long ago, I was working with a department head in an automotive-related industry who told me that the problem for him was, "Fear. I read a lot about psychological approaches to motivation and management, but I'm usually just too afraid to try anything out. I'm concerned I'll just make things worse if I start playing Dr. Freud."

That particular way of defining the problem is classic. Those words reflect the thoughts of many American managers who are very interested in psychology but somewhat afraid to try out management principles based on psychological dynamics. Yet this particular manager learned most of the intricacies of finding his way around the Internet in just 4 weeks the summer he put his mind to it. He learned enough to quickly become the company's rising star in international affairs in the finance office. He learned how to effectively parent kids the hard way—the way we all do—by having a couple of them, taking good advice, trying things out. This man is a competent and valuable individual who isn't worried about trying to be Bill Gates, Norman Rockefeller, or Dr. Spock in other areas of his life: Why should he worry about "playing Dr. Freud" when it comes to issues of motivation, teamwork, and human performance? Why shouldn't he find and use comfortable approaches to the psychology of leadership and management? In this age of information, it is self-defeating to reject the use of any area of knowledge that can help us run our work lives with greater clarity and greater quality.

The presentation of person-centered leadership developed here is strongly rooted in psychological perspectives (see Chapter 3), especially person-centered psychology developed within the clinical psychology field, the psychology of motivation, and some aspects of community and systems psychology. Although these influences are not always specified as the presentation proceeds, the reader will be able to notice them throughout, especially in Chapter 2 (considering the human being in the corporation), Chapter 4 (the role of the individual in this culture), the research methodologies (see the Appendix) supporting Chapters 7, 8, and 9, and the change strategies presented in Part III, which are based primarily on things we have learned about interpersonal psychological dynamics and cognitive psychology.

Organization of the Book

The book is divided into three parts: an introduction to the major ideas, a study of person-centered leaders in a variety of corporate organizations, and a discussion of strategies that leaders and managers can use when transforming a company into a person-centered organization. An exploration of theory and concept begins with this chapter and is followed in Part I with Chapter 2's discussion of the need to reintroduce the heart and spirit to the workplace. Chapter 3 provides a historical overview of the relationship of the individual to the corporation. The following chapter investigates the important question of the relationship of the individual and the team within the current U.S. culture and today's participatory management models. Chapter 5 talks about the response of new leaders to the problem of rapid technological and social changes that often outpace the development of cultural attitudes capable of guiding those changes safely and successfully.

The second part of the book is devoted to detailed descriptions of outstanding person-centered leaders. The introductory chapter in the second part is followed in Chapter 7 by a description of the person-centered model developed by Jim Mullen (1995), President of Mullen Advertising. Dean Kamen, President of DEKA Research and Development, is presented in Chapter 8, and the leadership approach of Robert Davis, President of Seaside Development Corporation, is described in Chapter 9. Chapter 10 provides important but less detailed descriptions of some of the person-centered strategies used by dozens of other corporate chiefs, many of them well-known.

Chapter 11 introduces the final part of the book, which illustrates a variety of person-by-person leadership and management strategies that can be used by those who want to begin organizational transformation. Chapter 12 concentrates on things that leaders can do to change themselves, and Chapter 13 focuses on strategies that can be used to change the system and to bring out the best in associates.

Much of the description of corporate leaders that you will find in subsequent chapters is provided in great detail. In addition, many of the transformation strategies described in Part III are quite specific. Thus, one of the goals of the book is to introduce readers to person-centered leadership by introducing them to some of the day-by-day actions that real leaders are taking to shift from more traditional management approaches toward leadership that is intent on building internal relationships. Throughout these discussions, the weaknesses of these new leaders get almost as much attention as do the strengths. One of the characteristics of good person-centered management is a commitment to owning up to individual weaknesses so that the system can compensate for them and authenticity can be reintroduced to the workplace.

Person-centered leadership is not a cerebral approach to leadership. It's based on a get-your-hands-dirty method that invests in human feelings just as it invests in intelligence and rationality. It's an approach that considers personal well-being and a few good laughs to be important company products.

Although person-centered management is by no means a completely developed paradigm, it is one of the most promising methods available to organizational leaders today. Its promise and influence are growing. Serious students of leadership and management as well as corporate leaders all over the country are turning back to the basics of human relationship to get prepared for the enormous challenges that organizations will confront in the next century.

References

Arnold, W. W., & Plas, J. M. (1993). *The human touch: Today's most unusual program for productivity and profit.* New York: John Wiley.

Block, P. (1993). *Stewardship: Choosing service over self-interest.* San Francisco: Berrett-Koehler.

Bradford, D. L., & Cohen, A. (1984). *Managing for excellence.* New York: John Wiley.

Cusamano, M. A. (1985). *The Japanese automobile industry.* Cambridge, MA: Harvard University Press.

Dinkmeyer, D. (1991). Encouragement: Basis for leader training and participative management. *Individual Psychology, 47*(4), 504-508.

Doyle, K. (1992, August). Who's killing total quality? *Incentive*, pp. 12-19.

Durlbahji, S., & Marks, N. E. (1993). *Japanese business: Cultural perspectives.* Albany: State University of New York Press.

Eisenberger, R., Fasolo, P., & Davis-LaMastro, V. (1990). Perceived organizational support and employee diligence, commitment, and innovation. *Journal of Applied Psychology, 75*(1), 51-59.

Evans, P. (1989). *Motivation and emotion.* New York: Routledge.

Florida, R., & Kenney, M. (1991). Transplanted organizations: The transfer of Japanese industrial organization to the U.S. *American Sociological Review, 56*, 381-398.

Frey, R. (1993). Empowerment or else. *Harvard Business Review, 71*(5), 80-88.

Garvin, D. (1987, November-December). Competing on the eight dimensions of quality. *Harvard Business Review*, pp. 101-109.

Griffin, A., & Hauser, J. R. (1993). The voice of the customer. *Marketing Science, 12*, 1-25.

Gyrna, F. M. (1988). Quality costs. In *Quality control handbook* (4th ed., pp. 4.1-4.30). New York: McGraw-Hill.

Handy, C. (1994). *The age of paradox.* Boston: Harvard Business School Press.

Herzberg, F. (1990). *One more time: How do you motivate employees?* (Manage people not personnel: The Harvard Business Review book series). Boston: Harvard Business School Publishing.

Hsu, F. L. K. (1983). *Rugged individualism reconsidered.* Knoxville: University of Tennessee Press.

Huey, J. (1993, January 25). Finding new heroes for a new era. *Fortune*, pp. 62-69.

Ivey, M., & Carey, J. (1991, October 21). The ecstasy and the agony. *Business Week*, p. 40.

Juran, J. M. (1989). *Juran on leadership for quality: An executive handbook.* Milwaukee, WI: American Society for Quality Control.

Katzenbach, J. R., & Smith, D. K. (1993). *The wisdom of teams: Creating the high-performance organization.* Boston: Harvard Business School Press.

Kerr, N. L. (1983). Motivation losses in small groups: A social dilemma analysis. *Journal of Personality and Social Psychology, 45*(4), 819-828.

Labovitz, G., & Rosansky, V. (1993). *Making quality work.* New York: Harper Business.

Larson, C. E., & LaFasto, F. M. (1989). *Teamwork: What must go right/What can go wrong.* Newbury Park, CA: Sage.

Levering, R., & Moskowitz, M. (1993). *The 100 best companies to work for in America.* New York: Doubleday.

Levinson, H. (1990). *Asinine attitudes toward motivation* (Manage people not personnel: The Harvard Business Review book series). Boston: Harvard Business School Publishing.

Levinson, H. (1994). Why the behemoths fell: Psychological roots of corporate failure. *American Psychologist, 49*(50), 428-436.

Loeb, M. (1995, January 16). Ten commandments for managing creative people. *Fortune,* pp. 135-136.

Maehr, M. L., & Braskamp, L. A. (1986). *The motivation factor: A theory of personal investment.* Lexington, MA: D. C. Heath.

Manz, C., & Sims, H. P. (1993). *Business without bosses: How self-managing teams are building high-performance companies.* New York: John Wiley.

Mullen, J. X. (1995). *The simple art of greatness.* New York: Viking.

Nohria, N., & Berkley, J. (1994, January-February). Whatever happened to the take-charge manager? *Harvard Business Review,* pp. 128-137.

Ouchi, W. (1982). *Theory Z: How American business can meet the Japanese challenge.* New York: Avon.

Pugh, D., & Hickson, D. (1989). *Writers on organizations* (4th ed.). Newbury Park, CA: Sage.

Rust, R., Zahorik, A., & Keiningham, T. (1994). *Return on quality.* Chicago: Probus.

Sabel, C. F. (1993). Studied trust: Building new forms of cooperation in a volatile economy. *Human Relations, 46*(9), 1029-1170.

Stead, W. E., & Stead, J. G. (1992). *Management for a small planet.* Newbury Park, CA: Sage.

Steininger, D. J. (1993). Why quality initiatives are failing: The need to address the foundation of human motivation. *Human Resource Management, 33*(4), 601-616.

Tjosvold, D., & Tjosvold, M. M. (1995). *Psychology for leaders.* New York: John Wiley.

Tocqueville, A. de. (1969). *Democracy in America* (G. Lawrence, Ed.; J. P. Mayer, Trans.). New York: Doubleday Anchor. (Original work published 1835)

Walton, M. (1986). *The Deming management method.* New York: Dodd, Mead.

Walton, M. (1990). *Deming management at work.* New York: Putnam.

Wilkinson, R. (1988). *The pursuit of the American character.* New York: Harper & Row.

Williams, K. D., & Karau, W. (1991). Social loafing and social compensation: The effects of expectations of co-worker performance. *Journal of Personality and Social Psychology, 61*(4), 570-581.

Wood, R. C. (1991, March 18). A hero without a company. *Forbes,* pp. 112-114.

Yost, J. H., Strube, M., & Bailey, J. R. (1992). The construction of the self: An evolutionary view. *Current Psychology: Research & Reviews, 11*(2), 110-121.

Zeithaml, V. A., Parasuraman, A., & Berry, L. L. (1990). *Delivering quality service: Balancing customer perceptions and expectations.* New York: Free Press.

PART I

Person-Centered Leadership:
The Fundamentals, the Past, the Future

2

Wholeness at Work

Hearts, Hands, Spirits, Minds

There is a revolution and a renewal under way in American culture. In a strange twist of irony, it is not being brought to us by the churches and synagogues, the government, or even the schools. It is being brought to us by the American corporation. For many, that is astonishing. The astonished are representatives of a majority that experienced the U.S. industrialized sector, almost from its inception, as the bastion of bureaucratic disinterest and heartless manipulation. Quite a few of these astonished people are those whose fathers and grandfathers worked at the pleasure of the company store, the captain of industry, the ineffective, paper-shuffling manager. Many of these average citizens—now third-generation postindustrial revolution—opted out of the corporate world. The hard-built savings of their parents sent them to medical school, law school, and liberal arts colleges where they ended up choosing careers in fields like social work, urban planning, architecture, and education as well as in our ubiquitous medical and government careers. Currently, we have a huge group of baby boomers from lower- and middle-class families who watched their parents suffer at the hand of American business and decided they wanted none of that kind of life for themselves and their families. These 30- and 45-year-old citizens of today are completely bewildered when they hear that there is a torrent of change working its will on U.S. corporate goals and management structures. They read and hear that U.S. companies want to produce goods of genuine quality that won't break down or wear out—and that these same companies want to empower their workers to make the important decisions and to develop their talents and personal growth at work. But they don't much believe it. Such has been the bitter taste that American business has left in the mouths of its citizens for the past 70 years (cf. Leach, 1993; Licht, 1995). Those who have not been associated with U.S. companies since the mid-1980s really haven't a clue about some of the most major cultural changes that are being spawned there. Even though they see the sequelae—customer-oriented business hours, U.S. goods that refuse to break down, neighbors who claim they "love" working for Herman Miller, Southwest Airlines, GE, or whatever—the revolution has come so quietly and from such a peculiar place that, unlike their corporate neighbors, they have missed the source of the changes. But, nonetheless, change has come.

Yet no program for organizational or cultural change of this magnitude could, of course, stand a chance of being effective if the motivators were solely things such as economics and international competition. No, this particular revolution and renewal is occurring because the individuals who work in businesses—at all levels of the organization—have suffered under traditional corporate structures and values and have welcomed the new management strategies and goals as—simply put—a good thing.

Summing Up

Although many are not yet aware of it, some of the most exciting contributions to human development currently are being created in corporations.

Finding a Place for the Heart Again

The changes that are sweeping through our corporate organizations allow people to be who they really are. In fact, some of the better transformation programs encourage and expect that. *Heart, feelings, truth, values, spirit, giving,* and even *love* are no longer dirty words at work. People like that. In fact, they have been starving for it.

Some in business may tentatively embrace the new participation models but still silently agree with one group of contemporary management researchers who continue to write such thoughts as the following: "Management then must get the involvement of employees. This is best done with facts, because facts overcome emotions" (Rust, Zahorik, & Keiningham, 1994, p. 143). But, in contrast, today's majority seem to find themselves lining up with people like Warren Bennis, who points out that this rejection of the human capacity to feel while at work is what got us into trouble in the first place. As Bennis (1989) puts it:

> The rebellion of the 1960s, the Me Decade that followed, today's yuppies, are all consequences of the mistakes and crudities of the organization men. Unable to find America's head or heart, many of its citizens seem to have declared their independence from it and from each other. (p. 19)

Stephen Covey, author of *Principle-Centered Leadership* (1992), writes:

> Life is, by nature, highly interdependent. To try to achieve maximum effectiveness through independence is like trying to play tennis with a golf club—the tool is not suited to the reality. . . . If I am emotionally interdependent, I derive a great sense of worth within myself, but I also recognize the need for love, for giving, and for receiving love from others. (Covey, 1989, p. 51)

Max DePree (1992), much-respected former chairman at Herman Miller, has written:

> In a society and a world that have serious problems and suffer all too often and far too painfully from heartbreak, each of us needs a haven.

> Part of the touch of leadership is to create such a haven. A good family, a good institution, or a good corporation can be a place of healing. It can be a place where work becomes redemptive. (pp. 64-65)

In fact, books written by Bennis (1989), Covey (1992), DePree (1992), and others such as Autry (1992, 1994) and Senge (1994) have been widely read for several years now. Although each author has a unique message and specific area of interest, what they have in common—and what is responsible for their astonishing popularity—is that when talking about work, businesses, and careers, they use words such as *joy, interdependence, integrity, humility, caring, self-respect, love,* and *letting go.* They do so without embarrassment or apology. Today's citizens not only appreciate that, they endorse it, praise it, and cling to the words with hope and shared vision.

People have long been ready to bring their hearts and values back to work. The worst thing about so many traditional U.S. corporations is that the leadership and the management structures gave workers the impression that if they wanted to come to work, they'd need to leave huge parts of themselves at home.

Summing Up

A work environment that ignores feelings and expects people to pretend they do not have them—the positive or the negative—puts a premium on the control of feelings. Inevitably, this distances workers from the organization. Genuineness and passion are left at home.

FALSE HEART: THE ORGANIZATION MAN

Relying on the intellectual legacy of theoreticians such as Max Weber and Frederick Taylor, early industrial models valued cool, considered, rational approaches to work at the expense of feelings. William Whyte (1956) provided a social science discussion of the results of that, titled *The Organization Man,* and Sloan Wilson (1955) produced a fictionalized version, *The Man in the Gray Flannel Suit.* Both revealed the workplace reality that personal and organizational control and efficiency had become more important than authenticity, creative risk taking, and emotional expression. In an atmosphere that ignores workers' feelings and expects people to pretend they do not have them—positive or negative—a premium comes to be placed on controlling one's feelings. Inevitably, this leads to distancing oneself from the organization. It leads to reduced loyalty, reduced caring about the company's mission and products. The message is clear: If the company doesn't want your real feelings around, then, obviously, it doesn't want your real self around. The need to control oneself in the workplace ended up as the intellectual anchor of one of the most widely read self-help books of all time, Dale Carnegie's (1941) *How to Win Friends and Influence People.* As I've pointed out elsewhere,

> One of the pioneers of the traveling corporate workshop, Carnegie tells the "rules" for getting along with others, indeed for "winning them over" to you in order to further your goals. The book indirectly conveys several messages. Among them are the beliefs that all people can benefit from and should learn the *same* set of strategies, that appearances are crucial, and that the other person needs to believe that you are more interested in him or her than you are in your own needs and opinions. (Plas & Hoover-Dempsey, 1988, p. 33)

Much of the Carnegie advice has to do with impression management, that is, how to withhold your real thoughts and feelings to manipulate and control what others think of you. People began to believe that at work it simply wasn't mature—and thus it wasn't safe—to reveal your less than noble thoughts and your uncomfortable feelings. Likewise, it wasn't mature to exhibit your positive feelings at work either. You wouldn't want to show frustration or ethical outrage; you wouldn't want to be too caring, joyful, energetic, or loving at work. In other words, it was wrong to connect your feelings to your organization. And we see how disastrous that line of thinking has been for U.S. corporations. Bennis (1989) writes:

> It was the mechanistic view that produced the organization man, and it was the organization man, as I have noted, who ironically enough has caused many of the problems in our organizations. It is the individual, operating at the peak of his creative and moral powers, who will revive our organizations, by reinventing himself and them. (p. 102)

One of the most important messages that psychology has to offer the world of work is the observation that people are connected and committed to the organizations and groups for which they have important feelings (Becker, 1964; Sabini, 1995). This fact of human personality seems to be so strong that it even applies to negative feelings (Becker, 1964; Miller, 1981). Thus, we've learned that although a child predominantly experiences anxiety, anger, and even abuse within a family, the fact of those feelings nonetheless is capable of creating strong needs to continue to belong to that family.

On the more positive side, of course, each of us realizes that it is our strong love and pride and joy in our families that create the strong commitments that we have to them. It is the emotions we experience that keep us connected to our recreational and political interests. The commitment that we have to our favorite college basketball teams each March and our favorite candidates each fall has everything to do with what we *feel* when we sit in front of the television screen as we "live, breathe, and die" with every questionable call of the referee and each perfectly executed slam dunk, or each report of the hour's most recent vote tallying. If our team wins, we win. If our candidate loses, we lose. That's how we feel. It's that simple. That's commitment. That's connection.

This basic fact of human psychology—the connection of our feelings to our allegiances—was largely ignored in work organizations during the early and middle part of this century. But at the close of the 1900s, we seem to be feeling that we've had enough. We're too weary from trying to hide what is authentically real—the messy stuff as well as the good stuff. We're too disillusioned to continue working in organizations that declare no values and devote pages of rhetoric to efficiency but none to integrity. We're bored within organizations that expect us to disconnect our passions from our work.

Because they can lead to spontaneous, nondeliberative action at times, we have felt that our feelings are dangerous. "Bad" feelings cause us to lose our cool and the "good" ones might get us too involved. But despite the perils involved, human feelings aren't going to go away. They're the great motivators in life (Janis, Mahl, Kagan, & Holt, 1969; O'Neil & Drillings, 1994; see also Cross & Markus, 1991). They're responsible for the need to wage the holy war, the battle on behalf of integrity. They're the very reason we like coming to work when we're lucky enough to be coming to a work environ-ment that encourages full human participation.

Summing Up

One of the most important messages that psychology has to offer managers is the observation that people are con-nected and committed to the organizations for which they have important feelings.

THE CORPORATE HEART REBORN

Encouraging authenticity is probably the most threatening, yet most important thing that new leaders must do. To encourage the typical worker to express what he or she truly feels and honestly thinks about the products, the rules, the environment, the customers, and the possibilities and visions is to encourage the worker to do no less than really come to work—heart, soul, hands, and mind. Rather than being something to be afraid of, there is something here to be very excited about. Hawley (1993) has observed traditional, bureau-cratic organizations for a good many years and like so many others he has grown to hate the silence. "Where's the roar?" he asks. "Where did the guts go? Where's the spirit?" (p. 8). In a wise response, Hawley tells us that "part of that flatness has to do with lack of truth" (p. 8). As he thinks about the new models of corporate leadership that are working their way into our organizations, he sees that

> the new game is like going home, with all that home entails: a warm hearth, a light left on for us, feeling understood, and being able to just *do* life without sweating it so much. The new game is the game that we have, at some level, longed to play all our lives: being able to set aside fear and live a life of more integrity. (p. 8)

And by "integrity" here, Hawley is talking about authenticity—integrating our personal, most real selves into our work lives. This is the kind of basic integrity that requires the risk of letting our true selves show up at work rather than some contemporary version of the affectless yes-men who dared not the original thought, said all the "right" things, and operated at work with the kind of cold, calculated efficiency that denies what true humanity is really all about—the possibilities of the heart.

In their recent *Fifth Discipline Fieldbook*, Senge, Kleiner, Roberts, Ross, and Smith (1994) use the word *intimacy* when describing what managers need to get good at to create atmospheres that produce authenticity. They directly respond to the anxieties associated with that term by saying:

> Some managers fear that if they act vulnerably they may unleash (or provoke) sexual overtones. Others are afraid of racism, or uncomfortable clashes of opinion. But intimacy is not sexuality in the workplace, nor does it mean giving free rein to every emotional impulse. Most people who have experience with intimacy know that expressing feeling is a skill, like any other. It improves with practice. A wide range of feelings can be expressed at work—from the genuine caring which we reserve for close friends to mutual respect for colleagues who contribute to the product or service. (p. 72)

Like so many others these days, Senge et al. realize that accepting feelings—and thus authenticity—into the workplace has passed the point of being an option that a manager may choose or choose to ignore.

> For whatever reasons, the generation of employees under age fifty appears to be more comfortable with this kind of expression. In many cases, they demand it. An organization hoping to attract the best of them has no choice but to permit the display of human feeling in the workplace, with consideration, but also with full acknowledgment of the whole person at work, not just his role. (p. 72)

Daniel Fishman and Cary Cherniss (1990), leaders at the Equitable Financial Companies Corporate Human Resources Department and affiliates of the organizational behavior program at Rutgers, have edited a provocative book on the need for organizational transformation that emphasizes the human side when it comes to corporate competitiveness. Even then, writing at the close of the 1980s, such contributors as Joe Radigan of Equitable could see the proverbial handwriting on the wall. Competition that creates vital products is very good. Competition that debilitates the human spirit is very bad. There is strength in caring. There is wisdom in bringing the concept of authentic caring back to the workplace, where it has always belonged. Like the Senge group, Radigan understands that words like *decency* and *caring* are hardly optional at work anymore and that, furthermore, the words truly have to mean something.

> Those of us who have not been mere armchair observers, but have been associated with major corporations that underwent restructuring and downsizing on a significant scale, can attest to the fact that without trust, respect, and mutual caring between management and its employees there can be pervasive cynicism, unpredictable outbursts of ill will, overt lack of cooperation, and destructive acts against the corporation. Employees want—yes, demand—decent treatment from employers, and when they don't perceive it is forthcoming, they vent their displeasure in unfortunate ways. (Radigan, 1990, p. 16)

Chris Argyris (1985, 1987), for many years holder of the Conant Chair in Organizational Behavior at Harvard, has spent a lifetime thinking about the influences of the workplace on the personal development of the individual. Argyris persuades us that personal development is dependent on the presence of a certain richness of environmental context that allows people to take risks, experiment, and feel safe enough to display their authentic selves. Given these standards, it is easy to see that American businesses have not heretofore allowed for the full development of America's citizens. Personal suspicions and mistrusts have been fostered rather than curiosity and passion. Argyris and Schön (1978) have made classic the idea of the managerial *theory-in-use* and have correctly identified the components of the typical managerial theory-in-use that dominated organizations just into the 1980s. Within that model, managers understood that they had to define unilateral goals, minimize the need to depend on others, minimize the generation and expression of their own "negative" emotions, and be "rationally objective" as they kept others from expressing feelings.

To grow, the human personality must make use of feelings as much as it relies on thinking. Thus, the lack of authenticity generated by all this—quite understandably—became too burdensome to continue to bear in business settings. It is not too much of a stretch to conclude that former management structures have been oppressive of the human spirit. As we've moved toward the close of this century, the people who have lived within those structures have seen a window of opportunity—for the most part the TQM movement and its sequelae —through which they now intend to pass. Why? Just because it feels right. What was formerly experienced in our organizations so often felt wrong.

Summing Up

Encouraging authenticity in the workplace is probably the most important thing that new leaders must do. Encouraging authenticity has passed the point of being an option that a manager may choose or choose to ignore.

THE SEARCH FOR SOMEONE TO BLAME

But as we review the damage that our former management models have wrought, it is misguided to blame business in general, or the architects of traditional management theory, or even specific CEOs and corporate presidents who may have perpetuated dysfunctional management systems. The phenomenon we are considering is a stage within a developing culture. If we had not made these particular mistakes during the formative years of industrial society, no doubt we would have made others. Human development and the institutions it spawns are, by nature, imperfect. The developmental paths that are created by human growth are sometimes circuitous, fraught with peril, or simply dead ends. In this case, in this particular country, the path of management development became too rigid. It concentrated too heavily on the products of the mind, such as rationality and objectivity, to the exclusion of the products of the heart—caring, passion, joy, pride, authenticity, and trust. So, newer models developed, in part, in response to older management models that couldn't provide enough flexibility for employees so that they could enjoy personal growth and keep us internationally competitive in such things as quality and output (cf. McFarland, Senn, & Childress, 1994; Morgan, 1993; Senge, 1994). Also taking a historical and developmental approach, Peter Drucker (1992) ends up seriously questioning the wisdom of blaming our cultural realities:

> Frederick Taylor has often been criticized for never once asking the workers whose jobs he studied; he told them. Nor did Elton Mayo ever ask—he also told. But there is also no record of Sigmund Freud's ever asking patients what they thought might be their problem. Neither Marx nor Lenin ever thought of asking the masses. And it did not occur to any High Command in World War I or World War II to ask junior officers or enlisted men in the front lines about weapons, uniforms, or even food (In the American armed forces this became the custom only during Vietnam.) *Taylor simply shared the belief of his age in the wisdom of the expert.* (pp. 106-107, italics added)

Just after the moment we've become markedly uncomfortable with the status quo, we will not leave the developmental path to which we've become accustomed and that has served at least some of the basic needs of the society and culture, unless circumstances abruptly reveal a better way. As Drucker (1992) further points out, "In making and moving things, partnership with the responsible worker is, however, only the *best* way—after all, Taylor's telling them worked, too, and quite well" (p. 107). Of course, after several decades of loading onto the corporate structure all the side effects of Tayloresque management, there inevitably comes a time when something like that form of management (which is far less than optimal) actually stops working at all or falls so significantly below threshold that its abandonment is imminent.

Using foresight, it is often difficult if not impossible to predict which cultural values can be seriously strained without significant damage as a group, country, or culture is growing and working its way through some hard developmental moments. Such is the case with the traditional U.S. management models. In 1900, 1925, and 1945, only the most wise and clever of observers and prognosticators could have predicted which of the American values would inevitably be responsible for the demise of the rational American management system that so dominated the world marketplace and the world's imagination. Now, in retrospect, we can begin to see that this management system grew out of and was held in place by a variety of sacred American values—some of them in conflict—values such as the separation of church and state, rugged individualism, personal initiative and effort, faith in education and expertise, and a Victorian approach to the sanctity of authority.

People of all cultures inevitably look at themselves through eyes that were created by the very culture they wish so much to truly see. So, the perennial problem of the social observer has always been how to get enough distance—in time or cultural perspective—to see what is really going on. Decades ago, who might have seen that this management system was a natural outgrowth of passionately held cultural values that had served the country well in so many personal areas of life but were somewhat at odds with each other and destined to eventually create problems of significant scope in our work lives? We can now see that Tocqueville, who clearly recognized our independent spirits and immanent alienations, was one such prognosticator. But there were few others.

Summing Up

Concentrating too heavily on the products of the mind to the exclusion of the products of the heart has created some of the rigidity in management models of the past. But if we had not made those mistakes, we likely would have made others. Human development and the institutions it spawns are, by nature, imperfect and nonlinear.

The Separation of the
Private Self From the Public Self

The single most important cultural factor responsible for the current legacy of pain and discomfort coming from our traditional corporate management models is not among the list of targets we have come most frequently to blame: collective greed, the erosion of ethics and values, the superficiality encouraged by some U.S. corporate marketing departments. Rather, the current problems we face are the inevitable result of something we as a culture are very proud of and have valued intensely—the separation of church and state. This separation was intended to purchase religious and personal freedom for a melting pot of citizens, drawn here specifically for that freedom, from nationalities and cultures all over the world. Many had come here from national situations where there was no distinction between the government and the representatives of God. Within the American merger, if peace was to prevail, no single spiritual voice could be permitted to speak for all the people. Government needed to be of the people, by the people, and for the people but independent of any need to bow to a certain kind of god defined by a certain religious persuasion. In a society that hoped to make room for the freedom of all, each individual's spiritual convictions and passions must—and could—be separated from the business of government and from the business of the marketplace in a society that hoped to make room for the freedom of all.

A good idea—a great idea—but the great problem that this good idea inevitably engendered resulted because the human spiritual belief—of whatever variety, even the atheist variety—is centered at the core of the human personality. *If one must separate one's spiritual self from the town council and the marketplace, one's true and whole self can then never fully participate there. The separation of church and state in the United States inexorably resulted in a separation of one's personal self from one's public self.*

Far from being an unnecessarily brutish form of management, the traditional American management structure was, in part, an automatic or almost unconscious response from a culture that was obligated to create a system that could keep diverse people out of trouble over basic differences at work as well as in the town council. Managers were expected to keep themselves and their workers operating rationally rather than emotionally. A strict line of authority was expected to prevent the upsurge of a variety of points of view that could erupt into those "unpredictable outbursts of ill will" that Radigan (1990) has warned us about. It would also serve to facilitate the rise of the well-motivated and the effortful, the Horatio Alger model citizen who develops talents, works hard, and is prevented by a strong societal and corporate system from allowing personal values to override the basic rights of others. If he chooses, Mr. Alger could, for example, start his own company, provided that it reflect his own beliefs in the value of hard work, honesty, and skill. He could not, however, ask his workers to kneel with him at the start of each day. All this makes sense to us; Americans endorse the ideas highly. But as Whitehead (1947, 1959) observed, all values are purchased at the price of exclusion—the exclusion of other things that might be of value. In Mr. Alger's world, both employer and employee found themselves leaving the most fundamental aspects of their selves and personalities at home, far from the workplace. Yet the gods we pray to, the styles of life we endorse, and the personal codes of conduct we believe in are our most precious possessions. From the beginning in American industrial society, we have been unable to bring these precious personal possessions onto the job.

This value of separation of church and state and the resulting fact of separation of the private and public self is so important to U.S. citizens that it is not available for question. This is so despite the fact that we tend to argue about everything else. In a country that is so fragmented by separations that mainstream groups, splinter groups, and countless individuals use media forums to debate just about everything, there is no voice that argues for an end to the separation of church and state. This is a voice you will not hear. Yet there are many voices now raised in protest of the separation of the private and public persona, the heart and the head. As we will see in subsequent chapters, the management and leadership literature these days is replete with this kind of call.

Tocqueville (1835/1969) was one of the first to observe—and to lament—the extreme individualism that this set of cultural mores must produce. "Each man is forever thrown back on himself alone," he wrote, "and there is danger that he may be shut up in the solitude of his own heart" (p. 508). Bellah, Madsen, Sullivan, Swidler, and Tipton (1985) have noted that

the most distinctive aspect of twentieth-century American society is the division of life into a number of separate functional sectors: home and workplace, work and leisure, white collar and blue collar, public and private. . . . Domesticity, love, and intimacy increasingly became "havens" against the competitive culture of work. (p. 43)

In fact, as Ann Douglas (1977) has pointed out, intimacy, love, and acceptance became so disconnected from the marketplace that the havens for these needs and personal expressions—the family and religion—became feminized as a result of the male having been predominant in commercial work while the female presided at family and worship. So, the situation may have become even more intense and conflicted for men in U.S. society as some of their most basic needs as people began to be associated with the feminine just as these needs were disassociated from the arenas in which men were expected to perform and achieve. Bellah's group (1985) further persuades:

Like the entrepreneur, the manager also has another life, divided among spouse, children, friends, community, and religious and other nonoccupational involvements. Here in contrast to the manipulative, achievement-oriented practices of the workplace, another kind of personality is actualized. . . . Public and "private" roles often contrast sharply, as symbolized by the daily commute from green suburban settings reminiscent of rural life to the industrial, technological ambience of the workplace.
   The split between public and private life correlates with a split between utilitarian individualism, appropriate in the economic and occupational spheres, and expressive individualism, appropriate in private life. (pp. 45-46)

Summing Up

A culture that separates church and state results in separation of the personal self from the public self. While supporting the need to keep religion and commerce distinct, organizations nonetheless need to create new ways to reunite the personal and the public—on behalf of the company's goals as well as the development of the individual.

34   THE FUNDAMENTALS, THE PAST, THE FUTURE

SEPARATION AND THE POPULAR CULTURE

Now we can understand the amazing rise of the popular culture. In his history of the American democratic experience, Boorstin (1974) hints at the answer from the first paragraph forward:

> A new civilization found new ways of holding men together—less and less by creed or belief, by tradition or by place, more and more by common effort and common experience, by the apparatus of daily life, by their ways of thinking about themselves. (p. 1)

In a culture that protects through separation, that guarantees individual rights by asking its citizens to leave their most personal selves out of government and business, something must fill the void. In the case of the United States, it has been the popular culture that has filled that void.

People seek kinship. They seek common ground and common bonds. Given the inability to connect the authentic self to the company's mission and goals or to the needs and desires of the faceless who answer the telephones in geographically distant organizations, we have had to struggle to find our meaningful human connections. The development of media and communication capability provided the answer. Now—because of television, magazines, newspapers, movies, and the Internet—we have something we can share. Maybe we cannot share what we're really thinking at work, but we can share our reaction to last night's episode of our current favorite sitcom. If we can't feel comfortable sharing our feelings about our colleagues— both good and bad—we can share how we feel about "the trial of the century." In the elevators, boardrooms, washrooms, and halls, the current stars that are rising and those that are falling—whether in sports, music, movies, or business—provide us the topics that we *can* bring up and discuss. And from that comes our sense of shared culture.

We are communal by nature (Aronson, 1965; Sabini, 1995). Although we cannot share our most important thoughts and feelings, we nonetheless need to share something. That there are bonds between us matters. Each person needs to belong to a community of work and of national heritage just as he or she needs to belong to a family. As we have seen earlier, it is these connections that provide the context for personal growth. This fact is part of the psychology of what it means to be human (cf. Becker, 1974; Koch & Leary, 1985).

The talk show hosts—to their credit, and to the credit of the culture that produces them—do not confine themselves to simple discussions of just exactly who is doing just exactly what. After some "facts" related to the day's topic have been shared, most of these hosts move quickly to the values and beliefs that provide the foundation for the actions under discussion. It is at this point that the audience gets involved. Audience participants are quick to reassure us that their perspectives on these issues do not derive from their religious backgrounds but represent general principles that all "good" or "smart" or "sane" people ought to endorse. They share their opinions about the principles that ought to govern attitudes and actions as if their lives depended on it—dare we say, as if they were in church? In a culture that has asked people to reserve the most important parts of themselves for their homes and religions, it is perhaps *not* to the discredit of our citizens that we've figured out a way to publicly share personal values and attitudes anyway. The profound pity is that absent the participation of our spiritual and most authentic selves, the result of all this popular culture discussion is often vacuous, superficial, irresponsible, and misleading.

Summing Up

In a culture that asks people to reserve the most important parts of themselves for their homes and religions, it is not surprising that citizens develop the so-called popular culture as a place within which to try to genuinely communicate with one another.

The Separation at Work. We have paid a high price for the traditions we have fallen into as a result of our desire to protect through separation of home and marketplace. Through these separations, we have protected the individual's right to worship and to value as he or she sees fit as long as there is no usurpation of the common good, that is, of the laws that protect that common good. These separations have made it possible for the person to preserve the sacred self, the unique self. But the result is that there are fewer arenas into which the individual can take this authentic self, once preserved. Most important of these excluded arenas has been the world of work, the place where the individual U.S. citizen spends more than 50% of his or her waking hours during each workday.

Stephen Covey (1989) quotes David Starr Jordan: " 'There is no real excellence in all this world that can be separated from right living' " (p. 15). Yet each of us has completely expected himself or herself to excel at work despite the fact that the personal version of truth, of right living, had to be kept private—discussed at home but not at work.

Many have cited the effects of all this on our working citizens. Bennis (1989) reports on the research of Frederick, who shows that people feel the company blocks their "personal values." A study of 6,000 executives revealed that 70% of them believe they have compromised their own ethical standards on behalf of the company. In a special message to his Chinese readers, Peter Senge (1994) has said:

> Yet, separation quickly became fragmentation and isolation. . . .
>   In the West, our primary social institutions are in a state of break-down because of fragmentation. . . . Virtually everything about our modern system of management is based on fragmentation, and the inevitable competition that results. Marketing departments are at war with manufacturing. Frontline managers have a hostility for corporate management that borders on hatred. People within the organization often compete more with one another than with external "competitors." (pp. 564-565)

In retrospect, we needn't be surprised. When people are asked to leave their feelings, unique values, and spiritual beliefs at home when they come to work, they will inevitably begin to distrust one another, because it is obvious that "what you see is not what you get." The organization becomes a place of anonymity where the comedienne Lily Tomlin's old but classic version of the telephone operator may be extremely funny, but its humor resides primarily in its sad commentary on the individual worker's emotional isolation from all those around her.

But, again, as the I Ching (Wilhelm & Baynes, 1967) might say, "No praise. No blame." American culture and American management are not to be derided for these current facts of organizational life. What we have here is a developmental phenomenon, the interaction of the basic psychological needs of human beings with an evolving culture composed of a variety of people from starkly different ancestral heritages. Human development has always involved "errors," travel down paths that showed themselves nonuseful. Progress in all of nature has never been exclusively linear.

It is energy-wasting to blame. Rather, now that we see where we have come, organizations need to be responsive and accountable for helping to create the new versions of leadership and management that can preserve the much-needed separation of church and state while allowing the individual to heal, to reunite the personal and public self.

Halal (1986) has said, "The key to restoring economic vitality today is to recognize that social goals and profit are not only compatible, but so interdependent that the firm cannot succeed unless it unifies these two sets of concerns" (p. 229). We might also say that this is the key to restoring cultural vitality and organizational vitality. It is no longer acceptable that the business organization be primarily and exclusively concerned with revenue and profit. Quality is equally as important. So is the developmental well-being of each person who is part of the company. Quality, employee development, and profit— these now form the only reasonable bottom line that a 21st-century company can responsibly endorse. For the past 75 years, American business organizations have been the only organizations exempt from the mandate to develop the nation's citizens. All other organizations—governmental, educational, sports, and all kinds of special interest groups—have overtly recognized a dual mission. As we get better at reuniting the personal and public selves, we necessarily will get better at recognizing that no important organization can be exempt from the mandate to further the growth of the people whose work creates the company.

Summing Up

Revenue and profit can no longer be the exclusive goal of the corporate organization. Today's citizens want a focus on quality and they want opportunities for personal growth and the development of personal well-being.

Summary: Ending the Separations and Healing the Splits

The fragmentations are arguably the biggest problem we currently face in the United States—socially, politically, and in the corporate organization. As people's public and private selves have been disconnected, so have the product and company policies been disconnected from ethics, morality, and responsibility. As so many have pointed out (e.g., Levine, 1995), in the past each corporate department and function has been divorced from the whole. This yields the typical infighting and internal competition we have found in many traditional U.S. organizations. The right hand not only hasn't known what the left is doing, it often has been caught sabotaging its work.

But the solution is not a marriage between church and state—far from it. The wisdom of our forebears on this point remains as viable today as it was at the inception of the Constitution. What is needed is a union between the personal and the private selves of each individual who comes to work. This does not mean that debates over religious and lifestyle persuasions need to permeate our offices and assembly lines. It does mean that people at work need to get the message that their hearts are as necessary to the company as their heads. Each person at work—executive, hourly employee, manager, secretary—needs to feel free again to use words like *caring, ethics, feelings, acceptance, dependence, joy,* and *love*.

The TQM strategies we are most familiar with are based on ideas of teamwork, interdependence, empowerment, cooperation, and communication. These processes cannot be viable in U.S. organizations unless the leadership learns how to replace rugged individualism with related individualism (see Chapter 4) and to give attention to the hearts as well as the hands and minds of the individuals who work with them. This means inviting people to come to work wholly again and teaching them how to get their individual needs met while working for a common cause. Those leadership models that are person centered in this way are the ones that are really working and show the greatest promise for development.

References

Argyris, C. (1985). *Strategy, change, and defensive routines*. New York: Ballinger.

Argyris, C. (1987). *Personality and organization*. New York: Garland.

Argyris, C., & Schön, D. (1978). *Organizational learning: A theory of action perspective*. Reading, MA: Addison-Wesley.

Aronson, E. (1965). *The social animal*. San Francisco: Freeman.

Autry, J. A. (1992). *Love and profit: The art of caring leadership*. New York: Avon.

Autry, J. A. (1994). *Life and work: A manager's search for meaning*. New York: Avon.

Becker, E. (1964). *Revolution in psychiatry*. New York: Free Press.

Becker, E. (1974). *Man's search for meaning*. New York: Free Press.

Bellah, R. N., Madsen, R., Sullivan, W., Swidler, A., & Tipton, S. (1985). *Habits of the heart: Individualism and commitment in American life*. New York: Harper & Row Perennial.

Bennis, W. (1989). *On becoming a leader* (paperback). Reading, MA: Addison-Wesley.

Boorstin, D. J. (1974). *The Americans: The democratic experience*. New York: Vintage.

Carnegie, D. (1941). *How to win friends and influence people*. New York: Simon & Schuster.

Covey, S. (1989). *The 7 habits of highly effective people*. New York: Simon & Schuster.

Covey, S. (1992). *Principle-centered leadership*. New York: Simon & Schuster.

Cross, S., & Markus, H. (1991). Possible selves across the life span. *Human Development, 34*(4), 230-255.

DePree, M. (1992). *Leadership jazz*. New York: Dell.

Douglas, A. (1977). *The feminization of American culture*. New York: Knopf.

Drucker, P. F. (1992). *Managing for the future*. New York: Plume.

Fishman, D., & Cherniss, C. (Eds.). (1990). *The human side of corporate competitiveness*. Newbury Park, CA: Sage.

Halal, W. E. (1986). *The new capitalism*. New York: John Wiley.

Hawley, J. (1993). *Reawakening the spirit in work*. San Francisco: Berret-Koehler.

Janis, I. L., Mahl, G., Kagan, J., & Holt, R. R. (1969). *Personality: Dynamics, development, and assessment*. New York: Harcourt, Brace.

Koch, S., & Leary, D. E. (Eds.). (1985). *A century of psychology as science*. New York: McGraw-Hill.

Leach, W. (1993). *Land of desire: Merchants, power, and the rise of a new American culture*. New York: Vintage.

Levine, D. I. (1995). *Reinventing the workplace: How business and employees can both win*. Washington, DC: Brookings Institution.

Licht, W. (1995). *Industrializing America: The nineteenth century.* Baltimore: Johns Hopkins University Press.

McFarland, L. J., Senn, L. E., & Childress, J. R. (1994). *21st-century leadership: Dialogues with 100 top leaders.* Los Angeles: Leadership Press.

Miller, A. (1981). *The drama of the gifted child.* New York: Basic Books.

Morgan, G. (1993). *Imaginization: The art of creative management.* Newbury Park, CA: Sage.

O'Neil, H. F., & Drillings, M. (Eds.). (1994). *Motivation: Theory and research.* Hillsdale, NJ: Lawrence Erlbaum.

Plas, J. M., & Hoover-Dempsey, K. V. (1988). *Working up a storm: Anger, anxiety, joy, and tears on the job.* New York: Norton.

Radigan, J. E. (1990). Setting the scene: Can a company be both pro-profits and pro-people? In D. Fishman & C. Cherniss (Eds.), *The human side of corporate competitiveness* (pp. 13-17). Newbury Park, CA: Sage.

Rust, R., Zahorik, A., & Keiningham, T. (1994). *Return on quality.* Chicago: Probus.

Sabini, J. (1995). *Social psychology.* New York: Norton.

Senge, P. (1994). *The fifth discipline: The art and practice of the learning organization.* New York: Doubleday.

Senge, P., Kleiner, A., Roberts, C., Ross, R., & Smith, B. (1994). *Fifth discipline fieldbook.* New York: Doubleday.

Tocqueville, A. de. (1969). *Democracy in America* (G. Lawrence, Ed.; J. P. Mayer, Trans.). New York: Doubleday Anchor. (Original work published 1835)

Whitehead, A. N. (1947). *The wit and wisdom of Alfred North Whitehead* (A. H. Johnson, Ed.). Boston: Beacon.

Whitehead, A. N. (1959). *American essays in social philosophy* (A. H. Johnson, Ed.). New York: Harper.

Whyte, W. (1956). *The organization man.* New York: Simon & Schuster.

Wilhelm, R., & Baynes, C. F. (1967). *I ching: Book of changes* (Bollingen Series No. 19). Princeton, NJ: Princeton University Press.

Wilson, S. (1955). *The man in the gray flannel suit.* New York: Simon & Schuster.

3

Historical Perspectives on the Relationship of the Individual to the Corporate Organization

In the 1950s, 1960s, and into the 1970s, a good company was often thought of as a hard-driving organization run by principled people who nonetheless understood that "business is business" and "nice guys may finish last." As Huey (1994) points out in retrospect,

> Corporate leadership used to be so simple. You had it, or you didn't. It was in the cut of your jib. And if you had it, you certainly didn't share it . . . the buck stopped with you. Your ass was on the line. Your job was to kick ass and take names. These were the immutable truths of leadership that you learned as you progressed from the Boy Scouts to officer candidate school to the Harvard B-school, and they worked. God was in his heaven, and the ruling class ruled. (p. 42)

Although there are relatively few corporate organizations left in America that are committed to that kind of leadership philosophy, most business organizations incorporate at least some of the traditional management strategies that were associated with that mindset. All useful descriptions of the various traditional organization models (cf. Chandler, 1977; Chandler & Daems, 1980; Drucker, 1992;

Mintzberg, 1979; Thompson, 1967) cite the same basic characteristics: mechanistic, bottom-line driven, bureaucratic layers of top-down management.

Stead and Stead (1992) and many others (e.g., Braverman, 1974; Nelson, 1992) have identified Adam Smith's economics, Max Weber's bureaucracy, and Frederick Taylor's scientific management ideas as being the stuff from which a mechanistic management paradigm was made. "Within this paradigm, organizations are viewed as goal-directed entities made of coordinated parts, those parts being people. The job of the manager is to make these parts work together more efficiently, cutting labor costs and improving profits" (Stead & Stead, 1992, p. 100). In many of these traditional management models, it was uncritically assumed that efficiency must have priority over personal satisfaction; cost cutting must at times be more important than quality. Above all, emotion must defer to rationality no matter what the decision of the day.

Person-centered leadership, at least in part, has been a response to uncomfortable ways of dealing with the individual in organizations. A historical look at the relationship of the individual and the corporation must consider the rise of the managerial role, quality improvement, participatory management development, and the rugged individualism that has culturally influenced the person-in-organization for so many years. Let us begin with a historical overview of American opinion and the corporate organization.

American Opinion and the Corporation

During the early part of this century, the U.S. corporation was not consistently lauded as of great benefit to the working person. In 1949, Elmo Roper wrote, "There is a large body of American opinion which is convinced that business at best is amoral and at worst greedy" (p. 55). As quoted in a *Harvard Business Review* article some 20 years later, in 1968 Gene Bradley observed that "the target of the New Left movement is what its members see as the 'depersonalized' industrialized state" ("Managing to Learn," 1992, p. 147). In the same article, he quoted a student protest banner that read, "Humanity will not be free until the last capitalist has been hanged with the innards of the last bureaucrat" (p. 147).

The early corporation often was seen as impersonal, dehumanizing, bureaucratic, autocratic, dishonest, greedy, immoral, amoral, and in many ways far more powerful than city hall (Brody, 1971; Chandler & Daems, 1980; McGill, 1988; Roethlisberger, 1942; Whitehead, 1933). The hated company store and company housing that dominated too many industrialized small towns came to represent the worst of what work could mean for quality of life. During the first half of this century, at least a little bit of that company store mentality was suspected of being part of every successful corporation anybody could name.

Despite only two generations' experience with it, we had come to despise the corporate organization (Dubofsky, 1985; Goldberg, 1992; Hoxie, 1918). Even though several states had yet to achieve an industrial presence, many Americans had come to the conclusion that working for big business was just barely better than not working at all. Although significant voices raised themselves in defense of the U.S. corporation (Berle, 1927; Drucker, 1954; Higgins, 1932), they weren't always persuasive. In 1963, Lyman Porter insisted:

> The popular assumption that bigness encourages the "organization man" has not been adequately supported in the literature to date. . . . Our findings indicate that big companies need not be apologetic either for their bigness or for their effects on their managers. ("Managing to Learn," 1992, p. 147)

The response of many working people to that kind of thinking ranged from incredulity to mirth. Nonetheless, Porter hit the nail on the head when he stated "bigness" was the most easily identifiable culprit when it came to the pains and disappointments of the modern workday world. Throughout the middle years of this century, many assumed—almost uncritically—that big was bad (Handlin & Handlin, 1989; Light, 1995; Whitehead, 1933). All of it—the whole package of distrust and disgust—was believed to result from that single factor: bigness.

Without questioning the premises, many executives, workers, and journalistic observers, as well as some academic scholars, tended to assume that the fact of *big* must necessarily result in the kind of im-personalization that can make workers feel as if they are things to be used rather than human beings to be cherished. Within the blame game that haunted U.S. corporations almost from their inception, even machines—quickly bought but often quickly distrusted—seemed to run a poor second to "bigness." The "company" and most of its dis-trusted executives were believed to care only about black on the bot-tom line, and the average worker's lament was some version of "this company don't treat me right, this company done me wrong."

The workers fought back. With their more constructive responses, they joined forces by founding unions and negotiating better condi-tions at work plus health and retirement benefits for their families (Blum, 1972; Taft, 1962). In more destructive modes, they stole the paper clips and all the replacement parts they could safely smuggle out of the factories. Or they didn't give an honest day's work for an honest day's pay. Or they connived to claim disability benefits that may not have been their due. In short, although they were perceived as hav-ing little power, average workers—much like average executives—were also sometimes perceived as dishonest, greedy, immoral, amoral, and probably not even competent (McGregor, 1960, 1965).

The characterizations just presented do not, of course, apply to all companies and all workers. Rather, they serve to illustrate perceptual tendencies that existed during those early years of organizational struggle—years that were sometimes marked by management-labor discord, union confrontations, and even violence (Braverman, 1974; Brooks, 1964; Rayback, 1959). Clearly, at the very least, many workers did not identify with their companies. They were not emotionally connected to them.

Summing Up

Working people became quickly dissatisfied during the early history of U.S. corporate organizations. They blamed the depersonalization that seemed to result from layers of management, bureaucracy, and bigness.

The Rise of the Managerial Class

As the possibilities and complexities of organizations increased, a new class of worker was created to deal with individual employees directly and to facilitate the flow of information and production within organizational infrastructures. Management positions became quite popular with workers. They seemed to represent a new development in corporate structure capable of attracting talented people and improving the corporate image (Drucker, 1954; Roethlisberger, 1942). A person could hope to gain a good management job—and thus a good income—through hard work and talent. As McGill (1988) puts it, "The democratic character of the managerial profession was particularly appealing to America's new aspiring middle class. It meant that any man could be a manager" (p. 10). By the end of the 1950s, after experiencing a decade of formula planning through management by objectives (Drucker, 1954; Waring, 1992) as well as the discomforts that quickly accompanied being stuck in the middle—between executives and labor—the management role no longer looked quite as vital and promising as it originally had appeared (McGill, 1988; McGregor, 1965, 1972). Of greatest interest for our discussions here, however, is not the development of the management profession but the development of the managerial mind-sets first described by Douglas McGregor in 1960. In *The Human Side of Enterprise*, McGregor asserted that each manager had come to believe in one of two sets of assumptions about the average worker. Those managers who endorsed *Theory X* tended to believe that people naturally do not like to work and therefore need to be controlled, threatened, or otherwise coerced into being responsible workers. Theory X managers, he said, believed that most people are not very ambitious and prefer to be told what to do. In contrast, McGregor talked about *Theory Y* managers, those who believed that people can get committed to work they respect and for which they are rewarded. These managers thought that people embrace work as a natural part of life and that workers will seek and accept responsibility as well as use creative energies on behalf of the managers and companies who place them in positive situations. At this point, many managers ceased to rely exclusively on management by objective strategies, experimenting instead with more people-oriented strategies. Theory Y management seemed to promise a better situation for all—more productivity for the company, better conditions for the worker, and a more comfortable job description for the manager.

Yet what Theory Y promised never seemed to materialize (cf. "Managing to Learn," 1992; Ouchi, 1982). As quality management initiatives began to be developed here, many turned to Japanese management models (Durlbahji & Marks, 1993; Hayashi, 1988) in an effort to understand the management philosophy that undergirded Japanese corporate successes during the 1970s and 1980s. Writing in the early 1980s, Ouchi (1982) described *Theory Z* management. Within that model, the idea is to clearly articulate company philosophy in all parts of the organization by relying on collective decision making and involving the worker as primary expert. With the rise of interest in quality improvement management strategies, U.S. corporations began the process of trying to create quality through the use of teamwork and worker-as-expert models. In many ways, these two mechanisms, teamwork and individual-as-expert, did not fit together naturally within this culture.

Summing Up

The management role enhanced the attractiveness of corporate organizations. In studying management and what managers ought to do, people began to look at typical management attitudes toward workers. Some managers believe people are motivated by coercion. Others believe that rewards and respect are all that is necessary. As quality improvement models were shown to be successful in Japan, some began to believe that management models are best if they rely on teams and operate in terms of worker-as-expert.

U.S. Culture, the Organization, and Rugged Individualism

Widespread awareness of the consequences of emphasizing teamwork in the absence of due attention to the worker is just now beginning to emerge (Arnold & Plas, 1993; Fletcher, 1993; Ford, 1992; Manz & Sims, 1989). Even though teamwork approaches are gaining in popularity, it is becoming more clear that any approach to organizational structure or functioning in this country that does not place the individual at the center of value may be doomed to failure or mediocrity. Slighted workers are capable of creating fewer products of lesser quality or of sabotaging company goals—unconsciously if not outright. This is a country that may not always treat its individuals with respect and caring (Handlin & Handlin, 1989; Wilkinson, 1991), but it is a country that cannot function in the absence (at the least) of the *ideal* of the sacredness of the individual (Bellah, Madsen, Sullivan, Swidler, & Tipton, 1985; Handlin & Handlin, 1994). But just what is it that turns a simple respect for the individual into a cultural phenomenon known as individualism—this cultural priority of the individual within law, religion, economics, and social intercourse?

Earlier in our intellectual history, Emerson, writing in the mid-1800s, was among the first to understand the country's passionate tendency toward self-reliance and individual achievement. "Trust thyself," he wrote, "every heart vibrates to that iron string" (Emerson, 1983, p. 289). A hundred years later, Bellah and his associates (1985) talked with hundreds of people in all walks of life, resulting in their highly provocative work on individualism and commitment in the United States. They wrote:

> The idea we have of ourselves as individuals on our own, who earn everything we get, accept no handouts or gifts, and free ourselves from our families of origin turns out, ironically enough, to be one of the things that holds us together. (p. 62)

Like Tocqueville (1835/1969), who coined the term *individualism*, as well as others who have given the concept much thought (e.g.,

Kulka, 1981; Varenne, 1977), Bellah and his associates talk about the country's ringing endorsement of those who "make something of themselves," "pull themselves up by their bootstraps," and "become one's own man."

Here, the development of one's self, progress with the self, is one's most important product. "Be all that you can be" is more than just a successful military marketing slogan, it is a statement of every American citizen's most important life task (Moore, 1993; Peck, 1979). Tracing the history of this fundamental Western value from Aristotle through the full development of Judeo-Christian culture is not as important for this discussion as is an understanding of the role of individualism in mainstream thought during this century. The fact that individualism shows no real signs of disappearing in this country in the near or far future (Terkel, 1995; Wilkinson, 1991) is more important for U.S. businesses than is the earliest history of the phenomenon.

As the century turned, U.S. citizens were exhorted to get in touch with their entrepreneurial spirits, to realize that Horatio Alger was more than just a story with a happy ending. It was a story that reflected the reality of what was possible if you worked hard and developed all the talents God had given you. Today, citizens are not only exhorted to get in touch with their entrepreneurial possibilities, they are urged to get in touch with their feelings, to find out what they truly believe, value, and need in their lives to become mature citizens and to pursue the happiness that is each citizen's constitutional right (cf. Autry, 1994; Hillman, 1989). Although the focus has widened over time to include these inner achievements in addition to community and business achievements, the central cultural message has not been altered: *You are unique. You are obliged to develop and prize that uniqueness. You must make that uniqueness make a difference in both your personal life and your professional life.*

Bellah and his associates (1985) make a crucial point:

> We want to make it clear that we are not saying that the people to whom we talked have empty selves. Most of them are serious, engaged, deeply involved in the world. But insofar as they are limited to a language of radical individual autonomy, as many of them are, they cannot think

about themselves or others except as arbitrary centers of volition. (p. 81)

In a society where one anchors oneself as a center of volition, two cultural outcomes are inevitable. First, people will revere achievement more than simple existence because willing something is rarely related to the status quo; it is concerned with bringing something into being. Second, people think of the self as of primary importance because it is the source of the willing and thus the source of achievement. A well-developed, mature self is capable of willing that which is good for the further development of society and family as well as what is good for the further development of one's own personal life. The strong, unique *individual* becomes the cornerstone of a safe, growing, reasonable society (Arieli, 1964; Kulka, 1981; Merelman, 1984). One's job or career becomes the means for gaining the financial resources to fund the personal development project as well as for the expression of oneself in the world.

Summing Up

Although individuals have not always received the respect they desire in U.S. organizations, the ideal of the sacredness of the individual is nonetheless part of the firm foundation of the culture.

Dysfunctional Belief Systems

In our recent book, *The Human Touch*, describing a person-centered management transformation in a major medical center, Bill Arnold and I (1993) began identifying a list of corporate translations of firmly embedded cultural beliefs that have had a stranglehold for a good many years on most everyone's organizational imagination. Several of these are outgrowths of Theory X thinking; others have been related to autocratic thinking, as in the following example:

Cultural Belief	Corporate Translation
One rotten apple spoils the barrel.	When something goes wrong, find your troublemakers and weak thinkers and get rid of them or you'll end up wishing you had (p. 201).
The lead dog always has the best view.	People in unskilled labor positions can never grasp the bigger corporate picture (p. 99).
Certain kinds of people are a dime a dozen.	Don't invest a whole lot in people who have ordinary jobs. They're easily replaceable (p. 179).
The more power you've got, the harder you need to be to find.	If you're the boss, get your assistants to protect you and insulate you (p. 213).
Keep it quiet.	The one with the most secrets wins the game (p. 245).

It can be argued that a good many dysfunctional business beliefs such as these derive from a single source—our cultural attitudes toward the general untrustworthiness of the average worker. It is somewhat ironic that a culture that prizes the individual also tends to distrust that individual. Some have suggested (Hsu, 1983; Kulka, 1981) that this results because rugged individualism carried to its extreme encourages people to value overachievement, to revere those who excel and who have power. More typical citizens are given less respect. Others (Bellah et al., 1985; Wiebe, 1975) think depersonalization has resulted in a tendency to value the individual in the abstract while distrusting the individual who is the stranger. But whatever the source of this phenomenon, there has been a tendency during this century for managers, executives, and workers alike to uncritically assume that people won't produce quality work if you don't watch them, order them, tip them, control them, and make them prove they've earned their merit pay. If you want people to perform, you have to give them quotas, directives, rules, and a firmly identified chain of command (Arnold & Plas, 1993; McGregor, 1960, 1965). Only recently have we begun to suspect that it's the system that has made the average worker look bad and that the organization itself may have been its own worst enemy.

Toward the end of the 1980s, Christopher Mathews (1989), a former political speechwriter and senior congressional aide, wrote a book titled *Hardball: How Politics Is Played* in which he identifies the "rules of the game." Among them are the following: "It's better to receive than to give." "Leave no shot unanswered." "Keep your enemies in front of you." Mathews talked about "hardball" in terms of aggressive, Machiavellian politics. "It is the discipline of gaining and holding power," he wrote, "but practiced most openly and unashamedly in the world of public affairs. It is the only game for grown people to play" (p. 42). Although Mathews made some defensible points—such as the desirability of playing cleanly and out in the open—he nonetheless carried belief in the untrustworthiness of the average person to one of its logical conclusions: Most people are your enemies; most people are only out for personal gain. Politics, then, isn't so much about working *with* people as it is about power *over* people. Throughout the middle years of the 20th century, many uncritically assumed that corporate leaders and managers who thought in terms of teamwork and shared glory were pie-in-the-sky idealists, naive at best. These were people who didn't understand how things really are, people who simply weren't tough enough to play the game the only way it can be played if you want to be a winner.

Summing Up

When overwhelming value is placed on rugged individualism, status differentials can result in dysfunctional beliefs about the value and roles of people who are not in positions of power—and *teamwork* can start to sound like a "dirty" word.

THE METAPHORS OF WAR AND HARDBALL

Images of games, hardball, winning, and war that so often have been the metaphorical tools of choice for Mathews and many other writers, managers, and executives are another major source of current dysfunctional baggage in the organization. Metaphors for aggressive competition using analogies like "hardball" have been far more common within organizations than have been metaphors that rely on cooperation and growth analogies. The tendency to consider war an apt and useful analogy to business has been particularly common and destructively dysfunctional. Companies that specialize in this cultural concept think in terms of winning or losing battles on the way to winning the war. They want to be seen as armed and dangerous, too powerful to challenge. They tell their people to give no quarter, leave no shot unanswered, and take no prisoners. These are the company managers who believe their job is to kick butt and take names—and to the victor go the spoils.

But war terms reflect warlike thinking. Competition within and between companies that gets viewed from a bellicose perspective forces people into a bunker mentality. Workers are on the lookout for the enemy. Lethal tactics not only seem viable, they get used. Ruthlessness becomes the only sensible approach to business. Your bosses and coworkers can be your enemies just as the competition is assumed to be your enemy.

Surely a warlike mentality is the only viable frame of mind for those engaged in war. For those engaged in business, it is limiting, adversarial, and self-destructive more than other-destructive. When we go to war, we do so gravely, knowing that some of our combatants are going to lose their lives but believing that our cause is so just, so dear, that it is worth the highest price of all—somebody's life, maybe my own. When we make such a decision, we intend to commit all the resources we've got to one end—conquering our enemy.

But businesses no longer tend to focus so strongly on destroying an enemy (Block, 1993; Greenleaf, 1977; Williams & Williams, 1993). Increasingly, business is about producing a quality product within a quality atmosphere with the goal of obtaining repeat customers and gaining prosperity and well-being for the company's associates and value for the shareholders (Bass, 1985; Peters & Waterman, 1982;

Ritscher, 1992). Good business is about making it possible to produce an ever-increasing higher quality of life by creating higher-quality products that customers will find useful as well as work atmospheres that make it possible for employees to find meaning in what they do to earn their living. War is concerned with preservation of the present and past. Business is concerned with creating the future.

Winner-take-all, warlike mind-sets and a general attitude of mistrust toward the average worker were simply givens within the corporate cultures of the majority of our companies during the earlier parts of this century (Blum, 1972; McGregor, 1960; Roper, 1949). Even within corporate cultures that did not specialize in these dysfunctional ways of thinking, these metaphors and attitudes were nonetheless ubiquitous, having insidious and lasting effects on attitudes and behaviors. As a result, we easily began to assume that business really is more like war than it is like farming, biology, or any of the other growth metaphors. Today, it is difficult for teamwork philosophies and cooperation metaphors to thrive in environments that still rely on more mechanistic ways of thinking and the metaphors that are associated with them. In these environments, it also is difficult for individuals in nonstarring roles to be seen as equally valuable.

Summing Up

Hardball, winning, and war metaphors have contributed to corporate agendas during the past 70 years. That resulted in suspicious attitudes toward the instincts and capabilities—and even the morality—of average people.

Participatory Management

Participatory management (cf. McLagan & Nel, 1995), a fundamental component of most quality improvement models, has become a particularly attractive management strategy that has captured the imaginations of leaders of both big and small companies. The high-profile participatory management success stories of Jack Welch at GE (Tichy & Sherman, 1993), David Kearns at Xerox (Reder,

1995), and Paul Galvin at Motorola (Collins & Porras, 1994) have been impressive and highly touted. But of even greater importance have been the hundreds of less publicized success stories that demonstrate widespread validity for the new participatory management movement. Without so many hundreds of reports coming from so many different kinds of managers, we would be tempted to conclude that the new leadership strategies may most importantly depend on charisma or a cult of personality of some sort.

The origins of the employee involvement movement were somewhat different in different countries such as Japan (DeMente, 1981; Hayashi, 1988), Europe (Emery & Thorsrud, 1969; Trist, 1987), and the United States (Levine, 1995; Manz & Sims, 1993), but all of them occurred about the same time, from the 1920s through the 1950s. In this country, of interest was an idea developed by a psychologist, J. D. Houser (cf. Landy, 1989), who was studying employee morale. He suspected that if workers were asked how they felt about their jobs, the asking itself might result in greater employee satisfaction. Despite the intriguing nature of that suggestion, not many companies invested time or resources in participatory management models during the midpart of this century. The first major investment in this kind of management method occurred in the 1970s after the theoretical management work of W. Edwards Deming (Walton, 1986) in Japan sparked increased interest here at a time that such solid companies as AT&T and Texas Instruments were experimenting with quality of work life (QWL) management ideas. In the late 1970s, *quality circles* (Levine, 1995), a management method that had its roots in the impressive Japanese manufacturing successes, seemed to hold much promise for success here. In this model, employees, usually volunteers, met each week to discuss process as well as problem issues with the goal being the improvement of plant operations, quality, and morale. McGill (1988) reports that by 1982, over 40% of businesses with more than 500 employees were experimenting with quality circles. Recently, management historians such as Levine (1995) have credited the demise of interest in quality circles to the realization here that within the Japanese management model, quality circles were but a component. Successes there have been due more to an overall cultural perspective than isolated model components. Through the 1980s, it became apparent that employee involvement was just one part of a quality improvement method. A variety of companies of various sizes and missions began experimenting with what has become known as Total Quality Management, or TQM, a comprehensive management model based on process improvement, customer relations, statistical graphing, problem solving, brainstorming, the establishment of priorities, information sharing, and interdepartmental communication (Creech, 1994; Gitlow, 1995; Walton, 1986). A growing number of U.S. companies have begun to focus on the participatory management component of TQM while deemphasizing other components.

Consider Monte Peterson and recent experiences at Thermos. Mr. Peterson is a representative member of this growing group of participatory leaders. Arriving at beleaguered Thermos in 1990, he tackled a heavily bureaucratic culture head on, creating an infrastructure that is built on interdisciplinary teams (Dumaine, 1990). Peterson developed an approach to participatory management that builds teams around markets rather than functions. In a very successful bid to move into a new market, Peterson's Lifestyle team created an outdoor electric grill that provides barbecue taste without having to rely on charcoal or gas. The grill won several design awards and an impressive market share. The Lifestyle team did it by concentrating first and last on the customer—and in between on team cohesion, spirit, and energy. In an interesting participatory innovation, leadership of the team consistently rotated depending on which aspect of product design, development, manufacture, and marketing was most pressing at that time. Team members have reported that the most substantial rewards they received and prize are the ones that accrued because "the team owns the project from the beginning to the end, and that gives us a sense of pride" (Dumaine, 1992, p. 109). Putting the pride back into the process is clearly one of the most important goals, tools, *and* rewards of many of the most successful new leadership models.

A key element of the new human resources program at Allied-Signal (Stewart, 1992) requires bosses to provide remedial assistance for employee weaknesses. Manager and employee participate in the strengthening of an individual's skills. In this way, a company can share responsibility for weaknesses rather than relying on more traditional corporate responses that use blame and reduced rewards as the great motivators for improvement.

There have been many examples of participatory management success stories. As a result, countless leaders today echo the empowerment sentiments of Barbara Levy Kipper, chairman at Levy, who has said, "There can no longer be rigid hierarchy, nor isolation of leadership. The people closest to any given situation know how to handle it best. The more voices that are heard, the stronger the organization" (McFarland et al., 1994, p. 64). A growing number of executives and managers at all levels are coming to agree with the former president of the University of California, David Gardner, that "the essential task of leadership is empowerment, which moves an institution toward its vision by fostering an environment in which individual excellence can flourish" (McFarland, Senn, & Childress, 1994, p. 64). But are the theory and practice of participatory management so effective that only success stories result?

Summing Up

The successes of quality improvement models and other new U.S. leadership models have been strongly related to participatory management. Although quality improvement strategies and empowerment strategies have not been universally successful, U.S. leadership continues to experiment with these models and to look forward to eventual consistent results.

RECENT FAILURES

It is becoming almost impossible these days to find a senior leader in a corporate organization who does not endorse at least some aspects of participative management and TQM ideology such as empowerment, shared vision spinning, teamwork, and systems thinking. Most senior executives have taken a stab at this kind of reorganization and reculturing. But whether the attempts have been wholehearted or faint, complete or partial, lately the number of failures seems to have risen faster than the number of successes (Brown, Hitchcock, & Willard, 1994; Howe, Gaedert, & Howe, 1995).

An Ernst & Young and American Quality Foundation report (American Quality Foundation, 1992) leads to the conclusion that many managers are very dissatisfied with the new management programs. Nohria and Berkley (1994) at the Harvard Business School studied managers in more than 90 companies in the early 1990s and reported that 75% of them were unhappy with the results in their organizations.

Hammer and Champy (1993) are the designers of the transformative leadership program known as "reengineering." In the final chapter of their most comprehensive explanation of the approach, they have written:

> Sadly, we must report that despite the success stories described in previous chapters, many companies that begin reengineering don't succeed at it. They end their efforts precisely where they began, making no significant changes, achieving no major performance improvement, and fueling employee cynicism with yet another ineffective business improvement program. (p. 200)

Also disconcerting is the now common knowledge that a sizable percentage of the early reported successes deriving from a variety of new leadership strategies eventually failed—including the successes reported by many of the companies of excellence cited by Peters and Waterman (1982). Uniformly, these were either failures at the bottom line or failures of confidence in leadership—or both.

In 1989, after almost a decade of effort, Florida Power & Light became the first U.S. company to receive Japan's Deming prize for quality. This success was heralded as proof positive that quality improvement and participatory management strategies could be adapted successfully in complex U.S. organizations. But shortly after the award was conferred, FP&L's senior executive quality motivator retired to "chairman emeritus" status, reportedly because the chairman of the holding company had become deeply disenchanted with the cost of the TQM program. He quickly dismantled the TQM programs and departments (Main, 1991; Wood, 1991). FP&L now gets listed in the failure category on TQM tally sheets.

The first company to win the prestigious Malcolm Baldrige National Quality Award in the small business category, Wallace Company, almost doubled its market share but incurred greatly inflated costs as it did so (Ivey & Carey, 1991). Only 4 years after the award was given, Wallace went out of business. Although these two stories of TQM and participatory management failure are more dramatic than most, they reveal just how bad things can and have become when it comes to instituting new leadership strategies such as these within U.S. company cultures.

Why? Why doesn't something that most everyone says is so great produce lasting greatness within most companies? How can some other countries get these management strategies to pay off at the bottom line? Why can't U.S. companies consistently make it possible for participatory management strategies to create growth and well-being for the company and its employees? Estimating that 50% to 70% of the organizations that institute a reengineering program fail to get the results they want, Hammer and Champy (1993) quote Tartakower, the Russian chess master, who once gazed at a newly set-up board and said, "The mistakes are all there, waiting to be made" (p. 201). No doubt that is true. But how do we avoid making the mistake-laden moves?

DISAPPOINTING SOLUTIONS

Hammer and Champy's perspective on the causes and solutions of failures includes admonishments to be sure not to try to just fix but to change processes and to be sure not to settle for minor results. In other words, if you start over, be sure to do reengineering *right* the second time. These authors are not alone in this approach to failure. No matter what version of the new management paradigm is being used, when it fails, it is likely that many will call for a recommitment to the basics of the program. Depending on the perspective in force at the time, management will be asked to refocus on the bottom line (Rust, Zahorik, & Keiningham, 1994), middle management (Troy, 1994), service (Henkoff, 1994), the culture (Rohan, 1994), or the customer (Elias, 1991; Walker, 1990) if they want to overcome failures with the new strategies.

Jacob (1994) has pointed out that some consultants these days are rushing to corporate America as fix-it agents, "a new kind of ambulance chaser: consultants who specialize in turning around failed quality programs" (p. 66). Many of these agents have focused on standard issues such as communication and failures of senior leadership commitment. Lately, a growing number of these consultants blame cookie cutter approaches and claim that failing organizations have adopted programs developed elsewhere rather than tailoring a bit, getting into their own kind of new leadership style.

Although all these approaches to the fact of failure seem to represent a wide variety of different attitudes toward the problems, fundamentally they all share a common point of view: *If your company is running into failure with these new strategies, you didn't follow the "rules" carefully enough.* Proponents claim that the best solutions demand a recommitment to do things more thoroughly, to involve more people. Simply put, the company needs to do it *right* the next time. For most fix-it agents—whether internal or external to the company—that translates into simply doing more of the same, only better. But more of the same probably isn't going to work any better the second time than it did the first.

Summing Up

Many companies redouble their efforts after failures with a variety of participatory and quality improvement management programs. The problems may not result from incorrectly implemented methods. It may be that an important ingredient has been missing from the models.

Roots of the Person-Centered Leadership Model

One of the most promising solutions to the difficulties and failures associated with participatory management is person-centered leadership, which not only empowers workers but also puts the *individual worker* at the center of company attention. Although participation models focus on the individual as they recruit workers as experts, person-centered leadership goes much further. In person-centered companies, development of individual associates is as important for the company as is revenue. Management does not convene teams of empowered workers simply for the purpose of solving problems. Teams are also to offer the opportunity for personal skill development and personal satisfaction. Management is concerned with recognizing and supporting personal and family needs, developing personal well-being, and listening carefully to individual complaints. Management proceeds person by person.

Historically, this method has its earliest roots in work that emerged from Harvard's Human Relations and Business faculties in the 1920s and 1930s—especially the work of F. J. Roethlisberger (1942, 1968) and others (Roethlisberger & Dickson, 1966) in connection with the now-famous Hawthorne studies at Western Electric in which workers increased productivity in response to attention. Taking an even broader psychological approach, Bernard Bass (1960, 1965, 1981, 1985, 1990) has been the widely cited proponent of transformational leadership, a method that puts quite a bit of emphasis on the individual.

PERSON-CENTERED MANAGEMENT:
PSYCHOLOGICAL CONTRIBUTIONS

Bass has been a leading organizational psychologist for the past 30 years. From that perspective, he has taken a close look at what actually happens when supervisors attempt to communicate with employees who do not believe they are being listened to or respected. According to Bass, transactional leaders recognize employee needs and expectations and act on them in a way that inspires trust. They create reputations for reliability and credibility because, among other things, they put energy into meeting workers' needs. Although he has emphasized other organizational dynamics, over the years Bass's eye has never turned away from the individual within the organization. Implied within all his major writings has been the idea that it is the individual worker who makes or breaks managers, leaders, and companies.

Much earlier, in the early 1940s, popular theoretical psychologist Kurt Lewin (1935; Marrow, 1969) designed field research that formed the foundation for modern thinking about motivation. Lewin was asked to investigate a unique cultural phenomenon because of his work with motivational conflict. The government was interested in encouraging protein substitutes at home so that meat could be used for the war effort. In an attempt to understand why sweetbreads were not as popular as the government hoped they would be, Lewin and his associates began to interview and try to motivate people in groups. The work led to the understanding that group dynamics could influence decision making and also to a recognition that an individual—in this case, the housewife—could be referred to as a gatekeeper because an individual is often responsible for group choices. In another series of classic studies, Lewin and others (Lewin, Lippit, & White, 1939) identified three basic types of individuals as leader: autocratic, laissez-faire, and democratic. They concluded that democratic leaders were more likely to inspire participation and that job satisfaction was one of the important results of that participation. The implications of most of Lewin's work were not lost on organizational theoreticians, and by the 1950s most good business schools were referencing Lewin's work as they considered issues of motivation, productivity, and group effort. Although the emphasis was usually on the group dynamics portions of Lewin's work, for many the focus on the individual as gatekeeper and leader was also intriguing.

Later, applied psychologists such as Hackman and Lawler (1971) and Guzzo, Jette, and Katzell (1985) as well as others (Hammer, Landau, & Stern, 1981) began serious investigations of the effects of autonomy in work settings. Results clearly showed that the more autonomy certain workers are given, the greater the productivity and the greater the reported job satisfaction. In retrospect, we can see that the focus on autonomy was a focus on the individual. The method gave attention and support to the individual as expert and decision maker.

Emery and Trist (1969, 1972), social psychologists, produced carefully designed studies that revealed the outcomes associated with self-directed work teams. When the teams work well, these outcomes include individual satisfaction as well as increased group production. Other psychologists and organizational behavior theorists have contributed organizational theory and research related to important aspects of motivation such as cohesion (Mullen & Copper, 1994), self-determination (Klein, 1987), feelings (George & Brief, 1992; Plas & Hoover-Dempsey, 1988), self-appraisal and self-esteem (Brown &

Smart, 1991), pay (Lawler, 1978), and commitment (Hollenbeck, Williams, & Klein, 1989; Wright, Farnsworth, & McMahan, 1993).

Of perhaps equal significance has been the work of Carl Rogers (1961, 1977, 1983), psychologist and psychotherapist, who popularized a type of psychotherapy that became known as client-centered, or person-centered, therapy. One might reasonably ask why a particular kind of therapy should be called "person centered" because all one-on-one therapy is ostensibly oriented toward the life and well-being of a single person. Isn't all therapy person centered? Rogers's response to this question was that his methods were really quite different than others because the focus on the client is so intense and so thorough that the client moves the therapeutic dialogue in critical directions while the therapist affirms and clarifies as the movement proceeds (Rogers, 1961, 1986; Seeman, 1990). This principle is based on a very careful and well-articulated method of *listening* to the client. Thus, we can see that this therapeutic method is analogous to the worker-as-expert model within the organization literature. In fact, topics getting attention in some current psychology journals (Cain, 1990; Raskin, 1990) mirror contemporary concerns in leadership and management theory, in which many (e.g., Natiello, 1990; Patterson, 1990) are talking about the positive effects for the company when individuals are heard and given opportunities to create self-esteem through work.

The investigations of personality and motivation theorists (Evans, 1989; Maehr & Braskamp, 1986; Weary, Gleicher, & Marsh, 1993) and their influence on the self-help literature (e.g., Simon, 1993; Williams & Williams, 1993) have been an additional source of influence on leaders and managers. It is difficult to find a popular management book today that does not think in terms of motivational dynamics and the needs of individuals. In a recent book on leadership and psychology, Tjosvold and Tjosvold (1995) present an important list of psychological and organizational behavior studies that provide understanding of leader characteristics, employee commitment, cooperation and competition, decision making, the expression of feelings at work, and other issues of importance. Tjosvold and Tjosvold also point out, however, that some contemporary managers are ambivalent toward psychology. Many are intrigued by the subject and its possibilities for providing the manager with useful perspectives.

Others are concerned that psychological knowledge appears too tricky to be used widely by organizational personnel who have not been trained in such things as personality theory, conflict, and motivation dynamics.

But despite the concerns, many contemporary person-centered leaders such as those who are introduced in Part II are among those who are getting more comfortable with the idea that psychological perspectives need to be part of a good manager's toolkit. In this Information Age, they believe that organizations must learn much more about how human beings create, produce, and develop commitment.

Today, the person-centered leadership approach is being inspired and crafted in the workplace by corporate executives and managers who claim they owe allegiance to psychological perspectives as well as to modern leadership and management theoreticians such as Peters and Waterman (1982), Warren Bennis (1989; Bennis & Nanus, 1985), Peter Drucker (1954, 1992), Gareth Morgan (1986, 1993), Peter Senge (1991), James Autry (1994), and others. Also getting a fair share of the credit are the corporate doers such as Paul Galvin at Motorola (Collins & Porras, 1994), Fred Smith at Federal Express (Trunick, 1989), and Jack Welch at GE (Tichy & Sherman, 1993). Some say that those who have had the most influence on them were people like Max DePree (1992) and Rosenbluth (1992), who offered written theoretical contributions while running companies at the same time. Many of the most promising success stories are being told by person-centered leaders. But how does a person-centered leader differ from other kinds of new leaders, especially other kinds of participatory leaders?

Summing Up

Roots of the person-centered leadership movement can be found in the early management literature, psychological theory and research, participatory management models, the general culture, and companies run by current corporate leaders who have experimented with these methods.

Participatory Management and
Person-Centered Leadership:
Similarities and Differences

Person-centered leadership is a very specific form of participatory management that achieves organizational goals by making the employee the primary object of attention. The personal and professional development of the employee are as important as the development of revenue and profit. Person-centered managers get the job done by concentrating on one individual at a time. But as leadership and management has developed in this country during the past 20 years, the relationship among participatory management, quality improvement models, and the newly emerging person-centered models has not been clear. Are these three models really the same approach under different names? If not, what are the similarities and what are the differences?

WHAT'S THE NEW LEADERSHIP
REALLY ALL ABOUT?

Because person-centered leadership, participatory management, and total quality improvement models are considered part of the new leadership initiative, let us precede a discussion of differences by identifying those characteristics that have come to be associated with what is referred to by the term *new leadership* (Sims & Lorenzi, 1992). The new ways of organizational leadership are many, varied, as yet uncategorized, and often misunderstood. Although they're not truly "touchy-feely" as some critics would have it, they are at this point fuzzy. We know there are a lot of people in a variety of different positions doing *something,* but we're not always certain just what that something is. Yet enough time has passed that certain commonalities of approach can be identified and described.

Although it is difficult to find many redundancies across all models, one thing that can be said of *all* these approaches is that they are, indeed, *participatory,* many based on *empowerment* (Cotton, 1993). The leader-manager makes sure that those who actually do the work participate in the decision making. These are the real experts. This is leadership by consensus rather than dictum, management through seeking input rather than being complaint repellant. *Teamwork* (Dumaine, 1992) structures are critically important, and often the specific goal of participatory management is the successful implementation of *continuous quality improvement cycling* (Creech, 1994). No longer are corporations satisfied with quality assurance mechanisms that guarantee the consumer's defective purchase will be replaced. Now it is mandatory that quality is continuously improved upstream in the manufacturing and service delivery processes so that defective products cannot be produced. *Systems thinking* (Pasmore & Sherwood, 1978; Walton, 1986) is crucial for many of these models. Use statistics; graph the processes and cycles; when the failures occur, blame the system, not the individual.

Organization charts go topsy-turvy for these new leaders (Arnold & Plas, 1993). Some version of an inverted pyramid works best for many; others use concentric designs. But in all cases, the people on the front lines, average employees, are represented so that the chart shows that management works *for* those who actually get the products and services out.

Learning (Senge, 1991) is more than just back in style—many new organizational structures put the learning process at the core of their culture. Because it's no longer possible to keep functionally abreast of all the information explosions that make a difference to the company and the individual worker, associates get trained in maintaining commitments to lifelong education. New thinking creates new opportunities, and people at all levels of the company are encouraged to develop their *risk-taking* skills. These new leaders don't want an organization full of "yes-men"; they want people who know how to take smart risks based on an informed approach to problems. Fundamentally, as Benson (1993) points out, the intention supporting these

> initiatives in the U.S. is the revamping of the corporate culture. The reasoning goes something like this: "If we can just weave the quality *mindset* into the way we think about doing business (and into the minds of everyone within the organization), then quality *practices* will become a way of life." (p. 40)

In the process of changing people's minds about the company, its mission, and its products, many of the most successful participative leaders have begun to revolutionize even the way people think about themselves.

Often, people have talked about the new leadership in terms of what it is *not* because it has been relatively easy to see that these forms of leadership have moved away from mechanistic, bureaucratic, top-down organizational structures. Yet as the list above shows, more and more these approaches are gaining recognition as standing *for* something rather than simply as movements in reaction to something.

IDENTIFYING DIFFERENCES

Quality improvement management models are not redundant with participatory management. Most quality improvement models do encourage the use of participatory management through expectations that the worker will be considered the expert and will be given much decision-making power. However, it is becoming more and more common to find companies that are developing participatory management methods although they are not committed to TQM methods in general (Cotton, 1993; Levine, 1995). That is, these companies may not be particularly interested in using strategies geared toward statistical graphing, upstream improvement, priority targets, and the other components that we've come to associate with conventional quality improvement initiatives. Likewise, it also is relatively easy to find companies that are run by person-centered leaders who do not use what are commonly thought of as quality improvement methods. It is unlikely, however, that you'll find a person-centered company that is not committed to participatory management because a person-centered focus results in an empowerment focus— participation is critical. So, although each of these labels defines a form of what is being called the *new leadership* or *new management*, they are not simply different terms for the same thing. But because there are so many terms and buzzwords used in reference to these and other management styles these days, it is important to identify differences and similarities as carefully as possible. In Part II, we will discuss individual person-centered leaders in some detail. A clear grasp of this particular form of leadership perhaps can be best gained by observing the kinds of things that person-centered leaders do. At this point, however, the reader may find it helpful to further investigate differences and similarities by consulting Table 3.1.

Summing Up

Although there are important differences among them, there is a tendency for most new leadership models to rely on participation, teamwork, continuous quality improvement cycling, systems thinking, participation-based organization charts, learning commitments, risk taking, and deliberate culture change.

Summary

Many of those who have helped to create new ways of thinking and leading during the past 10 years have tremendous success stories to tell. These new leaders are very sure these ideas are now at center stage, ready to capture the imaginations of those who are going to create the next century. Others will tell you horror stories of how they tried some of the new ways, and crashed and burned. Those leaders insist that concepts of TQM, servant leadership, the learning organization, and the like are nothing more than flavors of the month. Which group will prove to be the better prognosticators? Why can some leaders make the new ways work whereas others only seem to use the new ways to make bigger messes?

In the following chapters, we'll explore some of the reasons for the failures. Chief among these have been the difficulties associated with trying to maintain the cultural primacy of the individual while moving toward teamwork (Chapter 4) and the need to create new cultural perspectives that can guide and keep pace with rapidly evolving technological and social changes (Chapter 5). As we will see in Parts II and III, person-centered leadership can be legitimately seen as a response to the failures. It is a model that uses teamwork methods that are very compatible with the dominant U.S. culture.

TABLE 3.1 Person-Centered Leadership, Total Quality Management, Participatory Management: Similarities and Differences

	Total Quality Management	Participatory Management	Person-Centered Leadership
Sources	Management theory Culture: Japanese Development within QI network	Management theory Culture: Japanese, U.S., European	Management theory Psychological theory Culture: U.S. Corporate leaders
Current Descriptors	Continuous improvement Upstream priorities Participatory management Statistical graphing Customer focus	Shared decision making Teamwork Tendency toward flat organization Worker-as-expert	Focus on individual Dual goal: employee and revenue Teamwork-individual methods Participatory management
Current Locations	Large and midsize corporations (especially manufacturing and medical) Canada, Europe, Japan, U.S.	Large, midsize, small organizations (service, manufacturing, many entrepreneurial) Canada, Europe, Japan, U.S.	Midsize, small, some large corporations (private, entrepreneurial of all types) U.S., some Canadian and European
Successes	Japan, some U.S., Canada, Europe Recent failures—U.S., Europe	Japan, Canada, Europe, U.S.	U.S., some Canada, Europe
Current Popularity	Holding in Japan (model currently undergoing change) Declining in Canada, Europe, U.S.	Holding in Japan Gaining in Canada, Europe, U.S.	Gaining in U.S., Canada

References

American Quality Foundation. (1992). *The international quality study—best practices report.* Cleveland, OH: Author.

Arieli, Y. (1964). *Individualism and nationalism in American ideology.* Cambridge, MA: Harvard University Press.

Arnold, W. W., & Plas, J. M. (1993). *The human touch.* New York: John Wiley.

Autry, J. A. (1994). *Life and work: A manager's search for meaning.* New York: Avon.

Bass, B. (1960). *Leadership, psychology, and organizational behavior.* New York: Harper & Row.

Bass, B. (1965). *Organizational psychology.* New York: Allyn & Bacon.

Bass, B. (1981). *People, work, and organizations.* New York: Allyn & Bacon.

Bass, B. (1985). *Leadership and performance beyond expectations.* New York: Free Press.

Bass, B. (1990). *Bass & Stogdill's handbook of leadership: Theory, research, and managerial applications.* New York: Free Press.

Bellah, R. N., Madsen, R., Sullivan, W., Swidler, A., & Tipton, S. (1985). *Habits of the heart: Individualism and commitment in American life.* New York: Harper & Row Perennial.

Bennis, W. (1989). *On becoming a leader* (paperback). Reading, MA: Addison-Wesley.

Bennis, W., & Nanus, B. (1985). *Leaders.* New York: Harper & Row.

Benson, T. E. (1993). A business strategy comes of age. *Industry Week, 242*(9), 40-44.

Berle, A. A. (1927). Management power and stockholders' property. *Harvard Business Review, 33,* 14-18.

Block, P. (1993). *Stewardship.* San Francisco: Berrett-Koehler.

Blum, A. A. (1972). *A history of the American labor movement.* Washington, DC: American Historical Association.

Braverman, H. (1974). *Labor and monopoly capitalism: The degradation of work in the twentieth century.* New York: Monthly Review Press.

Brody, D. (1971). *The American labor movement.* New York: Harper & Row.

Brooks, T. R. (1964). *Toil and trouble: A history of American labor.* New York: Delacorte.

Brown, J. D., & Smart, S. A. (1991). The self and social conduct: Linking self-representations to prosocial behavior. *Journal of Personality and Social Psychology, 60*(3), 368-375.

Brown, M., Hitchcock, D., & Willard, M. (1994). *Why TQM fails.* Burr Ridge, IL: Irwin.

Cain, D. J. (1990). Celebration, reflection, and renewal: 50 years of client-centered therapy and beyond. *Person-Centered Review, 5*(4), 357-363.

Chandler, A. D. (1977). *The visible hand: The managerial revolution in American business.* Boston: Harvard University Press.

Chandler, A. D., & Daems, H. (Eds.). (1980). *Managerial hierarchies: Comparative perspectives on the rise of the modern industrial enterprise.* Boston: Harvard University Press.

Collins, J. C., & Porras, J. (1994). *Built to last: Successful habits of visionary companies.* New York: Harper Business.

Cotton, J. L. (1993). *Employee involvement.* Newbury Park, CA: Sage.

Creech, B. (1994). *The five pillars of TQM.* New York: Dutton.

DeMente, B. (1981). *The Japanese way of doing business.* Englewood Cliffs, NJ: Prentice Hall.

DePree, M. (1992). *Leadership jazz.* New York: Dell.

Drucker, P. F. (1954). *The practice of management.* New York: Harper & Row.

Drucker, P. F. (1992). *Managing for the future.* New York: Plume.

Dubofsky, M. (1985). *Industrialism and the American worker* (2nd ed.). Arlington Heights, IL: H. Davidson.

Dumaine, B. (1990, May 7). Who needs a boss. *Fortune,* pp. 52-60.

Dumaine, B. (1992). Payoff from the new management. *Fortune, 128*(15), 103-109.

Durlbahji, S., & Marks, N. E. (1993). *Japanese business: Cultural perspectives.* Albany: State University of New York Press.

Elias, K. (1991). A client's view of real estate services. *Vital Speeches, 57*(7), 214-216.

Emerson, R. W. (1983). *Essays and lectures.* New York: Library of America.

Emery, F., & Thorsrud, E. (1969). *New designs for work organizations.* Oslo, Norway: Tannum.

Emery, F., & Trist, E. (1969). *Form and content in industrial democracy: Some experiences from Norway and other European countries.* London: Tavistock.

Emery, F., & Trist, E. (1972). *Towards a social ecology: Contextual appreciations of the future in the present.* London: Plenum.

Evans, P. (1989). *Motivation and emotion.* New York: Routledge.

Fletcher, J. L. (1993). *Patterns of high performance.* San Francisco: Berrett-Koehler.

Ford, M. E. (1992). *Motivating humans: Goals, emotions, and personal agency beliefs.* Newbury Park, CA: Sage.

George, J. M., & Brief, A. P. (1992). Feeling good—doing good: A conceptual analysis of the mood at work—organizational spontaneity relationship. *Psychological Bulletin, 112,* 310-329.

Gitlow, H. (1995). *TQM in action.* New York: Prentice Hall.

Goldberg, D. A. (1992). Scientific management at Joseph & Feiss. In D. Nelson (Ed.), *A mental revolution.* Columbus: Ohio State University Press.

Greenleaf, R. (1977). *Servant leadership: A journey into the nature of legitimate power and greatness.* Mahweh, NJ: Paulist Press.

Guzzo, R. A., Jette, R. D., & Katzell, R. A. (1985). The effects of psychologically based intervention programs on worker productivity: A meta-analysis. *Personnel Psychology, 38,* 275-291.

Hackman, J. R., & Lawler, E. E. (1971). Employee reactions to job characteristics. *Journal of Applied Psychology, 55* (Monograph), pp. 259-286.

Hammer, M., & Champy, J. (1993). *Reengineering the corporation.* New York: Harper Business.

Hammer, T., Landau, J. C., & Stern, R. N. (1981). Absenteeism when workers have a voice: The case of employee ownership. *Journal of Applied Psychology, 66,* 561-573.

Handlin, O., & Handlin, L. (1989). *Liberty in peril.* New York: HarperCollins.

Handlin, O., & Handlin, L. (1994). *Liberty and equality.* New York: HarperCollins.

Hayashi, S. (1988). *Culture and management in Japan.* Tokyo: University of Tokyo Press.

Henkoff, R. (1994). Service is everybody's business. *Fortune, 129*(13), 48-60.

Higgins, J. W. (1932). Fine arts in mass production. *Harvard Business Review, 38,* 33-38.

Hillman, J. (1989). *A blue fire.* New York: Harper Perennial.

Hollenbeck, J. R., Williams, C. R., & Klein, H. J. (1989). An empirical examination of the antecedents of commitment to difficult goals. *Journal of Applied Psychology, 74,* 18-23.

Howe, R. J., Gaedert, D., & Howe, M. A. (1995). *Quality on trial* (2nd ed.). New York: McGraw-Hill.

Hoxie, R. F. (1918). *Scientific management and labor.* New York: Holt.

Hsu, H. L. (1983). *Rugged individualism reconsidered*. Knoxville: University of Tennessee Press.

Huey, J. (1994). The new post-heroic leadership. *Fortune, 129*(4), 42-50.

Ivey, M., & Carey, J. (1991, October 21). The ecstasy and the agony. *Business Week*, p. 40.

Jacob, R. (1994). TQM: More than a dying fad? *Fortune, 128*(9), 66-72.

Klein, J. (1987). Employee stock ownership and employee attitudes: A test of three models. *Journal of Applied Psychology, 72*, 319-332.

Kulka, R. A. (1981). *The inner American: A self-portrait from 1957 to 1976*. New York: Basic Books.

Landy, F. J. (1989). The early years of I/O: J. D. Houser and J.D.I. *Industrial-Organizational Psychologist, 26*(2), 63-64.

Lawler, E. E. (1978). *Pay and organizational effectiveness: A psychological view*. New York: McGraw-Hill.

Levine, D. I. (1995). *Reinventing the workplace*. Washington, DC: Brookings Institution.

Lewin, K. (1935). *A dynamic theory of personality* (K. E. Zaner & D. K. Adams, Trans.). New York: McGraw-Hill.

Lewin, K., Lippit, R., & White, R. (1939). Patterns of aggressive behavior in experimentally created "social climates." *Journal of Social Psychology, 10*, 271-299.

Light, W. (1995). *Industrializing America*. Baltimore: Johns Hopkins University Press.

Maehr, M. L., & Braskamp, L. A. (1986). *The motivation factor: A theory of personal investment*. Lexington, MA: D. C. Heath.

Main, J. (1991). Quality fever at Florida Power. *Fortune, 126*(8), 65.

Managing to learn, learning to manage: Harvard Business Review 70th Anniversary. (1992). *Harvard Business Review, 70*(5), 127-150.

Manz, C. C., & Sims, H. P. (1989). *Superleadership*. New York: Prentice Hall.

Manz, C. C., & Sims, H. P. (1993). *Business without bosses*. New York: John Wiley.

Marrow, A. J. (1969). *The practical theorist: The life and work of Kurt Lewin*. New York: Basic Books.

Mathews, C. (1989). *Hardball: How politics is played*. New York: Summit.

McFarland, L., Senn, L., & Childress, J. (1994). *21st-century leadership*. Los Angeles: Leadership Press.

McGill, M. E. (1988). *American business and the quick fix*. New York: Holt.

McGregor, D. (1960). *The human side of enterprise*. New York: McGraw-Hill.

McGregor, D. (1965). *Leadership and motivation*. Boston: MIT Press.

McGregor, D. (1972). An uneasy look at performance appraisal. In *Harvard Business Review* (Ed.), *Manage people not personnel*. Cambridge, MA: Harvard University Press.

McLagan, P., & Nel, C. (1995). *The age of participation*. San Francisco: Berrett-Koehler.

Merelman, R. M. (1984). *Making something of ourselves: On culture and politics in the United States*. Berkeley: University of California Press.

Mintzberg, H. (1979). *The structuring of organizations*. New York: Prentice Hall.

Moore, T. (1993). *Care of the soul*. New York: HarperCollins.

Morgan, G. (1986). *Images of organization*. Newbury Park, CA: Sage.

Morgan, G. (1993). *Imaginization: The art of creative management*. Newbury Park, CA: Sage.

Mullen, B., & Copper, C. (1994). The relation between group cohesiveness and performance: An integration. *Psychological Bulletin, 115*, 210-227.

Natiello, P. (1990). The person-centered approach, collaborative power, and cultural transformation. *Person-Centered Review, 5*(3), 268-286.

72   THE FUNDAMENTALS, THE PAST, THE FUTURE

Nelson, D. (Ed.). (1992). *A mental revolution.* Columbus: Ohio State University Press.
Nohria, N., & Berkley, J. (1994, January-February). Whatever happened to the take-charge manager? *Harvard Business Review,* pp. 128-137.
Ouchi, W. (1982). *Theory Z: How American business can meet the Japanese challenge.* New York: Avon.
Pasmore, W. A., & Sherwood, J. J. (Eds.). (1978). *The comparative impacts of sociotechnical systems, job redesign, and survey feedback interventions.* La Jolla, CA: University Associates.
Patterson, C. H. (1990). On being client-centered. *Person-Centered Review, 5*(4), 425-431.
Peck, M. S. (1979). *The road less travelled.* New York: Simon & Schuster.
Peters, T., & Waterman, R. (1982). *In search of excellence.* New York: Harper & Row.
Plas, J. M., & Hoover-Dempsey, K. V. (1988). *Working up a storm: Anger, anxiety, joy, and tears on the job.* New York: Norton.
Raskin, N. J. (1990). The first 50 years and the next 10. *Person-Centered Review, 5*(4), 364-372.
Rayback, J. G. (1959). *A history of American labor.* New York: Macmillan.
Reder, A. (1995). *Business practices for socially responsible companies.* New York: Putnam.
Ritscher, J. (1992). *Achieving excellence: Creating high-performance, spirited organizations.* Brookline, MA: Peak Dynamics.
Roethlisberger, F. J. (1942). *Management and morale.* Cambridge, MA: Harvard University Press.
Roethlisberger, F. J. (1968). *Man-in-organization.* Cambridge, MA: Harvard University Press.
Roethlisberger, F. J., & Dickson, W. J. (1966). *Management and the worker.* Cambridge, MA: Harvard University Press.
Rogers, C. R. (1961). *On becoming a person.* Boston: Houghton Mifflin.
Rogers, C. R. (1977). *Carl Rogers on personal power: Inner strength and its revolutionary impact.* New York: Delacrote.
Rogers, C. R. (1983). *Freedom to learn in the 80s.* Columbus, OH: Merrill.
Rogers, C. R. (1986). Reflection of feelings. *Person-Centered Review, 1,* 375-377.
Rohan, T. M. (1994). Culture change wins the Baldridge. *Industry Week, 243*(1), 41-42.
Roper, E. (1949). The public looks at business. *Harvard Business Review, 44,* 54-59.
Rosenbluth, H. F. (1992). *The customer comes second.* New York: William Morrow.
Rust, R., Zahorik, A., & Keiningham, T. (1994). *Return on quality.* Chicago: Probus.
Seeman, J. (1990). Theory as autobiography: The development of Carl Rogers. *Person-Centered Review, 5*(4), 373-386.
Senge, P. (1991). *The fifth discipline: The art and practice of the learning organization.* New York: Doubleday.
Simon, J. L. (1993). *Good mood: The new psychology of overcoming depression.* LaSalle, IL: Open Court.
Sims, H. P., & Lorenzi, P. (1992). *The new leadership paradigm.* Newbury Park, CA: Sage.
Stead, W. E., & Stead, J. G. (1992). *Management for a small planet.* Newbury Park, CA: Sage.
Stewart, T. A. (1992). Allied-Signal's turnaround blitz. *Fortune, 127*(14), 72-76.
Taft, P. (1962). *Organized labor in American history.* New York: Harper & Row.
Terkel, S. (1995). *Coming of age: The story of our century by those who've lived it.* New York: New Press.
Thompson, J. D. (1967). *Organization in action.* New York: McGraw-Hill.

Tichy, N. M., & Sherman, S. (1993). *Control your destiny or someone else will: How Jack Welch is making General Electric the world's most competitive corporation.* New York: Doubleday.

Tjosvold, D., & Tjosvold, M. M. (1995). *Psychology for leaders.* New York: John Wiley.

Tocqueville, A. de. (1969). *Democracy in America* (G. Lawrence, Ed.; J. P. Mayer, Trans.). New York: Doubleday Anchor. (Original work published 1835)

Trist, E. (1987). *Organizational choice.* New York: Garland.

Troy, K. (1994). *Change management, an overview of current initiatives: A research report.* New York: Conference Board.

Trunick, P. (1989, December). Leadership and people distinguish Federal Express. *Training and Development,* pp. 19-22.

Varenne, H. (1977). *Americans together: Structured diversity in a midwestern town.* New York: Teachers College Press.

Walker, D. (1990). *Customer first: A strategy for quality service.* Brookfield, VT: Gower.

Walton, M. (1986). *The Deming management method.* New York: Dodd, Mead.

Waring, S. P. (1992). Peter Drucker, MBO, and the corporatist critique of scientific management. In D. Nelson (Ed.), *A mental revolution.* Columbus: Ohio State University Press.

Weary, G., Gleicher, F., & Marsh, K. L. (1993). *Control motivation and social cognition.* New York: Springer-Verlag.

Whitehead, A. N. (1933). The study of the past—its uses and its dangers. *Harvard Business Review, 37,* 23-28.

Wiebe, R. H. (1975). *The segmented society: An introduction to the meaning of America.* New York: Oxford University Press.

Wilkinson, R. (1991). *The pursuit of the American character.* New York: Harper & Row.

Williams, R., & Williams, V. (1993). *Anger kills.* New York: HarperCollins.

Wood, R. C. (1991, March 18). A hero without a company. *Forbes,* pp. 112-114.

Wright, P., Farnsworth, S., & McMahan, P. (1993). Productivity and extra-role behavior: The effects of goals and incentives on spontaneous helping. *Journal of Applied Psychology, 78,* 374-381.

4

Teamwork and Individualism

While visiting an electric company I've worked with, I joined an initial meeting of a newly formed executive team composed of four people—an engineer, personnel department head, software specialist, and finance officer. The meeting had been in progress for about an hour when I arrived just as one of them remarked, "It doesn't seem like we're getting anywhere here." The statement was greeted with shoulder shrugs and silence as another said, "I think we've all got a pretty legitimate way of looking at this thing, so why don't we just go our separate ways and research feasibility for what we think is best and then bring that back to the next meeting?" Each of the four murmured assent and the meeting was over before I'd even removed my coat. Sound familiar? Unfortunately, that kind of teamwork frustration is all too familiar to most people who have attempted to forge a workable team in today's organizational environments.

The Cultural Priority of the Individual

One of our most widely read and respected investigators of U.S. organizational leadership, Warren Bennis (1994), has written that leadership is based on the assumption that leaders are people who are able to express themselves fully. By this I mean that they know who they are, what their strengths and weaknesses are, and how to fully deploy their strengths and compensate for their weaknesses. They also know what they want, why they want it, and how to communicate what they want to others, in order to gain their cooperation and support. Finally, they know how to achieve their goals. The key to full self-expression is understanding one's self and the world, and the key to understanding is learning—from one's own life and experience. (p. 3)

Bennis (1994) has maintained that true leadership is redundant with self-expression, that here a person can only be a true leader if he or she is a true individualist. He reports that U.S. leaders from all walks of life whom he has studied

> agree that no leader sets out to be a leader per se, but rather to express himself freely and fully. That is, leaders have no interest in proving themselves, but an abiding interest in expressing themselves. The difference is crucial, for it's the difference between being driven, as too many people are today, and leading, as too few people do. (p. 5)

Smith and Peterson (1988) have a somewhat different but no less important perspective on this issue. They appreciate Gergen's (1973) argument that much social and psychological research doesn't reveal ultimate truths so much as it reveals cultural truths. In reviewing the research on leadership, they conclude that

> the search by researchers for the "essence" of leadership must be seen as part and parcel of the culture of the individualistic societies which until recently have comprised the advanced industrial nations of the world. . . . Our cultural heritage makes it easiest to think of leadership as something which a leader does to a follower. Our attention is focused upon the leader as actor, not upon the subordinate or follower, who is seen much more dimly. (Smith & Peterson, 1988, pp. 13-14)

When I first present this point of view to senior-level undergraduate students in leadership seminars, they inevitably look at me blankly before someone offers up a remark that sounds something like, "Well, of course we study the leader if we want to study leadership. I don't get what you're driving at." And that, of course, is the point. Like the air we breathe, our fundamental cultural assumptions are so very present and dominating that we can't see them. To study leadership, we have believed we needed to study an individual who has been identified as the leader. When we look for leadership within teams, we often can't find it.

As Katzenbach and Smith (1993a) put it, "The difference between teams that perform and other groups that don't is a subject to which most of us pay far too little attention. Part of the problem is that *team* is a word and concept so familiar to everyone" (p. 111). So, unless we put a lot of effort into it, in this culture we can't even conceive of the reality—or even possibility—of group leadership and group responsibility, action that emanates from the whole rather than a part designated as "head." The only model of successful group functioning we seem able to turn to in our culture has been the sports team.

Teamwork in the American Culture

Although teamwork is a value that most Americans report they endorse, it is a practice that few engage in or understand outside the structure of a sports team. Businesses are rushing toward the team concept in record numbers. After initiating a teamwork model, many have failed to achieve (Huddleston, 1995; Manz, 1992). The problem? Corporations have assumed that U.S. citizens know how to work smart within work teams—and they don't. To this point, this is not a culture that equips people to do that. We load our pervasive and basic individualist attitudes (Bellah, Madsen, Sullivan, Swidler, & Tipton, 1985; Wilkinson, 1988; Wolfe, 1991) onto the work team while scarcely aware that these attitudes and values even exist. Then we wonder what went wrong.

Stewart, an entrepreneurship theoretician, provides a classic example of the kind of assumptions that will sabotage a teamwork project if left unchecked. When writing about something he calls team entrepreneurship, Stewart (1989) says:

> Individual leadership is a crucial part of the entrepreneurial process. The followers in team entrepreneurship, however, do not themselves have to see the overall main chance. . . . Is team entrepreneurship also

conceivable with a group of nonprofessional, low-tech, low-level employees? . . . Developing team entrepreneurship in such unlikely settings is only possible with entrepreneurial leaders. Increasing the supply of such leaders can, therefore, be an important contribution by the wider corporation. (p. 16)

In this model, the team becomes just another body with a head. The majority of team members can be looked on as "nonprofessional" and "low level." Teams won't function well that way—at least not for long and especially in this individualist society of ours that purports to value all persons, not just the identified leaders. Real teamwork is about shared responsibility and action as well as shared decision making. Difference of position does not mean inequality of position.

Hammer and Champy (1993) are considerably more sensitive to the fundamentals of teamwork, but much of their thinking about teamwork is derived from current cultural assumptions. A pivotal part of their popular reengineering model involves people working in process groups.

Process team workers share joint responsibility with their team members for performing the whole process, not just a small piece of it. They not only use a broader range of skills from day to day, they have to be thinking of a far bigger picture. While not every member of the team will be doing exactly the same work—after all, they have different skills and abilities—the lines between them blur. Each team member will have at least a basic familiarity with all the steps in the process and is likely to perform several of them. Moreover, everything an individual does is imbued with an appreciation for the process as a whole. (p. 68)

What Hammer and Champy (1993) are describing here are the ideal results of good teamwork, but not the methods for achieving them. Like so many others, they overlook the need to give a great deal of attention to the *just exactly how* of moving to a teamwork model. When these writers talk elsewhere (p. 200) of the many failures of companies who have attempted reengineering, their suggestions for remediation don't necessarily include a close look at the nature of the teamwork skills that U.S. employees have been unable to bring to bear. Thus, it is likely that Hammer and Champy, and others, are not looking so much at the failure of their particular models in specific settings as they are observing what happens when companies turn toward team approaches without understanding that typical U.S. workers in this ruggedly individualist culture do not yet know how to work effectively in teams. Most have not yet learned how to share group responsibility and rewards while not sacrificing individual identity and other psychological needs.

Larson and LaFasto (1989), themselves a collaborative team of an academic and a corporate executive, are among those (cf. Galagan, 1986; Katzenbach & Smith, 1993a, 1993b; Schonberger, 1986) who have given U.S. corporate teamwork a fair amount of investigative and theoretical attention during the past decade. After studying team achievement in U.S. companies for a few years, they reported that

> we now find it difficult to identify any goal that the collective "we" would be incapable of achieving. . . . On the other hand, we seem to lack the essential ability to work together effectively to solve critical problems. In fact, the potential for collective problem-solving is so often unrealized and the promise of collective achievement so often unfulfilled that we exhibit what seems to be a developmental disability in the area of social competence. The potential is there. The realization of that potential too often is not. (p. 13)

Even when confronted with evidence of U.S. weaknesses in group efforts, many sometimes still remain incredulous. Aren't we a melting pot country founded by many different kinds of people working together? Aren't our teamwork abilities responsible for the popularity and success of things such as the Olympics and Little League?

Summing Up

Leaders and managers turning toward participatory management have assumed that workers know how to work smart within teams—and many don't. Real teamwork is characterized by shared responsibility, shared decision making, and differentiated actions.

SPORTS AND TEAM SUCCESS

The phenomenal success of sports teams at capturing the national imagination may be one of the major factors responsible for our inability to see just how unskilled in teamwork we Americans can sometimes be. Imagine for a moment that there were no sports teams of any kind in this country—no college games, no professional games, no pickup games at the local corner sandlot. Conjure the image of a sportsless country; then look around at what's left in our culture in an effort to find other areas of outstanding American teamwork. Chances are you won't find many. Outside the newer attempts at participative management found in many of today's corporate organizations and good musical groups, you're not likely in your mind's eye to see any easily identifiable areas of teamwork achievement. Although other countries such as Japan rely on teamwork for most important achievements (Hayashi, 1988; Kamatu, 1982; Ohmae, 1987), we only seem good at it when we're playing games. It is these successes with sports teams that give us the false assumption that we're team players at heart.

In an effort to understand why U.S. workers can't carry teamwork skills off the court and onto the assembly line, I recently became involved in a research project with some senior leadership majors at Vanderbilt University, some of them athletes, some of them sons and daughters of parents who own their own businesses. They looked for literature on the topic of the relationship of sports teamwork to work teamwork but found very little of any quality. (See Martin, 1993, for a discussion of these issues from a perspective that is not based on person-centered or related individualism perspectives and principles.) They asked questions of leaders and employees in a variety of corporations as well as collegiate players in a number of sports. Then we considered and interpreted the anecdotal data they received, looking for factors that might discriminate between work and sports team performance and attitudes. Throughout our discussions, it became clear, anecdote by anecdote, that the most important factor by far is that people can get recognized for individual achievement within a sports team but not within work teams as they are currently constructed in most U.S. corporations.

INDIVIDUAL RECOGNITION

At first glance, it may appear that a U.S. sports team is fundamentally a group of interdependent players most primarily invested in their collective achievements. But although collective achievement is the goal—that is, winning the contest—individual achievements are as important for getting the job done as are teamwork episodes. Teams give America's individualists a chance to star. In most sports, for example, there is instant crowd recognition for individual performance. A forward pops in a three-pointer and the fans erupt. A soccer player uses a header to make a difficult pass and half the stadium goes wild with joy. In fact, in most team sports, it is possible for star players to get crowd recognition just for walking on the field or court.

Recruiting mechanisms in most sports are designed to attract individuals, to attract stars. The coach is supposed to get these high school or college hotshots working together as a team. There is a dance going on here, a delicate balance between working together and producing your own outstanding best—outstanding in the certain sense of standing out, of deserving individual recognition. There is much, much room in U.S. team sports for recognition of the individual, which develops even further the rugged individualist's point of view and valuable assets. Yet it is also clear that individual players need the team—and they certainly know that. Without team success, there are diminished opportunities for personal achievement. But although many athletes report that they originally got into sports because of the high they felt when producing an outstanding personal performance, many also report that somewhere along the line, pride in team performance, pride in the group, overtook them and became, at times, almost equally important. It is probably true, however, that although many U.S. athletes have come to love sports because of the team feelings, a sizable number never catch that fever and remain invested most primarily in the rewards that come from individual performance. But this is not to identify this latter group as selfish—not at all. Rather, they represent the cultural norm here, the rugged individualist spirit that emanates from the idea that you, the individual, deserve praise for your achievements and efforts as well as blame when you mess up. Part of being mature, here, means stepping up to take responsibility for your mistakes as well as graciously accepting the accolades when they come your way.

In contrast, our anecdotal data and a critical reading of some of the newer management literature (Katzenbach & Smith, 1993b; Nanus, 1992) suggest that in many of the new corporate teamwork settings, possibilities for individual recognition may be very limited. At times, individual recognition can come after a project is completed and relative contributions are inevitably sorted out—because in this culture people just don't feel right if that kind of thing isn't done at some point. Many feel uncomfortable until they recognize the contributions of others, making it plain that they have no desire to take credit for someone else's work. Yet this kind of recognition, although valuable, is nonetheless a delayed recognition. The experience is far different than the sports experience in which individuals can be singled out for applause several times during a 2-hour match or several times during a 3-hour practice. Even on the neighborhood playground, in the absence of an audience, many of the emotional kicks—at least for males—come from getting those slaps on the behind, punches on the arm, and "attaboys" that inevitably follow a good hit, kick, catch, throw, dump, block, or rebound. Even a teamwork-oriented assist can get some personal recognition delivered to you. But this is certainly not so at work, where one of the unwritten rules of the culture has been that you don't dish out a lot of praise. In an effort to understand the reasons behind all this and in connection with a previous major research project of a few years ago (Plas & Hoover-Dempsey, 1989), I discovered that when our rugged individualist society goes to work, people adopt the attitude that one shouldn't expect any "attaboys" for just doing a good job. Doing a good job is not something special; it's what's expected of you. Furthermore, people are afraid to praise for fear of looking like they're toadying up, or perhaps admitting their own lack of skills, or manipulating you to get points that can be cashed in later (Plas & Hoover-Dempsey, 1989).

All of this emerges, of course, from the individualist spirit that urges us to rely on our own evaluations of our work, not those of others. Our culture encourages us at work to become independent of what others think and independent of the need for applause. No wonder so many U.S. citizens like sports so much! Here is a place where our successes and individualist urges can be rewarded out-right. In work environments, those very same cultural urges are present but have been very frustrated. In the past, traditional management often overlooked the typical individual's needs, and now companies are moving inexorably toward group models of achievement. In one teamwork setting—the sports arena—Americans are richly rewarded for the individualism our society so much prizes. In another teamwork setting—the work arena—we are expected to give up that individualist spirit our society so much prizes. This double bind may have a lot to do with why so many Americans have come to love working in teams in the sports world but are learning to despise it in the work world (Frey, 1993; Katzenbach & Smith, 1993a; Latane, Williams, & Harkins, 1979).

Summing Up

Sports teams provide recognition for the individual at the same time they provide opportunities to work together effectively. These experiences meet both individualist and communal needs.

ROLE DIFFERENTIATION

A second critical difference factor those seminar students and I discovered was that, whatever the sport, teams have very clearly identified roles. Good sports teams are quite well structured. Each player knows what his or her job is, what the jobs of others are, and how all roles fit together in a way that gets the goals met. Working within different sports, a point guard and a tailback may not have much in common, but what they do share is a very clear set of expectations that they and their teammates will agree on how they're going to fit into the overall team strategy for getting the ball where the team wants it to be. No adolescent boy or girl walks into a high school locker room ready to suit up to play his or her team sport of choice without already knowing—sometimes in a rather sophisticated way—just exactly what moves are going to be expected given the position they've earned the right to play. But this is not so in the corporate world today. Most people armed with intelligence, enthusiasm, energy, and an M.B.A. walk into a new job and onto a work team with little idea of relative roles beyond a sense that each is supposed to produce a performance worthy of a star forward at the same time everyone is somehow expected to work together.

This lack of information about how to differentiate work team roles is an issue that cannot be taken too seriously. If you don't know that your job is to guard, you're quite naturally going to start trying to shoot baskets as often as possible. If you've got several people trying to perform the same task, you don't have a team, you have five individualists who haven't been trained in what teamwork must be all about—differentiation of roles and responsibilities. This is a valid and reliable fact about teamwork whether you're talking about an individualist or interdependent country and culture.

The issue of whether an individual actually needs the team came up in a sizable percentage of anecdotal responses to the teamwork questions those seminar students asked. Almost without exception, players said they definitely needed the sports team while workers said they didn't really see the need for the work team. The players couldn't even conceive of operating without the rest of the group. Many of the workers thought they could probably do a better job with less effort in quicker time if they were permitted to get the job done by themselves. After all, many Americans have always loathed committees. What is the differentiating factor? Team structure. On a sports team, the players know they've got to have their teammates functioning according to plan in the roles they've been assigned or they are definitely not going home with the win. In fact, as one young man put it, "If the quarterback doesn't have the guys producing pass protection who are supposed to be doing that, he's probably not going home at all!" In America's current work teams, with everybody assuming their job is to be a star, individuals quite naturally assume that if the others don't show up, there will still be somebody there to get the job done. In fact, we're often encouraged to believe that as individuals we can probably do it all. When everybody thinks they have roughly the same starring role, and could do all jobs if necessary, why would a team be needed?

This holds true even when the team is composed of a variety of people such as the engineer, finance person, computer specialist, and department head that were attempting to form the electric company team I recently visited. Each knew that his or her skills were different than those of the others. But just exactly who was supposed to decide what the group should work on first, who should contact the supply department, and so on, were not at all clear. The group members realized that they had no "leader," and that therefore the group was going to have to struggle toward a decision about the most basic of issues such as what their goals and agenda ought to be. The initial discussion was a classic example of what's going wrong in teams these days. All team members assumed—from their cultural individualist orientations—that each had the same role at that moment. Each was supposed to argue as cogently as possible for his or her point of view about what ought to be the group's goals and methods. Without question, each member believed that the best way to serve the team was to give it the benefit of his or her best thinking and persuasive powers. There were four would-be stars in that room. A fair amount of competition eventually began to grow beneath the surface of the dialogue. An even larger amount of frustration crept closer to the surface of the exchange.

Like many novice teamworkers, each of these bright and good-willed people assumed that process tasks should remain the responsibility of all members of the team and that the idea was to give your own ideas their best possible advantage before turning toward working with the ideas of colleagues. Eventually, a couple of them could see the need to differentiate some responsibilities along the lines of skill and expertise, but the idea of *differentiating group process responsibilities* never occurred to them. It seems that only when teams work together long enough for the possibility of role differentiation to occur does team success become a true possibility. How much more efficient might it be if there was a shortcut method of gaining the role differentiation that is so crucially needed for effective team functioning?

With the advent of so much insistence on a corporate team approach these days, colleges and universities, like high schools, have fallen in step to some extent, using task-oriented teams as part of instructional strategies. Students are often asked to "get in groups" to discuss an issue, problem solve, or produce a term project of some sort. Almost uniformly, students seem to find these experiences as disagreeable as do their parents who are struggling with work teams in their work environments. In these academic team exercises, the same problems prevail. People want recognition for individual achievements. They don't know how to get or give that. No role differentiations are provided. Everyone assumes that individual successes will definitely be measured, and each further assumes that individual success will get measured in terms of whether or not he or she can produce a star performance. Competition emerges. Social loafing (Kerr & Bruun, 1983; Williams & Karau, 1991) also emerges at times as somebody decides to rest while the others work. Things slip through the cracks because nobody assumed responsibility for certain critical parts of the project. Blame starts to fly around the group, though often indirectly. Most end up feeling disgruntled at best, angry at worst. The professors in these situations are like overloaded corporate department heads everywhere. Even if they have some understanding of teamwork skills, they invariably do not believe they have the responsibility or time to teach team skills as well as political science, French, finance, or whatever. And the product of these team efforts? Typically, it's inferior—the same as is often the case in the corporate world. Too often, this is what happens these days as companies turn toward the team as the possible solution to myriad quality and market position difficulties.

Summing Up

One of the keys to working well within teams is learning how to differentiate roles—process roles as well as task roles. Successful teams—no matter where you find them—are made up of individuals who know how to define roles for themselves and how to work with the roles that other team members have adopted.

Summary

While elementary schools are increasing efforts aimed at trying to teach children how to work well in teams (called *cooperative learning;* see Lefrancois, 1994), most adults are simply not exposed to this kind of training today. *The main reason people can't function well in work teams has been a disregard in business for the psychological needs of people (at all levels of the organization) who have grown up expecting themselves to succeed as individuals.* There is still much for us to learn about rewarding individuals within teams as well as training for role differentiation. But even though we may not know how to use them, teams can be a fundamental, valuable part of organizational life. Pressure is building for cultural change. One student who participated in my anecdotal study, who is also a student athlete, put it this way: "Americans just don't know yet that sports and work are no different from life. Looking out for number one really means looking out for the team. It can't be any other way."

References

Bellah, R. N., Madsen, R., Sullivan, W., Swidler, A., & Tipton, S. (1985). *Habits of the heart: Individualism and commitment in American life.* New York: Harper & Row Perennial.

Bennis, W. (1994). *On becoming a leader.* Reading, MA: Addison-Wesley.

Frey, R. (1993, September-October). Empowerment or else. *Harvard Business Review,* pp. 80-88.

Galagan, P. (1986). Work teams that work. *Training and Development Journal, 40,* 35-36.

Gergen, K. J. (1973). Social psychology as history. *Journal of Personality and Social Psychology, 26,* 309-320.

Hammer, M., & Champy, J. (1993). *Reengineering the corporation.* New York: Harper Business.

Hayashi, S. (1988). *Culture and management in Japan.* Tokyo: University of Tokyo Press.

Huddleston, K. (1995). *Back on the quality track.* New York: American Management Association.

Kamatu, S. (1982). *Japan in the fast lane.* New York: Pantheon.

Katzenbach, J. R., & Smith, D. K. (1993a, March-April). The discipline of teams. *Harvard Business Review,* pp. 110-120.

Katzenbach, J. R., & Smith, D. K. (1993b). *The wisdom of teams: Creating the high-performance organization.* Boston: Harvard Business School Press.

Kerr, N., & Bruun, S. (1983). Dispensability of member effort and group motivation losses: Free-rider effects. *Journal of Personality and Social Psychology, 44*, 78-94.

Larson, C. E., & LaFasto, F. M. (1989). *Teamwork: What must go right/What can go wrong.* Newbury Park, CA: Sage.

Latane, B., Williams, K., & Harkins, S. (1979). Many hands make light the work: The causes and consequences of social loafing. *Journal of Personality and Social Psychology, 32*, 822-832.

Lefrancois, G. R. (1994). *Psychology for teaching* (8th ed.). Belmont, CA: Wadsworth.

Manz, C. C. (1992). Self-leading work teams: Moving beyond self-management myths. *Human Relations, 45*(11), 1119-1140.

Martin, D. (1993). *Teamthink.* New York: Plume.

Nanus, B. (1992). *Visionary leadership.* San Francisco: Jossey-Bass.

Ohmae, K. (1987). How Japanese managers manage. In A. A. Thompson, Jr., A. J. Strickland, & W. E. Fulmer (Eds.), *Readings in strategic management* (2nd ed.). Plano, TX: EDS Business Publications.

Plas, J. M., & Hoover-Dempsey, K. V. (1989). *Working up a storm: Anger, anxiety, joy, and tears on the job.* New York: Norton.

Schonberger, R. J. (1986). *World class manufacturing.* New York: Free Press.

Smith, P. B., & Peterson, M. F. (1988). *Leadership, organizations, and culture.* Newbury Park, CA: Sage.

Stewart, A. (1989). *Team entrepreneurship.* Newbury Park, CA: Sage.

Wilkinson, R. (1988). *The pursuit of the American character.* New York: Harper & Row.

Williams, K. D., & Karau, S. J. (1991). Social loafing and social compensation: The effects of expectations of co-worker performance. *Journal of Personality and Social Psychology, 61*, 570-581.

Wolfe, A. (Ed.). (1991). *America at century's end.* Berkeley: University of California Press.

5

The Changing Culture

The Context for Business

When Mary Atwater went to work last Wednesday in Philadelphia's Center City, all she had to do was leave her kitchen and walk into the spare bedroom, a room that's been converted into a mostly full-time office. But Mary doesn't work at home because she works for herself. Actually, she's a salaried employee of an insurance underwriting company that has moved toward making it possible for some of their people to work full time from PC stations in their homes. On that particular morning, the first request from corporate headquarters had to do with company expenses related to birth weight, hospital days in treatment, and support services for premature infants. Mary produced some spreadsheets that revealed how many infants born to insured customers during the past 3 years had been placed in critical care immediately following birth. She inspected payout ranges for such expenditures as the purchase and use of life support equipment and medicines. She even found good statistics related to the number of hours of auxiliary nursing services that the company had partially supported. By 11 a.m., Mary had sent headquarters some very up-to-date statistics on what the company might consider current usual, customary, and reasonable expenses for premature infants of birth weight 33 ounces or greater. As she headed back to her kitchen for a midmorning cup of coffee, she muttered aloud that she hoped the individual child of concern to the company that morning had not been born below that weight. For if that were the case, the company's leadership was going to have to fly blind, making very difficult decisions without the guiding benefit of even company history, much less company policy.

The complex possibilities and demands of 20th-century life have grown, changed, and grown again with such speed that something important and unexpected has shifted within the very processes that govern human development itself. Many of our cultural attitudes and assumptions haven't been able to change as fast as the demands and possibilities—leaving us without a set of well-developed values capable of guiding our choices and actions within the new situations in which we find ourselves. One of the biggest victims of this situation has been organizational leadership. Some of our cultural beliefs and mores, and many of the leadership philosophies and strategies that have been available to 20th-century CEOs and entrepreneurs, have been far too inadequate given the kind of organizations these people have been expected to lead.

This century birthed the first generation of workers on planet Earth whose jobs were functionally obsolete by the time they hit midcareer. But even worse, the generation that takes over at the turn of the century, well before turning 35 years old, is going to find that not only the jobs but even the careers they've trained for have been so transformed as to be unrecognizable (cf. Kotter, 1995; Rifkin, 1995). *Imagine how dysfunctional it could be to assume that the cultural philosophies on which we base our actions will change automatically and with as much speed as do our job descriptions.* It would be dangerous to continue to assume that important cultural assumptions always and inevitably will change as needed, right on cue, immediately prior to a shift in action demands. Although that has been largely true in the past, life has moved off the trail and into the fast lane, which makes it very difficult for so many of our older cultural values and attitudes to catch up.

Culture refers to the identifiable set of assumptions, social habits, and behavior traits that characterize a given group of people. To make sense of this discussion, it's important to clearly define what is meant by the term *cultural assumptions*. Simply put, we're talking about beliefs about the "way things really are"—attitudes that are the foundation for action. We're talking about our group philosophy of life.

Culture is very much related to action. Our customary actions— such as wearing the expected and accepted kind of clothing—derive from a set of assumptions about what life is and how it ought to be lived. For example, what typical women in Tehran and St. Louis wear outside the home is almost completely dictated by cultural assumptions, by the groups' philosophies about the nature of women and their roles in the world. What people of both genders take with them on a managerial job interview is very limited because of the strength of cultural mores. Briefcases and notepads are expected and accepted; children, photo albums, and popcorn are not.

It is quite impossible to overstate the importance of our cultural assumptions about our behavior (cf. Johnson, 1985; Naisbitt, 1982). It's as fundamental as the fact that human beings need oxygen on a continuous and reliable basis. Bertrand Russell (1945) says it well as he talks about "philosophy as an integral part of social and political life: not as the isolated speculations of remarkable individuals, but as both an effect and a cause of the character of the various communities" (p. ix) in which we find ourselves. We do what we believe just as we are what we eat.

Summing Up

Cultural attitudes and values guide our actions. In the past, our cultural assumptions have changed slowly. Now, however, the demands and possibilities of life are changing very rapidly—in some important cases, much more rapidly than have the cultural attitudes that are needed to guide choices and behaviors.

EVOLUTIONARY CULTURAL CHANGE

Social scientists who study attitude development (e.g., Allport, 1935; Cole & Scribner, 1974; Koch & Leary, 1985; Lindsey & Aronson, 1985) have shown that although the processes of cultural attitude development and change are in some ways easy to understand and in other ways more difficult, it nonetheless has been clear that up until this point these processes have been time dependent. As people live their lives, they encounter novel situations. Based on these new experiences and their emerging adaptations to them, they form hypotheses about what the world is like, who they are, and how they ought to behave. Then they draw on their churches, institutions, and neighbors for models, support, and discussion of these attitudes. They take the revised assumptions back into their life experiences, refine them as before, and generally tend to drop the newer cultural attitudes from conscious awareness after a time. But even though they are not consciously aware of it, these attitudes guide their actions. Consider the example of money-lending, a practice that was considered immoral just a few centuries ago. Boorstin (1974) shows us that, in this country, attitudes toward the morality and value of money-lending changed rather radically but somewhat slowly, along with land development changes and the development of the automobile and early gasoline credit cards. Boorstin has demonstrated that by 1930 our attitudes toward the borrowing and lending of money were almost completely reversed from what they had been a century and a half before. *But that radical change took time.* It took many decades for us to experience the demands of a changing world in such a way that we challenged our previous assumptions about the morality of borrowing money. Many people experienced a great deal of chagrin and discomfort during the change process. But now we're experiencing what happens when life's demands and opportunities change so quickly that important cultural attitudes must change just as quickly—within years rather than decades, months rather than years—and sometimes within days.

CULTURE IN TRANSITION: AN EXAMPLE

We are the first generation faced with the incredible—and some might say impossible—task of having to intentionally create a set of cultural assumptions that can guide the new options that have quickly become available to us. Recently, while studying leadership in a large hospital, I dropped by the executive offices on a morning when chaos seemed to be at work and in control. The issue? A premature baby weighing less than 18 ounces had just been birthed and showed signs of being viable. The people in acute infant care were doing everything they could to keep the newborn alive but they needed special equipment and special expertise—lots of it. Much of what they needed could arrive within a matter of hours. Everybody was scrambling. The executive staff was being called on continuously to authorize and expedite vital purchases and personnel hours. Within a single hour, the cost of saving that tiny little life was projected to be well over $500,000 and many believed the figure would actually double or triple. The insurance carriers were contacted. Initial ruling? These were not usual, customary, and reasonable expenses. The contract carried maximums on several necessary categories of expense; no doubt, there would be severely restricted payouts.

Under the circumstances, a few doctors and nurses were volunteering their time. Several staff people did not volunteer but asked for pay—people for whom this would be a regular assignment for several days, staff members whose families seriously needed their regular paychecks plus overtime. The hospital did not have a large enough auxiliary nursing budget to handle this. There would be no temporary nursing services available for other acute operations for months if this one case used up all the monies now. The hospital's yearly capital-expenditure budget for life support equipment of any kind was, in total, not a great deal more than what the technologically advanced equipment for this single baby's life was going to cost. "What about the new technologies needed in acute cardiac care and the ER?" people wondered. What about those lives?

The parents, typical middle-class Americans, could themselves produce out of pocket and through borrowing power around $50,000. But that was only enough to keep their baby breathing for her first few hours of life.

Everyone involved with this tiny creature—whose fingers were not much bigger than a pencil point—believed that it might be very possible to keep her here, in life. But by the end of the first 2 days, it had become apparent that the total bill to pull that off was going to run well over a million dollars. Obviously, the parents couldn't pay that bill. The hospital, doctors, nurses, equipment suppliers, and computer and medicines suppliers couldn't pay it either. The insurance carrier, a modest-size company, had the money but didn't have enough of it to cover the birth of more than one such child and couldn't risk setting this kind of precedent without risking the business itself and the retirement funds of its investors. So, who should pay the bill? Should equipment be ordered that would ultimately never be paid for—despite any serious adverse consequences to the businesses of these suppliers? Should services be secured for which there would ultimately be no payment? When orders were placed, should the hospital risk delivery of the lifesaving equipment by telling the truth—that the supplier might not get paid? The list of heartbreaking issues went on and on. But the most important question was this: *What are the cultural values that ought to guide all the important decisions here?* Where can we find a set of agreed-on beliefs that are strong enough to get us successfully through this uncharted territory? The real and frightening truth is that the assumptions that guided that moment in the lives of all those people—and all the organizations that were touched—had to be created on the spot, the same as did the processes that saved the life (cf. Associated Press, 1995; Kolata, 1994).

Summing Up

This is the first generation in history that has found itself in the position of having to create—*intentionally*—sets of cultural attitudes and beliefs that can guide the new options that so quickly become available to us.

DELIBERATE CULTURAL CHANGE

Throughout recorded history, there have been people who have ruminated over the cultural beliefs handed down by previous generations. They have mused, commented, searched for the origins of those ideas, and pointed toward the emergence of newer beliefs that seemed destined to overshadow the old. Within Western history, the people of the ancient Greek city-states were probably the first to introduce the idea that this cultural speculation didn't have to be a game played only by formal philosophers (Durant, 1926). It could be fun for everybody, no matter what the occupation. Perhaps it was even a civic *duty* for all. Today, some 2,400 years later, we are bombarded from every source by the speculations of the average citizen concerning the cultural assumptions of our country and its people. The front pages of most newspapers consistently report the latest statistics that let us know what Americans think is the absolutely right way to think—whether the subject is sex, busing, or business ethics. This kind of phenomenon can make a contribution to the development of popular culture. Through media and now Internet contact, new cultural attitudes can be more quickly developed. They quickly begin to fill the void resulting from the fact that our ancestors couldn't pass down guiding attitudes about those things that weren't even an imagined possibility in their day.

So, while we watch what we do in this country, we're every bit as interested in watching what we think and say (cf. Robertson, 1980; Susman, 1984). Even Americans who don't seem directly interested in connecting attitudes with actions seem intuitively to know that there's a lot of power in our attitudes and that we need to give those attitudes a lot of attention. The other day on the Internet, I caught a bulletin board message from a man in Oklahoma who said, "Americans believe in the right to free speech—as long as it doesn't threaten their wallets." An eventual response from Des Moines said, "Not so, brother. Americans believe in the right to free speech even if it means letting somebody murder somebody. We're (most of us) going to let the people have their say and their vote rather than go on out and shut the damn things down." Speculation on the cultural philosophies that guide our actions has become so ubiquitous that most of the time we hardly realize we and others are doing it. Like Mr. Oklahoma and Mr. Des Moines, we're too busy using this speculation to make some sense out of the latest happening or some kind of point about something that matters to us.

The American pastime surely isn't baseball anymore. But the new American pastime may be playing the game of identifying the attitudes on which our neighbors ought to hang their actions. In fact, the currently most popular daytime talk show moderator, Oprah Winfrey, has risen to stardom because she's turned her talents to the service of revealing the typical assumptions that underlie the behaviors of our neighbors. On another recent daytime talk show, guests and audience almost feverishly pitched into a discussion of what attitudes ought to control the behavior of men who are married to one woman but fall in love with another. Other such shows recently got their guests and audiences deeply involved in naming those attitudes that ought to guide behavior when it comes to telling your boss what you really think about him or her and what your responsibility is when you find out your economically disadvantaged parents have a terminal illness—and all this before interactive television is even off the drawing board and into reality.

For the first time in the history of thought, we've come to a time when the rules of cultural change seem to have changed. Social and even religious philosophies are no longer a given for many individuals. The attitudes that are supposed to guide our actions seem all too often to be in a state of flux. A typical complaint of the average thoughtful American often sounds something like, "I don't even know how to *think* about this problem." Whenever you hear versions of that lament, it's likely that the speakers aren't talking about skills or abilities so much as they're talking about the values involved. Boorstin (1974) writes about the change in cultural assumptions by talking about "little-noticed revolutions . . . in homes and farms and factories and schools and stores, across the landscape and in the air—so little noticed because they came so swiftly, because they touched Americans everywhere and every day" (p. ix).

So many of our important experiences and actions are so new, so fresh, so different as to challenge current assumptions about life in the most profound of ways. Every day, we are faced with new demands and corresponding new actions that are guided by old attitudes because it all moves so fast that few have the time to do what it takes to create some new assumptions. We can't bear the burden of this kind of cultural crisis indefinitely. The solution involves—for the first time in Western history—the *deliberate* creation of cultural philosophy that can accommodate and guide the equally deliberate creation of new technologies, new skills, new sciences, and new discoveries. And because we know we can't count on the future to remain the same, we have to commit our philosophical energies to the near term. As astounding as that sounds, the new demands on organizational leaders nonetheless simply require no less. Fortunately, as we will see in Part II, we are witnessing the growth of a new set of leaders who intuitively have realized this need and have set about the task of creating cultural attitudes to fill the voids.

Summing Up

The rise in importance of the popular culture may well have much to do with the rapid change in social and technological possibilities. Rapid development of these things has prevented taking time for the slow, comprehensive cultural attitude changes that have been characteristic of past human cultural developments. The national pastime seems to have become the game of cultural speculation—discussion of the philosophies, attitudes, and values that ought to guide behaviors.

The New Culture Creators

Many of the observations about U.S. culture originally made by Alexis de Tocqueville (1835/1969) were accepted—both critically and uncritically. That has been true from the moment they were first published well before the Civil War to right up to yesterday. And incredibly, if we were to have considered him yesterday, Tocqueville could still have sounded right about us. Writing over 140 years ago, his keen powers of social observation led him to understand the basics about the rugged individualism he found here, the industrialization, and the character of the American community and people. Tomorrow, however, Tocqueville will only be right about us if the new leaders who are shaping our new cultural attitudes decide to make him so. But make no mistake about it, those new leaders who are going to make the most cultural impact are not government leaders. They are corporate leaders. These are the leaders who are in the position of having to make those hundreds of daily decisions that change the course of our culture. They are the ones who in record numbers have become fed up with the old ways of doing business here and have begun to create leadership models that are capable of replacing the old, inefficient, and painful top-down, kick-ass, take-names approach to organizational management.

Those who haven't been paying close attention to the corporation during the past 10 years have missed seeing it become the dominant change agent in our culture. Although the family, church and temple, school, and community have only held their own—or, as some would say, even *lost* ground—the corporation's influence over the way we think has increased dramatically (cf. Leach, 1993). The new leaders who are designing and implementing new management paradigms are asking Americans who come to work to change their fundamental thinking about issues such as risk taking, the proper location for blame when something goes wrong, the need to work together and to be rewarded within the group rather than as an individual, the destruction of traditional hierarchical forms of communication and authority, and a reemergence of trust in the average person. All of this has resulted in the creation of atmospheres that require that people do no less than reconstruct their basic attitudes toward the strengths and weaknesses of average people and be willing to become cocreators of badly needed attitudes that can guide behavior relevant to new technologies and social change. These new corporate cultures emphasize the development of the human being who works for the company as much as the development of the company's bottom line. Because of these new leaders, many U.S. corporations are now doing what government and the churches haven't been able to do. They're creating a kinder and gentler, more teamwork-oriented citizen.

> ### Summing Up
>
> Most of the important technological change and much of the current social change that are affecting us so much is occurring in corporations. Thus, corporate leaders are now in the position of having to deliberately facilitate the creation of attitudes and values that can guide how we relate to these developments. Many new corporate leaders are creating organizational cultures that encourage risk taking, values development, teamwork, and a new attitude toward the trustworthiness of the average worker.

Related Individualism

The development of a reinterpreted individualism within U.S. corporations is an example of the kind of culture creating that many new leaders have been put in the position of needing to undertake. In *The Human Touch*, a recent book chronicling the success of a person-centered management transformation in a large medical corporation, Bill Arnold and I (1993) came to understand, as have others (Bellah, Madsen, Sullivan, Swidler, & Tipton, 1985; Fletcher, 1993; Follet, 1995; Kauffman, 1995), that this country's culture has to meet the demands of tomorrow by moving from our old rugged individualist assumptions to something similar to what we have called *related individualism*, an approach that emphasizes the interdependence of strong individuals in a way that heretofore has been neglected in our culture.

Any Deming model reinterpretation for the United States that is seeking spectacular success must carve out a role for the individual person that is compatible with this culture's obsession with the individual. Yet it also has to transcend that obsession. Rugged individualism doesn't mix well with a simple systems approach to improvement of quality, but it will with *related individualism*, a systems approach that targets the individual. (Arnold & Plas, 1993, p. 74)

In that large medical center project mentioned above, people were recruited to a TQM orientation, person by person. The focus shifted constantly back and forth between system processes—graphing statistics, communication, flowcharting—and the individual workers who got *as much immediate positive recognition as possible for their complaints as well as their efforts and successes.* As the project matured, many had learned to provide attention and resources even when there was no possibility they would directly result in revenue. A basement office was redesigned because of a secretary's allergic reaction to environmental materials. Many personnel were routinely awarded days off for purposes of rejuvenation and family responsibility— with no questions asked and no recrimination.

In the beginning of that project, however, one of the biggest obstacles to overcome emerged when people attempted to move to a teamwork model, to shift from a praise/blame mind-set to one of simple encouragement and acceptance of team efforts. U.S. investment in the priority of the individual was too big a hurdle to overcome easily. In fact, being the American individualists Bill Arnold and I also culturally are, our closer inspection suggested that a person-centered approach was more likely to succeed if individualist needs were merged with teamwork goals rather than fought or abandoned.

> U.S. industrialization in this century developed both because of the individual and at the expense of that individual. The can-do worker got the job done but did so within an American mind-set that often focused on fault finding and worker blame when things didn't go well. Within contemporary TQM approaches, the blame is shifted to the system, in the process deemphasizing the role of the individual person. Yet most of us believe that America's focus on individual skills and initiative has been a major contributor to the strength of this country. Therefore, any reinterpretation of a Deming QI approach in the United States needs to pay careful attention to how to deal with the individual when the QI strategy is designed to blame or praise a system or a process rather than the individuals who implement it. (Arnold & Plas, 1993, pp. 74-75)

Although our individualist values need to be given renewed attention in this country, fresh attention also has to be turned toward the development of new ways of learning how to work together. The work-based management models that our companies are endorsing these days in record numbers are moving us in the direction of related individualism despite our current inability to be as successful at working together as we thought we would be. *Related* rather than rugged individualism is demanded by the reality of the shrinking globe if not by common sense. As Bellah and his associates (1985) have said:

> There are truths we do not see when we adopt the language of radical individualism. We find ourselves not independently of other people and institutions but through them. We never get to the bottom of ourselves on our own. We discover who we are face to face and side by side with others in work, love, and learning. (p. 84)

The participative management approaches that increase attention to the individual worker rather than reduce that attention are the ones that are succeeding. Even though these approaches are currently not the norm, they are increasing in number and influence as we get more experience with TQM and think more deeply about how best to go about implementing participative management in our corporate and service organizations. As the Bellah group has said, " 'Finding oneself' is not something one does alone" (p. 85). But it's equally true that, in the United States, one of the most important functions of the group is to protect and enhance the dignity, talents, and well-being of each individual citizen.

Summing Up

Moving from rugged to related individualism is an example of an organizational response to the need to create new values and attitudes that can support new possibilities and demands.

Summary

New technologies and the social interaction demands of a shrinking globe have radically affected the ways people have historically
gone about developing new cultural attitudes. Now, the speed with
which so many important things change has presented us with the
need for rapid development of cultural values that can guide the
decisions and actions that need to be taken. Because so many of the
rapid advancements are produced by and found within the corporate
sector, corporate leaders are finding themselves in the position of
having to facilitate cultural change that affects not only their organizations but also the society at large. Many new leaders, as we will see
in Part II, have embraced this social challenge with interest and vigor.
Among the cultural changes they are provoking are new attitudes
toward teamwork, risk taking, willingness to develop values, and
participation rather than authority-driven decision making. *Related
individualism* is an example of revised cultural thinking. It represents
a set of attitudes that replace the older reliance on rugged individualist mores with a more teamwork-oriented approach that nonetheless retains primacy and respect for the individual.

References

Allport, G. W. (1935). Attitudes. In C. C. Murchison (Ed.), *A handbook of social psychology.* Worcester, MA: Clark University Press.

Arnold, W. W., & Plas, J. M. (1993). *The human touch: Today's most unusual program for
productivity and profit.* New York: John Wiley.

Associated Press. (1995, September 24). Tiny victory. *Tennessean,* p. 6.

Bellah, R. N., Madsen, R., Sullivan, W., Swidler, A., & Tipton, S. (1985). *Habits of the
heart: Individualism and commitment in American life.* New York: Harper & Row
Perennial.

Boorstin, D. J. (1974). *The Americans: The democratic experience.* New York: Vintage/
Random House.

Cole, M., & Scribner, S. (1974). *Culture and thought.* New York: John Wiley.

Durant, W. (1926). *The story of philosophy.* New York: Simon & Schuster.

Fletcher, J. L. (1993). *Patterns of high performance.* San Francisco: Berrett-Koehler.

Follet, M. P. (1995). *Mary Parker Follet: Prophet of management.* Cambridge, MA: Harvard Business School Press.

Johnson, P. (1985). *Modern times: The world from the twenties to the eighties.* New York:
Harper & Row.

Kauffman, B. (1995). *America first: Its history, culture, and politics.* Amherst, NY: Prometheus.

Koch, S., & Leary, D. E. (1985). *A century of psychology as science.* New York: McGraw-Hill.

Kolata, G. (1994, December 27). Battle over a baby's future raises hard ethical issues. *New York Times,* p. 1.

Kotter, J. P. (1995). *The new rules.* New York: Free Press.

Leach, W. (1993). *Land of desire: Merchants, power, and the rise of a new American culture.* New York: Vintage/Random House.

Lindsey, G., & Aronson, E. (1985). *Handbook of social psychology* (3rd ed.). Reading, MA: Addison-Wesley.

Naisbitt, J. (1982). *Megatrends: Ten new directions transforming our lives.* New York: Warner.

Rifkin, J. (1995). *The end of work.* New York: Putnam.

Robertson, J. O. (1980). *American myth, American reality.* New York: Hill & Wang.

Russell, B. (1945). *A history of Western philosophy.* New York: Simon & Schuster.

Susman, W. (1984). *Culture as history: The transformation of American society in the twentieth century.* New York: Pantheon.

Tocqueville, A. de. (1969). *Democracy in America* (G. Lawrence, Ed.; J. P. Mayer, Trans.). New York: Doubleday Anchor. (Original work published 1835)

Thinking Creatively: Part I

1. Is there a difference between experiencing a feeling and expressing it? Do feelings *demand* expression?
2. Are there any particular feelings that you believe never ought to be expressed in a work setting?
3. Are there any occupations that *require* people to feel and express a certain kind of feeling?
4. In retrospect, what has been your own personal history with person-centered management?
5. What is the relationship between the individual and the groups within the organization with which you're currently most familiar?
6. Which is more important in communicating management messages: words? feelings? actions? other?
7. In your particular area of occupational interest, what has been the history of the organization's response to the individual?
8. To what extent is it desirable that individuals bring a more integrated self to the workplace? What are the advantages? What might the downside be?
9. In your experience, what have been the most important impediments to person-centered transformation?
10. In what ways do you think American leadership and management will change in the next 25 years?
11. Is it really desirable for corporate leaders to intentionally try to develop new cultural perspectives?
12. If cultural attitudes and beliefs cannot keep pace with technological and social changes, what might be the results?
13. Is it possible for leaders and managers to eliminate war and hardball metaphors in their companies? How could that be accomplished?
14. Person-centered leaders think that corporations ought to exist to promote the development of workers as well as to create revenue and profit. Do you agree?

PART II

Person-Centered Leadership:
The Basics, the Variations,
the Corporate Chiefs Who Make It Work

6

Person-Centered Leaders

An Introduction to the
Uniqueness and the Methodology

In my work as a researcher and consultant with person-centered executive leaders as well as companies that want to move in the direction of person-centered management, I have become most impressed by two things: the large amount of cross-country interest in all kinds of participatory management and the uniqueness of each person-centered leadership approach I've encountered.

Interest in Participatory Management

Despite the growing number of disappointments that have been associated with it (see Chapter 3), people continue to be very attracted by the possibilities inherent in empowerment management. As Larry Wilson put it in his Foreword to a leadership book a few years ago,

Every day, all over the business landscape, another company wakes up and realizes that its most underutilized resources are the minds and hearts of its people. It is people—those closest to the customer and closest to the work—who have the answers, who own the solutions. (Oakley & Krug, 1993, p. 9)

Executives and managers have responded to the simple logic of that idea in record numbers in the past few years. Then, they have discovered discouragement. The big payoffs failed to materialize. What we're coming to understand is that the individual who was to have been the focus of the continuous improvement and empowerment systems somehow has been lost.

Most versions of these new leadership models that have worked their way through large and small companies alike have suffered from the same design problem. They were not made to deal directly with the American culture or the needs of the U.S. worker they were designed to empower. Joshua Hammond, recent president of the American Quality Foundation, has been clear in saying that those at the foundation

believe that a primary reason for the less than overwhelming success of many quality initiatives is that they do not speak our language. They neglect the critical emotional component as they try to motivate us, and they promote methods and behavior that are un-American in the true sense. We are not calling for a wholesale scrapping of existing quality efforts, just a recasting, using U.S. players who are encouraged to act and speak naturally. (American Quality Foundation, 1992, p. 109)

The first thing that has been most noticeable, then, is the intense interest on the part of so many senior executives in figuring out a way to get participatory management to work in their companies. An increasingly large number of corporate executives have become convinced that these strategies can work, but they're equally convinced —for reasons they do not clearly understand—that the models aren't working like they should. As we saw in earlier chapters, in some cases they aren't working at all—despite good faith efforts on the part of senior leadership.

The Uniqueness of Each Person-Centered Approach

When one looks analytically across several companies in which the individual has been factored in advantageously, where person-centered leadership is up and running, very obvious similarities and very obvious differences can be found in the philosophies and styles of the person-centered CEOs who run these companies. They all have something in common, but each is doing it his or her way—that is, from a unique, almost idiosyncratic point of view. If Warren Bennis (1989) is right—and he probably is—we shouldn't be surprised by that. After studying dozens of top-notch leaders in all walks of life with the exception of politics, he concluded that the essence of leadership is the desire to express oneself, the commitment to share one's personal uniqueness with the organization one cares about and wants very much to influence.

Each of the person-centered leaders who is discussed in the following chapters is remarkably unique in the way he or she translates person-centered thinking into the strategies that form the management infrastructure of the company. These presidents and CEOs are so unique, in fact, that when some of them are written about in the popular press, people often come to the quick conclusion that the organization is run by a cult of personality of some sort. At times, some writers talk in terms of the charismatic leader as they describe these executives. Dictionary definitions of *charisma*, however, usually include the idea that the charismatic leader is one who possesses supernatural or at least extraordinary gifts and that followers respond because of the outstanding nature of the leader's personal appeal. But the leaders described here, for the most part, do not fall within a true definition of *charisma*.

When disengaged from the companies they run, these leaders are quite ordinary people, typical Americans in fact. If you were to meet one of them in a public place, you probably would have no clue at all that he or she is a successful leader of a significant U.S. company and that the employees think of these leaders as special people. When these CEOs do get labeled *charismatic*, it is always in connection with their specific roles in their organizations and invariably occurs because of a single factor—the ability to inspire people who work for them to give their best to the company. They have been able to engender trust and loyalty. The reason they inspire these things, however, has had little to do with what has been traditionally meant by *charisma*. Rather, it has everything to do with what true leadership is all about and what person-centered leadership, specifically, is all about.

These leaders are able to inspire their associates because of what they see in those associates, not because of what the associates see in them. Beyond that commonality, each personality is idiosyncratic. One may be detail-mongering; another is stubborn—perhaps, to a fault. A third is a servant leader who delays a decision beyond the point of tolerance in the eyes of some. This modest list of weaker traits is accompanied by a much longer list of strengths, and it is the strengths that their associates prefer to watch. Nonetheless, despite the variety of positive terms that their employees might use to describe them, the most important fact for these employees seems to be that each of these leaders uses his or her unique strengths and weaknesses to do the crucial things—release talent and creativity and serve the personal and work-related needs of each individual in the company. Despite their sometimes pedestrian personas, the success of their person-centered leadership strategies has made these leaders appear, at times, larger than life.

The Bennis notion that good leaders express themselves in and through their companies does not mean that they run roughshod over them. On the contrary, the leaders you will read about in Chapters 7 through 10 encourage others toward that same kind of productive self-expression. This is good leadership that works in U.S. companies—in large part because it is person centered.

The commonalities that I see across person-centered leaders have a great deal to do with how they treat the individuals they work with and what they expect from them. The differences beyond that are extraordinary. Certainly, there is no single "right" or even best way to translate person-centered leadership into an organization. But before we investigate the unique management strategies of a group of person-centered CEOs, it will be helpful to revisit the discussion of commonalities that was introduced at the close of Chapter 3.

Person-Centered Fundamentals

As in most continuous quality improvement programs, employee empowerment is primary—as is emphasis on teamwork and, to some extent, systems thinking. Using a mind-set similar to that of many basic TQM approaches, person-centered leaders are likely to look for glitches in the system before blaming an individual employee when things go wrong. They're also very likely to think of their companies as learning organizations, committed to enhancing the employee's capacity to stay ahead of the curve by knowing how to get the right information *before* it's needed rather than after. They tend to provide *all* employees with as much information as possible about corporate revenue and expenses as well as strategic planning. In other words, many of the specific management strategies in effect in these companies are not new. They amount to basic reinterpretations of now common continuous quality improvement and empowerment methods. But what *is* different is the dedication of the senior executives to the development of each corporate employee in addition to dedication to the product line, revenue, and profit. *Person-centered leaders have abandoned the idea that business ought to be just about business. They think of their companies as organizations of responsibility.* Their biggest cultural responsibility is the development of citizens who learn to make the most of their personal and professional selves. Indeed, most of these leaders want their employees to abandon those artificial distinctions. Person-centered leaders want their people to use the same values at work that they use at home. They want a single self to come to work.

Person-Centered Leaders:
Up Close and Personal

The three corporate presidents profiled in the following three chapters have been running person-centered organizations for a number of years. Their companies span a range of business interests. Jim Mullen is founder and president of Mullen Advertising near Boston; Dean Kamen is founder and president of DEKA Research and

Development Corporation in Manchester, New Hampshire; and Robert Davis is founder and president of Seaside Development Corporation in Florida. The differences in the approaches of these three to this kind of leadership illustrate the reality that people cannot possibly be exactly the same kind of person-centered leader because, by definition, the model develops the individuality of all employees —including the leader. A look at their unique leadership styles adds to the picture that Part II is primarily interested in developing—the picture of the possibilities inherent in a person-by-person management approach. But despite the differences, these three corporate presidents illustrate the basic attitudes toward the organization and toward service leadership that are common to all person-centered leaders and managers. In Chapter 10, many other leaders who have been profiled elsewhere are discussed in terms of person-centered leadership basics. These leaders range from Herb Kelleher at Southwest Airlines to Mary Kay Ash of Mary Kay Cosmetics. Thus, these are corporate heads with whom many readers are already familiar. But on closer inspection, these leaders are easily revealed to be running their companies person by person.

Methodology

A major part of my research in psychology-based corporate leadership has involved studying person-centered leaders in corporations that have a national presence—either because of their size or because their niche is so special that they have gained a fair amount of public attention and interest. My research methodology has relied on a number of qualitative models such as the Lincoln and Guba (1985) approach to naturalistic inquiry and the Gummeson (1991) approach to management research. The research model used to produce each of the following profiles involved some variation on the general strategy of naturalistic observation involving continuous time with the CEO on several occasions as he or she worked through a typical daily agenda. In addition, several private interview sessions of approximately 2 hours each were carved into the leader's agenda each day. I conducted these interviews in informal as well as formal sessions. Consonant with person-centered management theory, one of my research goals was to discover the personal side of the leader and the ways in which this personal self is translated into the organization. To discover the reality of the company, I also interviewed people at all levels of the organization—in impromptu and informal sessions as well as more structured situations. I also met with the leader's spouse and other family members, visited the home environment, and perhaps talked with friends. A fuller description of the research methodologies used can be found in the Appendix.

Summary

The methodological strategies used in this research result in leadership profiles that reveal the personal as well as professional side of these leaders. They also result in a clear picture of how the organizations experience their leader—what people think and feel about them, and what they believe their strengths and weaknesses to be. Thus, the following three chapters present person-centered research profiles that yield a three-dimensional look at leaders in a way that allows the reader to appreciate each as an individual, a very human person. Discussed here are three real people who are running very real organizations. Therefore, they are not even close to being perfect —as the following profiles show.

References

American Quality Foundation. (1992). *The international quality study—best practices report.* Cleveland, OH: Author.

Bennis, W. (1989). *On becoming a leader* (paperback). Reading, MA: Addison-Wesley.

Gummeson, E. (1991). *Qualitative methods in management research.* Newbury Park, CA: Sage.

Lincoln, Y. S., & Guba, E. (1985). *Naturalistic inquiry.* Beverly Hills, CA: Sage.

Oakley, E., & Krug, D. (1993). *Enlightened leadership: Getting to the heart of change.* New York: Simon & Schuster.

7

James X. Mullen

*Founder and President,
Mullen Advertising,
Wenham, Massachusetts*

To grow, you have to risk things precious.

—Joseph Grimaldi

Jim Mullen crewed aboard the top boat in the 1969 Admiral's Cup. He drove the Porsche that won at Sebring in 1983. He founded Mullen, one of the fastest growing advertising and public relations agencies of the 1990s. Yet none of these facts about Mullen's speed comes as close to capturing the core of who Jim is as does an oft-told story that has circulated through the Mullen agency for years. In the most common version of the tale, the young company is learning about the management style of its founder and president at the same time it's coping with a client load that seems to be expanding geometrically by the month—or maybe by the week. Jim's obsession with the looks of the agency's environment was already legendary in those days. But his obsessive investment in the idea that all employees ought to be treated with complete dignity and fairness wasn't yet quite such public knowledge. Nonetheless, Jim had been telling everybody that they ought to be cleaning their own cups and plates after lounge snacks. They ought to be pitching their own brown-bag garbage into the can. "The maintenance and housekeeping staffs weren't hired to be our mothers," he'd been known to say. "What kind of message does it send to people if we expect them to wash out our coffee cups for us? What kind of message does it send to clients if we work in a messy environment?" Jim was so serious about this that he wrote memos. He even used perfectly good staff meeting time to get the point across. Eventually, he figured the message had been driven home. So, he injected the principle into the company culture and got on with the business of creative advertising—until one fateful day.

Sometime during midafternoon that day, he passed by the sink in the staff lounge. It was full of dirty cups and mugs. Jim stopped. He reached out for a dirty cup. He stood there just looking at it for a second. Then he smashed it on the floor. In fact, he smashed all of them—cup by cup, deliberately, and with great frustration.

Today, Jim Mullen knows he'd handle the whole thing differently. He'd be less aggressive, less volatile, less impulsive—but perhaps not less angry. He says he'd use the opportunity to educate rather than confront. But even though his anger would be turned to more useful purposes now, he knows he'd still feel it. Within the essence of Jim Mullen is something that must be referred to, simply, as "standards." Jim has them in abundance—passionate standards for everything that matters to him. In fact, Jim doesn't think of himself as the boss or the president at Mullen. In print and in person, Jim refers to himself as Mullen's director of environment and standards.

Guideline 1: Treat all
employees with complete respect.

Velocity, Intensity, Cars, Boots, and Popcorn

In the fall of 1992, BMW of North America drove ripples of astonishment through the advertising world when it announced that it was going to ditch its 18-year relationship with New York's Ammirati & Puris, despite the fact that the Ammirati & Puris work had been instrumental in helping BMW put the concept of the "ultimate driving machine" into garages all over the country. Four months later, BMW went even further. It completely shocked the advertising world as it announced that it had chosen Mullen Advertising of Wenham, Massachusetts, to handle the creative portion of its $85 million per year account. Although Mullen had established a large enough national presence so that nobody exactly said, "Mullen who?" there were plenty who said, "Mullen where?"—especially within the Madison Avenue advertising establishment and especially because Mullen already held the Rolls Royce and Bentley accounts. "BMW's going with an agency that already markets an upper end car?!" they gasped. "BMW's going with a group that works out in the middle of next-to-nowhere?!" "You've got to be kidding—seriously kidding."

The middle of next-to-nowhere is actually a 50-acre estate located about 30 miles northeast of Boston. There gathers the Mullen team, in a stylishly redone 75,000-square-foot facility entered through a Jacobean mansion and surrounded by some of the most delightfully traditional New England landscaping you're likely to encounter. As you come up Essex Street, heading for Mullen off the interstate, the first thing you're likely to see is nothing much. Eventually, on your left, a tastefully discreet sign states, simply, *Mullen*. Were you not intentionally looking for an advertising agency, you might mistake the entrance for a horse farm or perhaps a boarding school for exceptional children of some sort.

This is an agency that stubbornly intends to define itself and to decide its own goals and methods. No one has ever called Mullen trendy or glitzy. Certainly it has never been known as "establishment." But the Mullen agency has been called cultish, quirky, elitist, and arrogant. The single most important factor responsible for these labels is the idyllic Mullen environment. This is Walden without the pond, the mountaintop without the mountain. Although most people recognize that there is no distinctive "look" that permeates the Mullen creative efforts, they nonetheless assume that any group who holes up off the beaten path must surely have a Waco-like mind-set, a drive toward conformity and protection from the outside world. Yet nothing could be further from the truth. As Paul Silverman, chief creative officer, says, "Our business is about being in touch with the world. Creativity is what we're selling. It's the in-touch individualists who can make the creative leaps." Indeed, the core of the Mullen creative program is a small, two-person team, usually a writer and a visual person. Eventually, teamwork on the part of dozens of people gets the products out and the quality up. But it's you, the individual, who's expected to create, to innovate.

Guideline 2: Encourage individualism.

The top-flight creativity of Mullen people has made their midsize, 175-person organization one of the most awarded agencies of recent years. Their work took Timberland from a smallish company to the international, complex corporation it is today. During the past 8 years, the Timberland ads may have received more print awards than any other advertising program produced by any agency of any size. In print, you've seen the panoramic picture of the dark and deadly roiling ocean, a couple pairs of Timberland shoes, and the heading, "What to Have on Your Feet When the Only Thing Dry Is the Heaves," or maybe the picture of the Timberland jacket, boots, and the barely recognizable feminine face bundled to the nose, with frost-encrusted eyelashes, and the lead statement, "In the Iditarod, the Idea That There Are Only Snowmen Is Abominable." During a TV spot, the camera, never more than ankle height, focuses on two pairs of Timberland-outfitted feet walking menacingly through the rain and muck toward one another. Only in the last frame do you see that one pair of shoes puts its owner on tiptoes as the two persons meet. Presumably, she and he are enjoying the kiss for which they couldn't wait. This is the kind of advertising campaign most of us like. It's fresh. It's real. It's something with which we can identify. It's fun.

For Veryfine juices, Mullen took on the colas by taking on Pepsi. On television, you see the lonely Pepsi machine standing like a forgotten cowboy in the street as a brand-new Veryfine juice machine comes to town. Suddenly, there's a reason to party—and the camera cuts out as the guy who delivered the machine breaks into that full-of-pride laugh many of us would like to feel a bit more often than most of us actually do.

For *Money* magazine, Mullen produced a series of top-notch ads that appealed to the visionary and imaginative side of each of us. In one of them, a beat-up, partially paint-primed 1958 Mustang convertible is surrounded by nothing—standing stationary beneath a dusky, darkened blue sky: "Some see scrap metal. Bob Horgan sees a gleaming red hood, a perfectly restored engine, and a sun-drenched, winding country road. *Money*. Where American Dreams still come true." In a visually stunning Bentley ad, you see the grille of a speeding Turbo R heading straight for you. The caption reads, "Heroes do not buy their chariots off the rack."

This kind of gut-level, emotional work is what Mullen clients have come to expect from their agency. Other corporations on the Mullen client list have included Boston Whaler, Cellular One, Colgate, Digital Equipment, Gitano, Hewlett-Packard Medical, J&B, Polartec, Puma, and three divisions of Reebok. But possibly the most talked about program Mullen has produced during the past few years has been the smart and sassy campaign that brought Smartfood from a $35,000 per year popcorn popper to a $150 million brand that was snapped up by Frito-Lay. In the beginning, Mullen concentrated on a guerilla marketing campaign that employed college students dressed as Smartfood popcorn bags. They infiltrated games, beaches, and concerts and gave away free bags of the client's product. Witty and irreverent ads followed, appearing in mostly black and white with the tag line, "You can't get it off your mind." We see a family praying together at bedtime. But the little girl isn't praying; she's thinking about Smartfood white cheddar popcorn. We see a couple who look a lot like Marilyn and Dan Quayle. She's thinking about

Smartfood. His thought balloon is empty. The caption reads, "Smartfood is air-popped popcorn smothered in white cheddar cheese. It's a great concept. Even if it's a little over Dan's head." There were many, many more, and Mullen's Smartfood work became the most awarded print campaign of 1990.

But it wasn't always so. Originally, Mullen Advertising was a one-person show that Jim ran off his kitchen table.

To Go Sailing on an Honest Sea . . .

Throughout the 1960s, the sea was always rolling somewhere within Jim Mullen's young heart and mind. As the 1960s came to a close, Jim figured it was probably now or never. If he was going to chase his dream, he'd better start chasing. The dream du jour for Jim centered on building an extremely fast and worthy sailboat in which he could tramp around the world. The only problem was that he didn't have enough money to buy somebody's old castoff, much less money for building something elegantly new. To earn the requisite capital, Jim convinced his employer, Hood Sailmakers, that because of his love for sailing and love for words, he'd be the perfect person to produce some ads that could sell their sails. Mullen will bill more than $155 million this year; in 1970, Jim billed Hood Sailmakers around $25,000. They were his only client. Nonetheless, he figured his sailing dream might come true. Not too long after, however, Jim's client list started to grow. Mullen Advertising had to move off the kitchen table and into a suite of two rooms at the back of a building in Marblehead. Jim and Jeanne Ridgeway, his newly hired secretary-treasurer-accountant-general manager, shared a bathroom with the optometrist across the hall.

"In those days, he'd come to work with cutoffs and no butt," recalls Jeanne, now a Mullen vice president.

As well as I knew Jim then, I had no idea that he had any desire to be big, to grow a company of this size and reputation. When we got another creative person on staff, he and Jim would spend the afternoons in a harbor bar eating lobster and drinking beer. Maybe they'd write copy. Maybe they wouldn't. Meanwhile, I was in charge of everything else—including cleaning the toilet and bailing out his dog when it got caught stealing ice cream from kids around Marblehead. Jim's the last person I would have figured to turn out to be a workaholic—especially a workaholic with a suit on. I'm not sure he even owned one back then.

Jim never did get his sailboat built, never sailed around the world—because he fell in love. Much to his surprise, really, he fell so much in love with advertising and with business that he's been at it ever since. But the part of the around-the-world dream that was all about risk taking and individualism never let go of him. At Mullen, even the secretaries and maintenance people are shining individualists, not just the creative types. Yet within this team of obvious individualists, Jim Mullen still stands out as the reigning iconoclast.

The shattering of icons has pretty much been a Mullen goal since the early days in Marblehead. In the U.S. advertising business these days, an iconoclast of any seriousness eventually has to begin telling the truth about the client's product and telling the truth about what we tend to really think and feel about ourselves, each other, our leaders, our lifestyles. Although most of us may groan about it, it's nonetheless true that we don't trust very many contemporary advertising messages. Right now in the advertising business, being different means you're very likely to be refreshingly honest. Mullen advertising does that kind of thing with disarming directness and a considerable amount of panache. As a result, they make money for their clients.

Truth isn't something that gets produced only for the clients at Mullen. It's built into the fabric of the organization. People who come in contact with Mullen employees may quickly find themselves getting a dose of truth when perhaps they least expect it. During my first phone conversation with Jim, a 20-minute romp through a fog of topics, I eventually got around to asking him how things were going with BMW. At that time, the Mullen-BMW alliance had been in existence only for about 3 months. Jim didn't skip a beat as he answered my question with the statement, "It's rough. If we can both not die from what's been going on these first few months, we're all going to enjoy it a lot."

What was *this?* A corporate president was admitting tension with a major, much ballyhooed client relationship?! "What's the real problem?" I immediately shot back. Again, Jim didn't hesitate:

> They've got an organization that's as complex and smooth running as their automobiles. Their structure and ways of doing things have been in place for decades. We're a bunch of creative people who make ourselves think differently. We work best when we're loose. BMW and Mullen aren't communicating right now. We aren't even speaking the same language.

But Jim had no doubt that Mullen and BMW were going to very quickly start singing off the same sheet music—with excellent results. He hadn't tried to hide the current problem, nor had he seemed embarrassed by or afraid of it. That kind of confidence and honesty is fast becoming a Mullen trademark.

Guideline 3:   Share the truth.

The Leader

Jim Mullen is a passionate man; in a low-key kind of way, he's mostly proud of that. Across his three-plus decades of productivity, Jim's passionate interests have multiplied and their intensity deepened. Of greatest importance for his company is the fact that, in the end, his greatest passion has turned out to be his love for a certain "style of business." Despite a genuine and rather deep streak of humility about his accomplishments and opinions, you don't have to spend more than 10 minutes with Jim before you get the picture that he believes he knows how a good business ought to be run. He has no doubts about this. Leaders have to change themselves and control themselves—not their companies. They have to achieve a very specific set of standards, a particular style of thinking and behaving. As far as Jim is concerned, these standards dictate how you deal with your employees and how you deal with your environment. Jim Mullen is rigid in his attitudes toward these two sets of corporate issues—the people standards and the environment standards. He has parlayed this personal rigidity into corporate success.

DEPENDENT INDIVIDUALISTS

When it comes to the people stuff, Jim expects himself to run an organization that encourages individuality and develops teamwork. Sound contradictory? Unfortunately, for too long in American corporate history, those two needs have seemed at least paradoxical if not downright impossible to achieve within the same organization. That's probably why we've endured so many flavor-of-the-month management strategies lately. What is most desirable—teamwork-dependent individualists—has seemed out of reach to a sizable portion of our corporate leadership.

Jim Mullen requires teamwork but he also requires unique thinking. His person-centered approach to management yields both. Jim asks, "Why pay someone else for your own opinion?" He wants corporate communication dynamics that yield the truth rather than somebody's idea of what's likely to be accepted, what's politically correct. So, how does he create a climate that will produce unique thinkers rather than corporate yes-people? He gets it by insisting on winning. Not competition. Not intraoffice politics. *Winning.*

WINNING

Mullen Advertising's people are always out to win. As you walk from floor to floor at Mullen, it sometimes seems like the desire to win is so pervasive it's become part of the very air you breathe. Or maybe it's in the drinking water. But these are not people who are out to best each other. Rather, the focus is almost totally directed outward toward winning the new client, some new market share for an old client, the old client's continued admiration, photography awards, graphic awards, copy awards—whatever the bust-your-butt award of the month might be.

When Jim talks about winning, he talks in terms of going for it with all you've got, taking risks, making mistakes, taking more risks. He makes it clear that if you're not making mistakes, you're not doing good work and you're probably not going to be part of a Mullen win. He talks about using all the tools you've got to make that happen. He insists—and this is crucial—that personal *judgment* is one of the most important tools available to any employee. Mullen employees are not expected to represent the company—because they *are* the company. An individual is paid, in large part, to exercise personal judgment on behalf of personal productivity goals as well as the company mission. As smart people do learn to develop and use personal perspectives, positions, and opinions, they develop the individuality that is so prized and cultivated in all corners of the Mullen operation.

When hiring a secretary, maintenance person, account executive, or any other employee, Jim looks for the same four qualities: intelligence, passion, entrepreneurial skill, and a sense of fun. People who enter the organization need to know how to think, how to care, how to find ways to get the job done, and how to be joyful and enjoyable people.

Paul Silverman says that "people come here to add imagination. We hire individualists who can solve problems." Once they're in, as Margie Brandfon, corporate communications manager, says, "people can't be obsequious. They need to inspire confidence in order to be successful." The standards for personal productivity and the quality of that productivity are extremely high. "Working at Mullen is like training for the Olympics," Margie says.

> Sometimes you pull a muscle. Most of the people here have stretched themselves too far from time to time and failed as a result. But that's part of the process. At Mullen, we learn from a mistake; we don't expect ourselves not to make them.

Margie talks about the idea of the teamwork-dependent individualist with a pride that she doesn't try to hide. She grins as she says, "Most people here are stars." Then she quietly adds, "Loners hardly ever make it at Mullen."

Guideline 4: *Hire people who can think for*
themselves and then ask for and support risk taking.

During the months when Mullen was going after the BMW account, the entire agency caught the fever—the *entire* agency. Most of
the maintenance staff people, for example, made it their business to
check in with the creative types on a fairly regular basis. "How's it
going with you guys? Are you coming up with anything? Are we
going to nail this one?" As the weeks wore on, some of the maintenance workers noticed that the creative people seemed to be drag-
ging a bit as one good idea after another wasn't working. A lot of
hard work was ending up on a graphics room floor or in a recycling
bin. On some days, these men and women couldn't seem to get beyond just plain tired. So, some of the maintenance men got creative
themselves. They grabbed some buckets of paint and some artist
supplies and headed for the parking lot. It was so brutally cold that
they had to tent the project and rely on the fragile warmth of a pro-
pane heater. One of the guys had a broken leg. Nonetheless, within
a couple of days they'd produced a facsimile of the BMW emblem
that completely covered the center of the agency's main parking lot.
As the graphic artists and writers got out of their cars each morning,
they got hyped. The message was clear: "BMW is going to be ours.
You people can do this. You're going to do it. We're with you all the
way." The emblem was still there when the auto company's executives arrived to see and hear the Mullen pitch. Their surprise quickly
turned to interest and satisfaction. About a year after Mullen had
won this account and just after I'd finished my work with Jim Mullen
and his agency, I happened to be walking through a BMW showroom
in Atlanta. I noted the catchy and compelling ads all over the walls
and commented on the Mullen work. A salesperson quickly replied,
with a good deal of interest and delight, "Yeah, that advertising
agency painted a BMW emblem on their parking lot before they ever
won the account. BMW loved that. Pretty clever, huh?"

Indeed, that's teamwork. That's a team of real individualists at work. For me, perhaps the most striking example of Mullen team-work occurred about 6:30 in the morning a couple of hot summers ago. I was staying that week in the Mullen carriage house near the agency's mansion headquarters. A large, 19th-century stone struc-ture, the carriage house can provide ample temporary housing for a number of Mullen guests-in-residence. During those particular days, I was sharing the guest house with only one other person, Harold Kobakof, a newly hired senior account executive who came in late at night and left early. I never got the chance to meet him or even to see him. On this particular morning, I'd risen early and wandered in the dark out onto the spectacular Mullen grounds to watch a New Eng-land sunrise break through the trees. Eventually, I realized I'd snapped the carriage house door shut without bringing a key. I was locked out, without the possibility of my faceless, silent partner's reentry assistance for I had heard him leave about 5 a.m. Perplexed, I stood in the middle of the Mullen parking lot, on the spot where the BMW logo had once been. Now what? Suddenly, a small red car came toward me up the winding driveway. The driver wasn't even able to get out of his car before I was in his face introducing myself and asking if he could help. Phil Nuccio, a maintenance man with Mullen for some 7 years, was more than just pleasant; he was proprietary. In a very low-key way, he didn't act so much like he worked for Mullen but like he owned Mullen. Phil announced that he already knew who I was and what my business was at the agency. He assured me that he had a key to the carriage house. As we headed over there, I began to explain that I had been sharing the space with a newly hired vice president who had left quite early that morning and was thus un-available for the rescue operation. Phil replied, "Ah, yes, Harold had to drive down to an emergency meeting today with a major client in Jersey. He might be back tonight but probably not till late." Here was another refreshing Mullen surprise! Even though this man's major responsibilities were in plant maintenance, he not only knew where a new senior executive was going to spend his day, he knew what the issues were that had prompted the meeting with the client. And he knew the VP by his first name, which was amazing but typical.

In this corporation, everybody is part of the action. The background people root for the front office associates and those lead people rely on and appreciate the centrality of the support staffs. Phil Nuccio is as much Mullen Advertising as is Jim Mullen or Harold Kobakof. This ownership produces the teamwork that allows individualism to work to the benefit of the organization rather than to its detriment. The result? Mullen tends to win.

Guideline 5: Empowerment—all individuals are important members of the team.

But make no mistake about it, this is not a simple romantic or idyllic love-your-neighbor kind of thing. At base, all Mullen people want to win because they're going to share in the rewards of that win. At all levels of the organization, everyone connected with a project in any way realizes substantial profit-sharing rewards when profit is made. Generalists as well as experts are nicely built into the profit-sharing structure. Over the years, the cash profit shares for all employees have averaged about 25% of salary. A long time ago, Jim came to the conclusion that *substantial* profit sharing is not only a fair way to operate, it is a smart way to operate. The emotional highs and satisfaction rewards are also a very shared experience. Jim has proceeded over the years to give the company away in many ways that range from profit sharing and stock acquisition to shared decision making and completely disseminated information on all aspects of the financials. And everybody attends the victory celebrations. They're all throwing the party—in their own honor.

If you were to spend a few days observing the Mullen organization, you might get the idea that this dance between teamwork and individualism is a very natural and easy thing for a corporation to come by. Yet from personal experience, most of us know that such is not the case. There are many organizations that reward the hotshots and punish the lowly. Others—especially these days—insist on business by committee, and heaven help the person who wants to sing counterpoint. If someone asked you to identify 10 top-notch corporations that insist on teamwork-driven individuality, chances are you'd have a hard time doing it. If somebody asked about ever having worked for such a corporation, most people, without hesitation, would have to reply, "No. Afraid not."

The steps needed to build this kind of desirable organizational mind-set are nontraditional—but simple and highly effective. At *all* levels of the organization, start with smart, passionate, fun-loving people. Then, make sure that you personally believe that both goals—the teamwork and the individualism—are equally important. Then, just ask for what you want. Jim asks his people to cooperate, work together, and bond within client-focused work teams. He also asks them to use their personal judgment, to create, and to think independently. He lets people figure out how to create the dance. Jim doesn't get compulsive over the details of how this synchrony gets created; that's not his job. You can't very well tell people you want them to think independently and work together and then tell them exactly how they're supposed to do that. Jim Mullen has roughed in the outlines of the company culture at Mullen. It's all the rest of them who have made it into a work of art.

Guideline 6:   Always keep your eye
on the goal—a creative balance
between individualism and teamwork.

FEELINGS, NOTHING MORE THAN FEELINGS

The Mullen manual does not state, "Passion required. Emotional flexibility rewarded," and nobody ever told a Mullen employee that he or she had to bring some feelings to work. Yet they are there. Paul Silverman seems neither proud nor ashamed of this part of the Mullen culture. He quietly and without fanfare says, "We share grief and we share joy." Ian Hunter, Mullen's maintenance director, projects a very relaxed attitude toward the range of Mullen feelings. He'll tell you, "We don't expect people not to have moods from time to time." Jeanne Ridgeway has heard colleagues come right out and say, "I love you" to someone who has meant a lot to them over the years or in a special circumstance. As is the case with most forms of art, it's the presence of the feelings that creates the masterpiece—cultured feelings. Mullen certainly bears little resemblance to one of those corporate free-for-alls where people posture and vent, giving free expression to any emotion that emerges. The loudest person is not the winner at Mullen. This is not management through anger. Rather, this is an organization that is maturely self-aware. This staff knows what kind of business is being run here. This is a very competitive organization working with client-imposed deadlines, performance stresses, multimillion dollar deals. People who take their work and this company seriously are bound to have a considerable range of human emotions to contend with—their own and those of the people who work alongside them. The difference between most of the people who work at Mullen and those in so many other organizations is that these people expect their feelings to show up at work from time to time. They expect what's real. They don't hold onto some idyllic notion of the perfectly wise, perfectly controlled, perfectly functioning adult who comes to work only to serve, who always does the right thing.

Joe Grimaldi, chief operating officer, takes a very down-to-earth approach to emotions in the workplace. As long as you truly respect your coworkers and acknowledge your debt to their skills, he believes you can be honest and forthright—even humorous—when your frustrations get in your way. When his crackerjack administrative assistant does some things he has difficulty with, he searches her out at the end of the day to say, "Linda, you're ruining my life!" Conversation—real dialogue—then proceeds. Recently, a senior person choked up after getting the news that a project she'd worked on for several weeks had crashed and burned. As she tearily walked down the hall, heading for an exit, several people—men and women alike—stopped her to offer support, a tissue, a commiserating look. No one she passed seemed the least bit put off or afraid of her strong emotions. Yet all this genuine wisdom about expecting and accepting the reality of human feelings, foibles, and passions does not create a perfect corporate environment anymore than does a cool, automaton mind-set. Human feelings are generally pretty messy. The uncomfortable ones can create tension as well as cleansing. The comfortable feelings can just as easily get you off track as make life worth living. No, the Mullen approach to feelings does not create a utopian climate; it's just more realistic than some.

Guideline 7:   Human feelings are just as important as human minds.

Within the Mullen reality, the truth is that the organization is not really run by Jim Mullen. It's operated by a triumvirate: the creative director, Paul Silverman; the chief operating officer, Joe Grimaldi; and the president. As Jim puts it, "This agency is amiably run by a Jew, an Italian, and an Irishman." Although the word *amiable* seems to work for Jim, the term really is far too superficial for adequate description of the complex dynamics within the Mullen leadership team. This triumvirate is so representative of the culture of the entire organization that no single word can adequately do its dynamics justice. This group of three men is perfectly exemplary of the most treasured Mullen characteristics—individualism, teamwork, and feeling.

Each of these three men has clearly identified responsibilities within the organization. Paul has the last word on creative decisions. Joe has the final word on all aspects of operations, including many financial decisions. Jim has the last word on standards, client acquisition, the books, the buildings, and the grounds. What happens is that these three strongly positioned individualists bring their final words to the triumvirate meetings. Each of the three uses the word *defend* when telling how decisions get made. Each of them puts forth a position, defends it, and then listens to the other guy's truth. The resulting discussions are often enthusiastic, heated, and intense. Others in the organization describe them as "loud." Each member of the triumvirate, however, is careful to point out that he does not yell. Yet each is also careful to recognize that their Mullen leadership trio does not operate without feelings. As Paul puts it, "Not one of us is beyond a reality that allows for human conflict and human error." Joe points out that he doesn't have to hesitate if he wants to tell Jim "to shut up and listen," and he expects the same in return. Jim says that when "the other two are in agreement even when I know I'm right, I've got to figure I'm likely to be wrong."

Because of the intensity each of them has brought to the Mullen leadership team, each man—who thought of himself early on as a rather timid type—has developed the individualized style that now characterizes him in the eyes of so many at Mullen. The need for the teamwork created the need to develop the individual style. They couldn't have worked together if they hadn't developed their individually strong positions and personalities; there would have been an unfortunate imbalance. The converse has also been true. On many occasions, it was the safety of the team approach that allowed each of them to overstate a position so as to be personally creative, to push the limits as far as they could. If any one of the three of them had been afraid of the range of human feelings, they would not have been able to craft the unique and effective leadership team that is currently guiding Mullen toward an apex of quality and success within the world of American advertising and marketing.

Guideline 8: Related individualism means creating an environment where individualists can work together—exploiting their differences to the benefit of the company and themselves.

THE QUALITY OF WORK, THE QUALITY OF LIFE

Jim's second self-delegated major responsibility, environmental quality, cannot be considered apart from the company's attitude about the broader issues involved in today's corporate movement toward quality improvement in general. His interest in issues of quality is intense, but he's got his own take on those issues. "You don't measure success by the financial consequences," he says. "You measure it by the quality of the decision, the quality of judgment." When I asked a woman who was about to clean a bathroom what she thought Jim Mullen's best quality was, she replied, "He wants to get things *right*." That's TQM at its best.

Like most of the others who are profiled in this volume, Jim did not get interested in quality improvement after his organization had come into its own, or experienced a crisis, or came in second in a battle for clients or market share. For Jim, quality has always been the priority. When he thinks of environmental quality, he includes not only the facility but also "the working environment—the civility in the way we treat each other, the freedom people have to be their best, the atmosphere that encourages fun." Yet his interest in the quality of the *physical* environment is almost obsessive. He is convinced that the excellence of the surroundings is strongly related to the excellence of the work. In fact, he believes the former causes the latter. Like everyone else who enters these grounds to work for a living, Vivian Christiano, production director, *"feels* the beauty." As Ian Hunter says,

> The quality of life here draws the best from you. That's why we're a top ad agency. Like a lot of others, it's more important to me to be happy in my life than just go to work. Driving up that drive through those trees and shrubs and flowers is a happy thing.

If Jim is Mullen's president of environmental standards, then Ian is Mullen's environmental standards CEO or, perhaps better put, Mullen's CES. His job is to direct the landscaping and to direct Mullen's constant "reconfiguration" of space. In addition to being beautiful, Mullen's accommodations are efficient. This is not an organization where you have to wait 6 weeks before the paperwork goes through on your request to redesign some office space. Within hours of your request, you can expect Ian or members of his staff to be on the scene to assess your needs, to create cost and time estimates as the staff shifts into high gear. If you've produced a carefully defended case for your redesign, it's not unlikely that someone could start knocking down a wall within 72 hours of your having put the issue on the appropriate desks. Being responsive is just as important as being beautiful. Not only do Mullen employees not have to be concerned about the threshold quality of the toilet tissue, the technology, and the paper clips, they can count on things like solid brass, real marble, genuine mahogany, and a plant operations staff that will come in record time to help them rethink and redo when they need all that wood, brass, and marble rearranged a bit. Ian and Jim—and everyone else at Mullen—believe that if the leadership provides an environment of beauty and responsive excellence, the staff will provide output that is of the very highest quality possible. No special TQM program so far has been needed at Mullen.

Guideline 9: You cannot expect individuals to produce high quality—to produce their best—if you do not provide them a high-quality environment in which to work.

THE MULLEN MANTRA

It is extremely rare to find individuals at all levels of a corporation who *invariably* communicate the same idea when you talk to them—especially in person-centered organizations where people tend to think for themselves. Yet at Mullen, person after person reacted in exactly the same way to many of my questions and observations—whether I spontaneously struck up a conversation with someone in a hall or was well into a scheduled interview. It didn't make any difference whether the employee was a longtime vice president, a newly hired graphics technician, or a cafeteria cook. Young, old, man, woman—all Mullen employees reacted in exactly the same way when I asked them about their accomplishments at Mullen, their particular place within the organization. By the time my work with the Mullen group was drawing to a close, I could quietly predict to myself how many conversational minutes might elapse before I heard the "Mullen Mantra" escape from an associate's lips. The average amount of time turned out to be 7 minutes. But more important is the fact that this issue is of crucial and almost primary importance in the minds of everyone who works at Mullen.

What is the issue? It is humility. At Mullen, everyone is going to tell you that they

"don't deserve the credit,"
"couldn't have done it all alone,"
"contributed much less than the person in the office next door."

No single person at Mullen will take credit for anything or even admit to having been a pivotal, crucial, or necessary component for one of their many successful outcomes. My first reaction was to be a bit suspicious of that much liberally applied humility. But the genuineness with which Mullen people give others all the credit is not to be denied. Jim gave me my first introduction to the Mullen humility index the first morning I met with him. As I began to explore who he is and how he fits with the company, he began to get uncomfortable: "This is not an organization that reflects the philosophy and ideals of a single individual," he said. "This is a company that could get along very nicely without me. This is an organization of personally egalitarian individuals." Then he began to list associate names with associated characteristics and accomplishments. One person has "a blinding productivity." Another associate has "innate warmth and passion." Another is "America's best barometer of its tastes and lifestyles." It took an inordinately long time for him to yield to my desire to talk about himself in terms of his contributions to his organization. But rather than being atypical in this trait, Jim turned out to be representative of the Mullen staff. Ian Hunter wanted to make the point that the idea that everybody is an *important* part of the team is "no bull." But his own contributions were certainly "not deserving of undue credit." When I offered a compliment to Paul Silverman about the turn of one of his phrases, he immediately replied with, "But, my secretary can say something more intelligent than I most of the time. I'm good, but she can make it better." He added that "hierarchies are related to closed minds, not open minds," as he went on to make another point about the effectiveness of the Mullen team approach to things.

Conversation after conversation found me chasing these very creative individualists down one blind alley after another as I vainly searched for someone who would admit to being responsible for something. Finally, the Mullen Mantra, "I'm not the one to praise, it's everybody else who did the good work," became its own topic of investigation. What was going on here? Were associates unrealistically devaluing their own contributions? Were people *afraid* to take too much individual credit? Why did this kind of person-centered management structure produce such humility as a by-product?

Joe Grimaldi gave the issue some provocative thought in terms of the fundamental goals of the Mullen Corporation. First, he believes that everybody truly wants to provide excellent client service. Beyond that, the most important thing usually feels like a group thing—"the betterment of the group," as he puts it. As Margie Brandfon silently struggled with the issue of the Mullen Mantra, she reflected the dynamics involved. As her thinking began to coalesce, her posture and facial expressions cycled from pride to humility and back again. Eventually, she offered some very revealing insights. "I'll bet there are two reasons behind this," she said.

> On the one hand, quite frankly, most of us, deep down, probably think, "I'm good at my job so I can afford to be humble." On the other hand, we also know that the people we work with here are really *excellent* at what they do. Deep down each of us also knows that we wouldn't be this much of a star if everybody else weren't so good, too, helping to make the stardom possible. Whatever it is, though, I know we get a genuine sense of pleasure out of other people's successes.

Guideline 10: When individualists from all parts and levels of the company learn how to work well within a creative, risk-taking team, genuine humility can become a reality that replaces arrogance, pushiness, and insecurity.

Lots of people you might talk with at Mullen will give you some version of the idea that "Jim Mullen is one of the best things about this place." After you hear this a half-dozen times, you might get the idea—as I did—that the statement is not just an affirmation of Jim's value to the company. It's also an affirmation of the reality that as highly as Jim is thought of within this company, he's just *one* of the good things about working at Mullen. He is a unique individual; he's the leader. But he's also no more or no less than one of the very valued members of the team.

8

Dean Kamen

Founder and President,
DEKA Research and Development,
Manchester, New Hampshire

---

*Have fun doing whatever it is that you desire to accomplish . . . and do
it because you love it, not because it's work.*

—Paul Westphal

When Dean Kamen was a youngster, his teachers complained that he
couldn't do multiplication and division very well and wasn't a good
reader. He also didn't pay attention. When questioned by his parents,
Dean reported that he did, indeed, pay lots of attention. But he "paid
attention only to what he was trying to understand," which, often,
was the rules. He'd get all hung up on the rules, usually trying to
figure out how to get them not to contradict one another. An unques-
tioned faith in the rules for sounding out words and for doing long
division rather quickly gave way to a sincere skepticism about the

validity of all rules. He became "belligerent," one of those difficult children many teachers find hard to love. After he got to high school, still "paying attention only to what he was trying to understand," he figured out how to make a switching device that allows circuits to control high-power light and audio systems. He sold a few of these inventions for quite a few thousand dollars. Then, his older brother, a resident in a Harvard Medical School program, asked him if he could create a particular kind of syringe pump needed for a research experiment. Dean complied, producing an infusion pump that reliably permitted delivery of small doses over a long time period. His brother's physician friends saw it and wanted some for their patients too. Eventually, the National Institutes of Health called to say they wanted 100 of them and they'd pay $2,000 apiece.

Dean gave his parents a vacation trip to Europe, and while they were gone, he jacked the family home up on stilts so his basement workshop could be enlarged. Eventually, before he was very far into his 20s, Dean sold his infusion pump and syringe company to Baxter International for a reported $6 million. Today, Dean Kamen owns several businesses, the most loved of which is an elegantly run research and development operation in New Hampshire known as DEKA Research and Development.

Old Buildings,
Bad Kidneys, Young Minds

DEKA and two of Mr. Kamen's other businesses are located in a series of refurbished buildings in Manchester, New Hampshire, along with some Motorola offices and several other high-tech companies—most of them also entrepreneurial. In the previous decade, these riverside buildings housed one of the largest millworks in the world. When Mr. Kamen, now 45, acquired them a few years ago, they were run down and mostly empty. Today, through his real estate company, he has reclaimed them. Having concentrated on showcasing the original materials, the buildings now house office, design, and manufacturing operations that are beautifully located within spacious, arched window areas boasting exposed woods and bricks. Occupying several floors of the 1874 building is DEKA, a design and technology firm that has predominantly specialized in medical apparatus research. Management per se is not the primary focus of activity at DEKA. This is a company of very bright, high-energy people who very intensely work on solving difficult engineering problems.

Mike Ambrogi, one of DEKA's design engineers, calls Dean "the ultimate rainmaker." His sentiments are echoed by every person at every level in the organization. What they mean is that their boss has an outstanding ability to inspire confidence. Within a group of very bright, well-trained minds, Dean Kamen's "judgment is respected beyond everyone else's." If Mr. Kamen says it can be done—that the seemingly impossible can be created—he does so with remarkable enthusiasm and confidence. Usually, whatever it is, indeed, gets done.

Guideline 1: Have faith in talent and perseverance— your own and that of every person who works with you.

A case in point is the new breakthrough in peritoneal dialysis that Baxter International has begun to market—a machine that Baxter asked DEKA to create a few years ago. Prior to the creation of the new DEKA technology, the old state-of-the-art dialysis machine used a relatively cumbersome pump, 15-pound valves, and a cantilever-beam balance to gauge fluid volumes. Weighing in at 180 pounds, trained technicians were required to mast-hang fluid bags and route tubing through a system that had to rely on a crank handle. When Baxter asked DEKA to improve the apparatus, Dean figured that the best approach was to think about the whole process from scratch—as if you were creating the first dialysis machine ever to exist. If that were the case, what would you want? The answers were obvious: lightweight portability with guaranteed reliability and enough ease of operation that patients could operate it themselves. The Rainmaker convinced his staff they could create such a thing—and within

3 years they had done it. Baxter's new Home Choice PD System weighs about 27 pounds and has eliminated the possibility of user error. DEKA's dialysis team created the design of the housing so that it could fit comfortably beneath the seat of an airplane. For the first time, peritoneal dialysis patients can leave their home cities without worry that they'll lose access to the support machine that keeps toxic wastes from building up in their systems, the machine that literally keeps them alive. Although the many problems that the DEKA design group encountered are of interest for a variety of reasons, there are a couple of aspects of this design process that are particularly important for students of leadership and management, especially person-centered management.

At a critical point in the process, Doug Vincent, a young systems engineer straight out of MIT and the newest member of the design team, was asked to figure out how a flexible sheet of PVC could be attached to a rigid ABS cassette manifold. In retrospect, Doug now talks irreverently about the conventional wisdom that says that you can't join rigid and flexible, thick and thin, PVC and ABS materials. "Here," he says, "we don't take the conventional wisdom all that seriously—unless we personally learn we absolutely have to." With these words, Doug identifies one of the strongest management as well as design principles at DEKA: Tailor-make things so that they fit the needs of the job rather than the rules that somebody has told you are inviolate. Later in this discussion of Mr. Kamen's leadership methods, you'll see how this principle is one of the most often used strategies in his person-centered approach.

---

*Guideline 2: Never accept conventional
wisdom as a substitute for personal experience.*

Another management philosophy component that had direct bearing on the development of this portable dialysis machine is embodied in the person of Richard Lanigan, the member of the team who is responsible for having engineered the design of over 90% of the very intricate pathways and spaces in the disposable cassettes that are critical for machine operation. Richard has been with DEKA for over 10 years and has had significant engineering responsibilities on this and other projects. But he was originally hired as an apprentice machinist. In this company, interest and talent dictate what you can work on—not credentials or job titles.

========

Guideline 3:   Put people where they want to be.

========

U.S. FIRST

The development of scientific and technological interest and talent is such an important goal for Dean Kamen that he now finds himself devoting a relatively large amount of his time to it on behalf of the United States. Early in the 1990s, reacting to his discovery that most kids can tell you the names of the sports stars but cannot name a single living scientist, he started *U.S. First* (for Inspiration and Recognition of Science and Technology). This nationwide project for schoolchildren is designed to stimulate enough interest in science to rival their current interest in sports. With Dean Kamen as its principal founder, U.S. First is a coalition of business, education, and government leaders whose goal is to motivate through projects and competitions. The most well-known of these is a series of gymnasium competitions held around the country each year. Building on a commitment to teamwork and the natural enthusiasm many children have for sports contests these days, interested kids team up with interested scientists and engineers from the corporate sector. These adult-child teams create innovative devices from standard parts supplied by U.S. First. Then, they prepare for elimination matches held on specified target days. The idea is to make scientifically creative processes fun, popular, and available to average kids everywhere.

---

*Guideline 4:   Obligate yourself to take advantage
of every opportunity to develop interests and talents.*

If you were to observe Dean Kamen on typical days at DEKA, as I did, you'd probably notice that he creates no distinction among his many interests, preferring not to split himself into artificial parts. He does not relegate some of his interests to business categories and others to personal or philanthropic categories. So, Dean takes phone calls and other interruptions related to U.S. First activities with as much frequency and enthusiasm as he responds to all other requests for his attention.

Speaking passionately, he'll tell you that today's kids can't tell the difference between celebrities and heroes. He thinks that our culture prepares kids to want the ability to create wealth rather than the ability to create designs, products, and services that offer value to the culture in addition to wealth for the individual. In fact, he laments that the culture is encouraging the accumulation of wealth when, at the least, "it should be teaching average people how to accumulate well-being." Clearly, well-being for Dean Kamen is closely associated with achievement, with devoting your life to having fun because you're doing the things that "you get off on," things that provide self-expression through creativity and production. Mobilizing attitudes about all this through the media is one of his prime projects these days. He wants our culture "to convince kids to be smart." He doesn't want them to settle for being only athletic and sports-minded, or to settle for a dream that includes wealth without achievement and little sense of personal well-being. In the Rose Garden three springtimes ago, while recognizing the accomplishments of U.S. First gymnasium competitions around the country, President Bill Clinton said that "Dean Kamen's energy is the single most inexhaustible thing I've seen in the United States of America." This energy level, which his associates at DEKA often reference with the term *Turbo Dean*, is one of the most outstanding traits of his leadership style. But it is the substance and not the style that most distinguishes his person-centered approach to corporate leadership.

The Leader

The most remarkable thing about DEKA's management system is that there is none. This is one of the flattest organizational structures you're ever likely to encounter. It is difficult to find organizational titles among the 70-odd core personnel that DEKA currently employs. In fact, there are basically two levels in the company. There is the president, and there is everyone else. Dean is dead set against the concept of middle management. When one or two of his former companies got so large that they could not function well without middle managers, he sold the companies. For him, the problem with middle management is not the role and functions; the problem is the distance it creates between the president and the rest of the company's associates. Dean's need to maintain close contact with all employees derives from a variety of personal characteristics as well as philosophical principles. On one side of the ledger, it emerges from one of his acknowledged weaknesses, a tendency to want to micromanage. On the positive side of things, it emerges from his fiercely person-centered orientation to leadership.

Guideline 5: Do everything you can to eliminate
distance between bosses and employees—even if you have
to do something drastic like getting rid of middle management.

Dean Kamen has one of the most elegant open-door systems in the country today. It is a simple system—his door stays open. He makes it clear that he wants each person to drop by when there is something he or she wants to say. He makes numerous reconnaissance visits throughout the company every day. Thus, at first glance, his system seems no different than any other open-door policy we might study. There *is* a difference, however, and that difference is in the attitudes of the associates who work at DEKA. Unlike many other associates at many other open-door companies, these people clearly understand that the boss is sincere when he says, "Drop by to talk when that's what you and I need to do." They feel remarkably free to do so. In fact, *because there is no middle management to go to,* they are forced to do one of two things: Either drop by the president's office when something needs the kind of attention he can give it, or make decisions on their own.

People in a variety of roles at DEKA told me that one of the biggest advantages of this system is that it gives them the opportunity and the blessing to make big and small decisions themselves. Dean's tendency toward micromanagement is generally not of the variety that finds him wanting to have a say about everything. In fact, he prefers *not* to get involved in most of the day-to-day decisions that the staff has to make. Rather, his micromanagement gets troublesome for his staff in those areas where he gets particularly interested and enthusiastic—the design and machinist problems. Occasionally, he just doesn't want to miss out on the fun of being one of those who comes up with the most elegant way to create some new method of doing something. So, these are the areas where he's likely not to let go. As a result, when he's out of town or out of the office, people have no president to turn to and no management to consult. Things can get a little frustrating at these times. But overall, the people at DEKA will tell you that the autonomy and open-door policy are two of the big reasons their jobs are as much sheer fun and as rewarding as they usually are.

---

*Guideline 6: Require and expect that people will
make big and small decisions on their own. Don't keep
people from acting because they're dependent on management.*

Another method of reducing distance between the president and the company is captured in the physical layout of the organization. Unlike most organizations, at DEKA the finance people are not placed strategically near the president's office. In fact, they are the farthest from it. Directly across from his office, Dean Kamen has housed what, for him, is the most important part of the operation. Many visitors have been completely startled as they walked out of Dean's office, pulled open the set of doors directly opposite, and realized they had just walked into the machine shop. Making design become reality is the most important, most pressing, and most enjoyable aspect of the business for Mr. Kamen. Therefore, he has placed the machine shop in the most central position in the company. All employees have access to it through a variety of entries that are proximal to most of the company's other work areas. This positioning allows teams to go from design to prototype within a matter of days. That kind of rapid development of ideas means that making mistakes becomes an accepted part of the process rather than a disaster. As one of his staff members commented, "The ability to recover rapidly from bad ideas is what creates our excellence." The innovation reflected in DEKA's physical layout is typical of the innovation found everywhere here—in the leadership as well as the products.

Guideline 7:   Make it easy for people to
feel OK about making mistakes and provide
mechanisms so they can rapidly recover from them.

THE BASIC INNOVATION: LEARNING

During the initial hours I spent with Dean Kamen and the associates in this company, I was constantly distracted by a certain intensity that regularly seemed to be reflected in each person's face and posture. DEKA associates—whether secretaries, machinists, software people, or design engineers—claim that they love their jobs primarily because they have so much fun. They talk about one another's sense of humor. They talk about practical jokes and cleverly humorous in-jokes. Given how much of this kind of thing they describe, I was consistently surprised that I rarely saw it. I certainly saw *evidence* of fun posted on walls, doors, and bulletin boards; but what I regularly actually *saw* was people staring intently at one another, listening as the other talked softly. I was puzzled.

Eventually, however, I realized that this organization is deeply committed to learning. No matter the role and responsibility, each person soaks up learning like a sponge—and people learn from one another. That's what all the intensity is about.

Jennifer Coon, Dean's secretary, claims he has one of the best senses of humor she's ever encountered. Yet when Jennifer talks with Dean, she is never ready to be entertained; she's habitually intent, always ready to learn. Dean Kamen seems to teach and to learn with most of the breaths he takes. When Jennifer arrives with a letter they've received that she doesn't know how to respond to, Dean gives her a copy of a report to read. He fills her in on the legal and government-related issues that form the background for the letter writer's comments. Intentionally, with Jennifer and with everyone else in the organization, Dean establishes a priority for the act of learning.

Donna Tamzarian is a former DEKA secretary who is now one of the computer software specialists and the primary person responsible for writing and producing the technical manuals that accompany the company's products. She says her boss "knows how to combine practicality and intelligence in the business world." Donna thinks that one of the most practical things that Dean does is to encourage people

> to take all the time they need to learn whatever they want to learn—even if it doesn't look like it's related to anything we might be doing. He never minds if we're spending time learning rather than *doing* something.

Mike Ambrogi talks about *"The Dean Kamen Test,* the 50 questions that he asks each job applicant to see if they can come out alive." Mike says that

Dean always seems to ask exactly the right questions that somebody with this person's training ought to be able to think about. Most people think it's all just part of a job interview, but I don't think it's ever really just a test. Dean always wants to learn something; he wants the person to teach him.

When I first began to question people around the organization about all the intensity and almost unblinking regard of one another as they talked, each looked at me blankly for a few seconds and then explained with a statement like, "Well, I'm just listening. I need to hear what he's saying." Eventually, it became clear that people were telling me, *"I need to learn."*

This is a company where people do not talk over one another or interrupt one another. Not once did I hear two or more people talking at the same time or fighting for airtime. DEKA has its own communication rhythms. These rhythms reflect the energy involved in creating knowledge. Doug, the youngest member of the team, declared that "my learning curve has been off the scale all 4 years I've been here." There is an excitement here—almost a reverence—for all that is possible to learn and for each colleague who is so often the source of new learning.

Guideline 8: The most viable
organizations are the ones that understand
that taking time to learn is never a waste of time.

THE LEADERSHIP INNOVATION: RELATIONSHIP

If you ask Dean Kamen what his management philosophy is, he'll tell you that he doesn't like the word *management.*

You manage projects; but you lead people. And you can't lead people with 5-year plans. You have to get people to take advantage of the moment. Having a 5-year plan for everybody is like getting stuck in a continuous do-loop with no hope of access.

The relationship Dean forms with each person and with the teams is at the center of his leadership philosophy and methodology. In every way, this is person-by-person leadership. Although people at DEKA are not *directly* encouraged to express themselves in their work or to bring their whole selves—personal and public—into the company offices, they do nonetheless. Perhaps the major reason the message is communicated so effectively is that it is an indirect message that is part of every communication that associates receive. Even more important, this integration is modeled by the company president.

Dean Kamen owns 25 pairs of jeans and 25 blue cotton chambray shirts. These 50 pieces of clothing constitute the entirety of Dean's wardrobe. He owns nothing else that he might wear. When the not-yet-married Mr. Kamen takes a woman out for the first time, shows up at work, or takes a client out to dinner, he is wearing a pair of jeans and a chambray shirt. When he attended the Rose Garden festivities where the president of the United States honored him and his work with U.S. First, he was wearing jeans and a chambray shirt. His approach to his wardrobe represents a personal consistency that has become somewhat of a trademark for all people at DEKA. But it's not that all employees wear jeans to work each day. Rather, all employees feel pretty free to bring their authentic selves to work. It is very difficult to find professional rather than personal selves in that organization. Dean expects that each person's unique idea of his or her real self will show up at work and will enter into a real relationship with him and the others who work there.

Guideline 9: Authentic people will get interested, develop their talents, and produce innovative excellence. People who are trying to be what they're not, cannot.

All this is reflected in the absence of personnel policies. Dean says that if someone were to ask if he or she could go on vacation, he'd

say, "How would I know? Can you?" There are no policies about
vacation, sick days, or holidays. In fact, there are no company policies
about anything—not even hours of operation. People come to work
and leave work when it suits their personal habits and the needs of
whatever they're working on that week. Each person has access to a
budget or controls a budget with a remarkable degree of autonomy.
Because much of the activity at DEKA is self-directed, only the individual is in a position of knowing which supplies are necessary and
how much of an area budget or project budget ought to be spent on
them. Dean comments that "if there's too much waste after a couple
of months, they know they have to answer for that. But how could I
tell anybody on the front end what they do or don't need?"

Richard Lanigan thinks the relationships at DEKA create the excellence. He says, "What Dean wants for us is to be happy. That's just
obvious. He works at trying to make us happy people." Recognizing
that the openness at DEKA seems to result in people working at all
odd hours of the days, nights, and weekends, Dean says, "I think that
the way we work around here is sometimes hard on the spouses and
the kids more than on my people. It's the families I especially like to
try to keep happy." Consequently, he stages elaborate and regular
outings for families. For example, he's flown all employees and their
families to Disney World for a long weekend at the attractions. It's
obvious Dean is particularly pleased with the success of the Disney
trip because his eyes just dance when he talks about how hard it was
to get enough buses to meet them at the airport so they could get to
the amusement areas.

This president's commitment to the relationships in the company
is somewhat legendary at DEKA. For example, once Dean agrees to
hire someone, he will not fire that person. Donna says that she has
seen him "devastated" over individuals who didn't work out in the
positions for which they were hired. Dean's eventual response to this
situation is to ask the person, "Where should we put you so that you
can be comfortable here?" His commitment to working with a person
until he finds a good spot for his or her talents and interests can
sometimes cause difficulties for other associates who might be more
likely simply to let the person go if they were in charge. But they are
not. The individual in charge is a very person-centered leader who

believes that if a person is not working out in a particular job, it's as much his own fault as the employee's. For, after all, it was Dean's judgment that placed the person in the current position. Thus, he feels partial responsibility and is willing to accept that responsibility by working with an individual until an appropriate spot in the organization can be found.

Another aspect of Dean Kamen's responsibility to work relationships is so important that it ought not be overlooked or treated superficially. It emerges from the fact that Mr. Kamen has a temper and finds himself unable to completely control it in some situations. For example, if a colleague tells him that they ought to go back down a blind alley that caused them some lost time and money on a project in the past, he might begin to express some feeling as he demands that the person provide an excellent rationale. If the associate wants to resist being argued out of the position, some hot and heavy words are going to be exchanged. Dean's attitude about all this is that he doesn't want any "yes-men" around—he wants people who will argue passionately with him. If he's going to argue passionately, he's going to feel things like enthusiasm, conviction—and anger. Therefore, as far as he's concerned, his relationship and leadership responsibilities require that he warn new associates in advance that he's going to argue, expects them to do the same, and is likely to lose his temper during a heated exchange.

Doug Vincent talks freely about his encounters with this style. He describes himself as having been a young, overly confident engineer when he first came on board at DEKA. Dean lost his temper so many times with Doug that the young man lost count and found himself in the middle of an attitude adjustment phase in his life. Doug and Dean say that those were very difficult days for the two of them— especially because they were all under a lot of stress at the time with the demands of the dialysis machine project. Eventually, Doug says,

> Dean learned to accept my weaknesses and me, his. We were usually direct, honest, and there was always caring. But he could be plain brutal. I might not have stood it if I hadn't known that his people are the most important people in the world to him.

Doug said that those struggles 5 years ago were unbelievably diffi-cult and that on a day he felt himself choking up over the latest brutal thing that Dean had said, he decided he'd better just apply to gradu-ate school. But he didn't go through with those plans. Dean kept losing his temper a little too much, and Doug kept being a little too cocky from time to time. But they stuck it out and kept talking it through. Today, Doug grins from ear to ear as he says, "We worked hard at our relationship so that now we can just say to one another, 'Look, Shit-for-Brains, you're ticking me off!' "

Guideline 10:   Leadership grows out of relationship.
Each person deserves a personal investment.

Doug Vincent is not the only person at DEKA who is proud of his relationship with his boss and proud of the company and the work they do. He is one of many. Dean Kamen's leadership style involves building relationships one at a time and using the relationships to produce innovative, quality work. He encourages risk taking, always responds authentically, provides abundant opportunities for learn-ing, and keeps the distance between the worker and the boss at a minimum. Some parts of his method of person-centered leadership may not be useful for those who cannot do without middle manage-ment. But the genuineness, respect, and eager willingness to learn and to teach that he brings to each of his relationships is something that can pay off in excellence for any leader or manager intent on developing a very person-centered style.

9

Robert S. Davis

Founder and President,
Seaside Development Corporation,
Seaside, Florida

Linger on the details. They're the part that reflects the change. There lies revolution.

—Holly Near

On a hot day early in June a couple of summers ago, a group of 12 Auburn University architecture students arrived in caravan at a prosperous and thriving Gulf of Mexico resort and fishing village. Even though they were coping more or less badly with the early summer heat, these creative kids were ready to energetically present 5 months of their hard work to the town council and interested citizens. Robert Davis, the well-known and celebrated developer of nearby Seaside, Florida, had been invited to come comment on the students' work. They had been asked to redesign a couple of miles of harbor property so as to attract tourist visits to that area while leaving normal harbor

153

activities undisturbed. When Robert Davis and I arrived—Robert, typically later than most—the front of the room was crowded with graphic displays of 12 project designs, each hooked visually to its neighbors. Beneath these visual images were hundreds of small cardboard and wood mock-ups that provided a small-scale view of what the projected building and common areas would look like if student plans were to be accepted by the town's political powers-that-be. The young students were obviously tense but excited. The project had occupied the major portion of their attention, both in class and out, since the early part of January. Each person's contribution was unique. Each student's personality had been projected lovingly onto the scale models and drawings.

Robert Davis did not speak to anyone as we entered the room; instead, he went immediately toward the models and graphics. Throughout the students' verbal presentations, he moved from one end of the display tables to the other, his dark eyes focused and roaming as if he were a gunnery officer trained to capture every detail of a new terrain.

The architecture students had known that Mr. Davis might attend this presentation. The chance to have an urban planner of his reputation comment on their work definitely added more spiced adrenalin to the occasion. For an hour, they explained. For an hour, Robert Davis launched silent visual sorties in the direction of their tiny models.

The students talked about the desirability of small, intimate areas as opposed to intimidating high rises. They cited the need to protect the beautiful trees in the area. They frequently compared and contrasted their ambitious designs with Robert Davis's Seaside, an urban project that is fast becoming a gold standard for this kind of ecological and person-friendly urban planning. Eventually, the students fell silent. The time for comments had arrived.

Robert was standing at the edge of the presenting tables when he first spoke. Many in the room expected that he'd direct his initial remarks to singling out those plans and designs that he found most appealing. But he didn't. Others no doubt expected him to comment on the overall effort that had been involved and the student group's obvious respect for the newer ecological and user-compatible architectural styles. He didn't do that either. Robert's gunnery sergeant eyes

had found a worthy target, and with his first remarks, he attempted
to destroy that target—or at least to render it impotent. "Where did
you get the idea that you had to work with an 80% retail, 20% residential ratio?" he pointedly asked the students. "Did the town council ask you to work within those parameters? That's way too much
retail."

A just noticeable buzz rippled through the room as Mr. Davis
continued.

> There are too many parking lots and not enough parking spaces. Did
> the town Planning Committee tell you that you *had* to work with pe-
> destrian bridges connecting the parking lots on the north side of the
> highway to the harbor on the south? People don't like to use pedestrian
> bridges across highways and they won't use them. Where did you get
> the idea you had to work with foot bridges?

By this time, several people were on their feet. Four or five folks
started talking at once. At least two of the speakers were attempting
to salvage the feelings of the architecture students. After about 15
minutes of heated conversation, Robert stopped in midstride in front
of the refreshment table. An inner struggle made its presence briefly
known as his face darkened and turned downward. When he looked
back at the people in the room, he said, very slowly, "I guess I'm being
hypercritical." Then he stopped speaking. The brevity of that remark
kept its meaning from connecting with his listeners. They dove across
the comment as if it hadn't been uttered as they continued attempts
to shore up the students, pitching compliments at them from all corners of the room. At the same time, many used some hard-nosed
persistence to shore up the self-esteem of the town council's Planning
Committee—and its respect for "practicality."

Within that hour, in great graphic relief, Robert Davis had revealed
one of his most outstanding strengths and probably his greatest current weakness. As is the case with most others profiled in this volume, Mr. Davis's strengths and weaknesses are constant compan-
ions, often emerging from a single trait, often appearing to the public
much like a set of complementary bookends.

Robert Davis is a visionary who will not settle for anything less
than what he believes ought to be. Robert thinks that when he dies,

the most important thing anyone could say about him would be that he was a visionary who kept pushing his dreams until they became reality, an idealist who stood firm in the face of pressures to abandon the possibilities. A single, unuttered statement drove the mind and the performance of the man that humid afternoon: "It doesn't have to be this way."

Guideline 1:   The development of the individual's ability to create visions ought to be one of the most important goals of the company.

Robert does not just take these things on faith; he knows that we don't have to force people to relate to buildings and highways in ways that are uncomfortable for us. It is possible to make profit by catering to the community and residential needs of people rather than by overcommitting to their commercial needs. It *is* possible to create parking areas that don't degrade the ecology or the spirits of the human beings who use them.

As we drove back toward Seaside that afternoon, Robert talked about his embarrassment over his performance in the same way a kid tends to talk about the medicine he knows he has to take. The subject was obviously very distasteful, but he figured only a fool wouldn't admit to the obvious. In response to my baffled looks over what had gone on, he tried hard to help me understand that, for him, the important issue that day was not how well the students had used their creative talents to express the town's wishes, but how shortsighted the Planning Committee might have been in overlooking possibilities for improving the conventional ways we've gone about urban planning in this country. Unlike the typical person in that community center that day, Robert Davis assumed without hesitation that it would be possible to figure out a way to get large groups of people safely across a four-lane highway without badly disrupting traffic or using an overpass foot bridge. When the people he's working with can't think beyond conventional and "obvious" limitations as they plan urban environments, Mr. Davis just digs right in—and keeps pushing.

So Robert concentrated that afternoon on a vision of what *could* be. In the process, he ignored the feelings of every human being in the room. Students, planners, interested community observers—everybody was strafed by his words. Because Robert is doggedly developing his commitment to person-centered leadership, he eventually self-corrected, realizing that his passion for the vision had once again gotten his cart before his horse. Robert says that across the past decade, he's learned that a commitment to better urban living has to include a commitment to the very real feelings of the people he's working with right here, right now, in whatever setting he finds himself. But this gear-shifting in the midst of the passionate moment is not easy for Robert. On some days, he feels like he's fighting a losing battle—not only with urban planning committees but also with himself. If Robert gets embarrassed while at work, it almost always follows a moment when he ignores the emotional components of a situation—emotional factors that seem to be obvious to everyone else. These are the times when he engages in his personal version of the age-old strategy of kicking-oneself-for-being-such-a-jerk. Sometimes he kicks pretty hard.

Robert's persistence borders on the bullheaded; he doesn't give up. He's committed to the continual development of a corporation and a town that will increase employee and citizen participation, stay committed to quality, and eventually change the fundamental values of the American urban culture. A few years ago, Robert realized that if he was really going to have a shot at changing urban realities, he might just first have to change himself—and the way he leads his organization.

Guideline 2: Company executives
cannot achieve leadership excellence unless
they are willing first to change themselves.

By the Sea, by the Sea, by the Beautiful Sea

In the late 1980s, after inheriting 85 acres of land on the beautiful Florida Gulf Coast, one of the first things Robert Davis did was to tramp around Europe a bit. Then he tramped around the South a lot. His goal? Identifying the factors that provoke a certain kind of feeling, one he couldn't completely describe but nonetheless wanted to create in a new town that he would build on those acres by the sea. With Miami architects Andres Duany and Elizabeth Plater-Zyberk, who subsequently won significant awards for their work with Seaside, he went from one residential community to another, looking for the architectural details that could revive that sense of freedom and joy he'd felt as a child when visiting this part of the Gulf of Mexico. Slowly, Duany, Plater-Zyberk, and Davis began to get a fix on things—the warm breezes, wraparound porches, outdoor showers, rocking chairs, and tin roofs. By 1980, Robert had the outlines of an entire town more or less in his head. When he stood on those sandy, scrub-filled acres, he truly saw that town as if it already existed. In those days, he owned most of the dreams, all the possibilities, and all of the town. Today, he owns relatively few acres in town, shares the dreams, and has a lot of neighbors. The story of his successful urban planning efforts has become almost legendary.

Seaside has been discussed and acclaimed in most major U.S. media outlets, many professional outlets, and dozens of foreign publications. The *Wall Street Journal* has commented that "Seaside stands as a model for the possibility of reviving the public realm, pedestrian life, neighborliness and community." *Travel & Leisure* claims that Seaside

> has seized the attention of urban planning theorists and brought them down to see for themselves. It has become the subject of seminars among municipal officials across the country, and it contains the seed of a land-development philosophy that could influence the way America lives in the 21st century.

The Prince of Wales has asserted that "the lessons they're working out at Seaside have very serious applications, both in rural areas and in our cities." In a 1990 article, *Time* writers suggested that "Seaside could be the most astounding design achievement of its era, and one might hope, the most influential."

A new Seaside citizen, Kenneth Scoggins, is a successful investment counselor who got fed up with urban living a few years ago and set out to try to find an island of some sort for himself and his young family. One summer as he was looking around, the family decided to opt for a Seaside vacation. Sight unseen, they made long-distance arrangements for a week's rental of a house named *Sandcastle*, a crisply trimmed, pale-pink, three-story Victorian on Tupelo Circle at the eastern edge of town. Mr. Scoggins told me how they had arrived in Seaside late at night in dense fog. The tired family dumped themselves and their beach gear in the house and collapsed. Early the next morning, a thick fog still enveloped the town as Mr. Scoggins roused himself at dawn to go exploring. He began to walk west from *Sandcastle*, down Grove Avenue. As he moved through the wispy white silence, one stunning Seaside house at a time broke through the fog, presenting itself as if the whole thing were an arranged private performance—complete with the fog-muffled sound of shore birds and the very real presence of jasmine vines and English roses. The astonishing deep pink of the wide-porched *Savannah Rose* on his left gave way to the delicate sun-colored splendor of *Mellow Yellow* on his right. Across the street, the riot of wildflowers in front of *Precious* bobbed their heads in his direction as he looked up—and up—at the multileveled and multidecked pewter handsomeness of *Topisaw*. By the time he'd gone two blocks, Mr. Scoggins pretty much knew he'd found his "island." "It just felt right," he says. "The main thing about Seaside is that it somehow feels so 'right.' "

Guideline 3: Companies ought to concern themselves with what employees and customers feel as well as what they think.

You and Me, You and Me—
Oh, How Happy We'll Be

Seaside returns you to the kind of life you once saw when you were a little kid peeking through screen door summers. Yet the houses in Seaside have been designed by leading architects from all over the country and sophistication runs unabashed all over town. But the sophistication is casual; it's about homeyness, friendliness, neighborliness—and fun. There are traditional houses, nouveau houses, bungalows, and the ubiquitous multistory Victorians. But despite the breathtaking quality, it isn't really the architecture that steals the show. Seaside's colors are outrageous. A house called *Plum Crazy* is the most vibrant shade of violet you're likely to see outside a teenager's closet. Sound awful? It's not. With lots of crisp white trim, it becomes delightful. Another home is painted the most perfect shade of robin's egg blue any nonbird is likely ever to achieve. Houses with multicolor paint schemes are everywhere and they're completely charming. You might find a pale peach Victorian next to a more conservative buff-colored bungalow, but each is likely to be trimmed with various shades of blue, green, and rose in addition to the ever-present white. Seaside's Architectural Review Committee monitors color scheme plans so as to avoid duplicates in close proximity and color schemes that potentially could be side-by-side disasters if located on the same block. So, while the range of creative color combinations that has evolved within Seaside may well be the most ambitious you're likely to find anywhere in the country, the whole thing has been pulled off with exquisite good taste.

The town codes mandate that houses have substantial porches. Even more important than their mandated existence is the requirement that on most lots those porches must be only a few feet from the street so the neighbors will be encouraged to drop by to sit-a-spell as they stroll around town. Strolling is, in fact, one of the chief pastimes in Seaside. With Duany and Plater-Zyberk, Robert Davis intentionally designed the town to be inhospitable for automobiles. Attached garages are prohibited. In fact, any kind of garage at all is considered somewhat gauche unless there's a guest house nestled on top of it. Most people do keep a car or two tucked somewhere on their property, but overflow parking for guests is provided in a large half-circled parking area that surrounds the outdoor amphitheater grounds in central Seaside. Although quite a few people bicycle around town, from early on the entire place was designed to be one gigantic labyrinth of foot paths. Foot paths have been constructed between houses and you'll find foot paths replacing alleys between streets. Urban planners have discovered that most people will walk a quarter mile to get groceries, entertainment, and other necessities, but not a whole lot further. As Seaside has evolved, there are few houses that are more than a quarter mile or so from its commercial center. But it's not that there's anybody telling you to walk anywhere. It's just that you automatically start walking. That's the kind of urban planning for which Robert Davis has become famous. The kind of planning that gets you wanting to do what you know you should do —exercise, relax, make friends, help your neighbors, notice beauty, enjoy your family, laugh. Robert also believes that this planning principle is equally important for constructing a corporate organization.

Guideline 4: Good leaders create environments for employees and customers that encourage a sense of community, sharing, and opportunities to play as well as work together.

The Leader

Robert Davis's umbrella company, Seaside Development Corporation, currently owns most of the commercial property in town, the honeymoon cottages, a few apartments, the town's major home sales and rental agency, some recreation areas, and a few as yet unsold residential lots. Within the last few years, SDC has become operations rather than sales driven, but the corporation currently is making plans to develop a Grand Hotel on the beach. No one connected with SDC will be satisfied unless the new venture ends up providing nothing less than a redefinition of what a Grand Hotel is all about. That's the "Seaside way," relentless implementation of the grand vision.

Like many visionaries, Robert has had to endure a fair number of years of hearing his corporate suite referred to as "The Ivory Tower," a phrase that many people tend to use when they're afraid they can't implement what's coming out of the boss's office. But if Robert Davis does occupy an Ivory Tower, you can bet it's a tower with a twist. For, unlike many visionaries, Robert's passionate investment in the dreams is equalled by his passionate investment in the details. This is a dreamer who has one eye on the grain of sand beneath his feet while the second gazes at the stars. This detail mania of his is greatly responsible for the success that Seaside is now enjoying. It also drives the people he works with crazy.

Robert doesn't meander around when talking about the heart of his vision. He'll put it to you directly. He was intent on creating an environment that could induce a certain kind of feeling within the people who inhabited it: "How does it look? How does it sound? How does it smell? How does it feel?" He believes that attention to detail is what brings dream into reality—and he can be tyrannical about the details. That's how he gets the quality into the enterprise. Robert will spend the extra dollar and the extra hour to get whatever it is to look softer, cleaner, or more vivid, to get it to smell more pungent or to taste more like something for which we might be willing to die.

Beth Folta, the corporation's general manager of development, leaned back at her desk and smiled broadly as she talked with fond resignation about this particular Robert Davis trait. She describes the time Robert let her know about the unacceptable noise level of the machines that keep Seaside's streets so spotlessly clean. He'd given the matter some thought and realized that these machines were going to have to go. They didn't represent "Seaside Quality." Seaside is all about the sound of the Gulf and the sound of kids playing. He wanted the machines replaced, as Beth puts it, "by an army of teenagers who would walk around town pushing brooms." The first time he brought this up, Robert refused even to consider the twin issues of cost and practicality. As she warmed to this topic, Beth's eyes started to twinkle. Eventually, she recalled the time "a building already had been roofed when Robert realized that the back wall needed to be raised a foot" to complete the visual picture it was supposed to be anchoring in that part of town. The wall was rebuilt. She laughingly tells how the Grecian arch over by the family pool was repainted at least five times until just exactly the right shade of sienna had been achieved. It is obvious that Beth Folta is fond of her boss. It's also obvious that she believes her town's standards of quality could not possibly run second to any other—because of Robert.

Guideline 5: Quality is in the details and quality is essential—whether one is creating a town, an organization, or a life.

On a warm summer morning, Robert walked me over to the north side of town, where he could show off Seaside's simple but stunning tennis court design. As we passed one of the junior town architects, Robert stopped in midsentence to talk with the man, pointing out that the sign identifying the tennis courts was visually misplaced at the left of the footpath. He asked the young man if he agreed that it would be better if the sign were moved to the right, directly in front of the bike rack. Although others might assume that the idea was to hide the bike rack, in Seaside that kind of thing is hardly ever the case. At Seaside, you're not likely to find ugly bike racks in need of camouflage. Rather, Robert is always looking at a complete picture, so in this case his focus was the relation of the sign to the visually dominant small tree in the area. The sign and the tree needed to be proximal.

Attention to this level of detail is not something with which the average person is prepared to cope. Robert easily admits he's "a perfectionist with a mania for getting it right." Although he doesn't say so, you get the impression that Robert genuinely can't understand why all the rest of us aren't like that too. But because he knows the people he works with don't share with natural enthusiasm his concern for detail, he began to realize a few years ago that his leadership style needed some alteration. He hadn't believed he had a particular aptitude for teaching people how to appreciate the grand importance of the little things. Without education, people were getting confused. They often didn't know what he wanted and then worried that he'd be critical if they didn't get it right. His coworkers were getting a little timid with him, a little afraid. So, Robert found himself needing to take on this "hypercritical" thing of his, this tendency to quickly evaluate the less than perfect performance and product. To become a person-centered leader, he first had to transform himself. By all reports, Robert has achieved substantial success with this goal during the past few years. But everybody, including Robert, knows he's got a ways to go.

PUSHING THE TEAMWORK ENVELOPE

At the head of the corporation that has created and developed Seaside is a man who has passionate interest and substantial ability in areas that lie at the outer edges of most people's skill bases. Crusading on behalf of the details as well as the visions is not typically a part of a corporate leader's package of managerial skills and interests. Robert had to improvise in the leadership area to get himself and his corporation working together. Investing in and appreciating his own humanity and the human strengths and weaknesses of others may have been the most important thing he's learned to do as a leader. He doesn't expect people to kowtow or eat their anger. He doesn't expect himself to be perfect. Certainly this person-centered leadership approach has had a lot to do with making it possible for the people of Seaside Development Corporation to accomplish all that they have—including development of their abilities to work brilliantly with and for a detail-mongering visionary.

Guideline 6: Accepting weaknesses is crucial. A leader must be kind when addressing his or her own faults just as it is necessary to be considerate and careful with the weaknesses of associates.

In the early years of corporate history, there were more than a few frustrating moments for all concerned as production delays, dropped balls, and communication snafus seemed almost the norm during several critical periods. SDC suffered. Then they started to develop some teamwork. Robert's leadership style now contains a fair number of team-development strategies. He's built teams that can "do it all themselves" without any direct input from the company president. One evening, in the midst of a laid-back conversation with me about life, in general, he leaned forward abruptly and intensely to say that he finds team building "intrinsically interesting. It's all about human development rather than urban development, but some of the most effective principles are precisely the same."

If you were to attend a meeting of the Seaside Architectural Review Committee, the only two things you'd be likely to notice are the blueprints and the teamwork. SAC is the group that translates the town building codes into practical action. Every 2 weeks, Seaside's architects in residence, the directors of development and construction, and Robert spend an afternoon reviewing architect and owner plans for lot development in Seaside. There are three goals: to interpret and implement the Seaside codes, to protect the rights of existing homeowners, and to help the petitioning owner realize his or her plans and dreams. The way this group functions during the meeting is so smooth that a good rap musician could lay some sound tracks beneath the words and perhaps get a hit disc as a result. Although there is no formal chair of the group, it is subtly obvious that Robert is the bandleader. But every member of the team is carrying a heavy contribution load and they're all reading off the same sheet music. No one in the group even announces a topic for discussion. Rather, someone opens a set of blueprints and the rap begins. Quickly, the first to speak points out a badly designed roof deck with the comment, "That's a liability nightmare." Someone else announces that the overall design "will do good things for the lot." A third person wonders if a chimney "ought to be expressed in brick or block." With an almost magical coalescence, the group fixes on a common element, the issue of a stovepipe chimney that plans call for hiding by boxing it in with clapboard.

"Pretend stuff never works."

"Better to run the stovepipe up and let it represent itself."

"No boxing, no faking. Let the most natural expression complement that wall."

As the unheard but nonetheless dominant background rap rhythm continues, someone unrolls a new set of plans for a covered deck connecting the main house and a guest house on an already developed lot. By this time, the SAC team is not just reviewing, they've kicked it all up a level and they're creating, seeing things through the eyes of the deck's architect and through the heart and spirit of the homeowner. Town codes don't permit such covered connecting decks because the idea is to keep as many open spaces between buildings as possible to protect Gulf views. But why not put a small deck a few feet to the north that could carry a second-story deck off the master bedroom? "What a great view of the Gulf they'd get from that upstairs location and they'd also get their covered deck." As one, the team murmurs assent on the downbeat and all five go to work redesigning on behalf of codes, the neighbors' rights and needs, and the petitioner's dreams. When it's all over—in a typical visually artistic moment—Robert suggests they put a duplicate deck on the other side of the house. "The balance on the back side would be very effective if they added a mirror image," he concludes. The group moves on to another set of plans—and the rhythm continues without a missed beat.

Guideline 7: You know you have achieved real teamwork when the room is full of individuals working together with little sense that any single individual is "in charge."

One of the strategies that Robert uses to develop teamwork involves a simple approach to fairness. The number of times he brings it up and the intensity in his voice convince you pretty easily that he's passionately concerned about justice. But for Robert, the essence of justice isn't about a fair-minded approach to tit for tat. It isn't even about judgment or mercy. Rather, a just man is one who makes it his business to try consistently to see issues from the other person's point of view. A just organization is one that encourages its personnel to crawl inside the other person's mind when a dispute arises. For Robert, justice is about balancing your own perspective.

Guideline 8: Values are an important part of good business. Everyone in the organization should feel free to discuss and develop the values that are meaningful for them.

Another strategy Robert uses to get the best out of people is to take them seriously. He wants to pay attention to the good ideas that people want to share. Furthermore, within his organization, he wants to be known for that kind of thing. Robert can be so good at taking his people seriously that it sometimes creates confusion. When he hears a good idea, he'll almost always question further, think about it aloud, and maybe even take notes in a small notebook that is his constant companion. After this kind of interchange, his associate sometimes walks off thinking that Robert is going to implement the idea because he's spent so much time thinking it through and taking it seriously. But that's not always the case. Most likely, Robert's been thinking, not deciding, during that kind of conversation. Chewing things over conversationally is part of his approach to teamwork and decision making.

Guideline 9: It is not possible to lead if you are unwilling to listen. A good leader spends more time listening than talking.

In addition to the teamwork and fairness observations, Robert peppers his discussions of the organization and its functioning with references to the growth of his associates. He's not embarrassed to use such terms as *self-actualization* and *personal growth*. He proudly mentions Donna, who originally cleaned rental houses but asked if she could hang around the sales office and learn. Soon, she became a sales leader. He reminisces about Beth Folta's initial introduction to the corporation years ago. She had come on board as a construction supervisor for a couple of houses, a young woman with a lot of talent and potential but not much people experience. Robert says he's watched her self-actualize over the years, developing into the corporation's most savvy politician:

> The kind of political understanding that Beth now has is mystifying to me. I don't fully understand that kind of thing and I don't enjoy it. I rely on Beth. I know I can count on her judgment when it comes to state and local political factors. I do not second-guess her. Political know-how has become one of her major contributions to the team.

Guideline 10: Provide opportunity and encouragement for the development of each associate's unique interests as well as strengths.

When Robert talks about his leadership skills, he tends to deprecate them. When he talks about his twin passions—the grand visions and the little things—he gets intense, focused, and brilliantly articulate. He shines. First and foremost, Robert thinks of himself as an urban planner. He wants urban environments to exist for people, not for automobiles. He wants people to enjoy residential areas that can help create good neighbors. He wants people to invest in their community and to learn to take governance seriously again so that we can create sensible towns in which to live lives of genuine quality. He wants our kids to grow up in environments that surround them with unspoiled natural objects and events, visual artistry, balance, and the kind of pure sophistication that results when the truly beautiful meets the truly casual. Robert smiles a little shyly as he asks, "Wouldn't it be good for people if residential living were always like camping out with great style?" Creating the kinds of visions that can bring these dreams to reality is always a developmental process. Although many people believe that his design for Seaside was present from the first weeks of inception, Robert knows better. Good community visions are developed by a variety of people, not just one. They can exist only if you let time work on your team and if you can allow it to come to work long enough to demonstrate which of the possibilities deserves the investment. Above all, Mr. Davis believes you've got to be as obsessive with the details as you are with the overall plan. A commitment to an ambitious vision of a good, connected, fulfilling community life is critically important for us at the close of this century. But, in addition, Robert knows "it's just as important what butter tells you and what the soap smells like." This compulsive dual focus of his may be the reason his dreams—as opposed to some other fantasy spinners'—have come to fruition. Robert Davis is a fine example of that extremely rare breed, the visionary-who-makes-it-happen. Others might do well to heed his advice: Be sure you're trying to create something that people or the environment truly needs, and be sure to be very respectful of the human needs of those who share your goals and with whom you work. Also be sure that you do, indeed, "sweat the small stuff."

Guideline 11: The most important thing leaders and managers can do is to express themselves—their strongest visions and beliefs about the development of quality living—through their companies and departments. Work ought to be all about expressing within your organization your finest visions for humanity.

10

Leading Person by Person

Multiple Variations on the Theme

As the Mullen, Kamen, and Davis profiles reveal, there is no single "right" or best way to translate a person-centered approach into a leadership style. The marriage of participatory management fundamentals with a rigorous insistence on one-person-at-a-time management is actually most effective when translated through the personal values and styles of the organization's leaders. There are as many unique interpretations as there are people who adopt this kind of approach. Look closely at a number of the good companies and the highly touted CEOs who run them and you will see that the secret of their success lies in senior leadership attitudes toward the value, dignity, and intelligence of the average person who comes to work. But these leaders don't stop with empowerment; they offer something even more culturally precious within the United States. They have a commitment to the values inherent in individualism. They give their associates *attention,* an opportunity to be the best they can be and to get rewarded for it—social rewards as well as financial rewards. An inspection of currently stellar U.S. corporate organizations reveals that the people who run them are individuals who encourage the individualism of their employees. Each may give attention to different human characteristics and potentials, but there is a single action all have in common—they pay attention to their individuals every bit as much as they attend to their revenue sheets. Many highly touted U.S. companies tend to credit their successes to such strategies as teamwork, statistical graphing, upstream improvements, and other TQM and participatory management methods. Yet for the majority of these special companies, a closer inspection of popular reports—such as those on which the following discussion is largely based—is likely to reveal that something even more fundamental for U.S. corporate success is taking place. That basic strategy is persistent attention to individuals, one at a time.

Listening to the Person at the Front: Southwest Airlines

Herb Kelleher, CEO of Southwest Airlines, has been called such things as "brazen" ("Flying Straight," 1994), and reports of his successes almost always make reference to his "unorthodox" methods and "antics." But as pointed out in *Fortune,*

> Behind his clowning is a people-wise manager who wins where others can't. In an industry that has been losing billions, Southwest is rapidly expanding. . . . The bond of loyalty between employees and company may have vanished elsewhere in America, but it is stronger than ever here. (Labich, 1994, p. 46)

Kelleher is showing how a large, publicly held company can concentrate massive attention on the individual and can make that pay off in terms of profit, growth, and employees who feel their jobs are adding much to the overall quality of their lives.

Southwest's remarkable achievements have been much heralded (Hartley, 1994), including their ability to turn an airplane around at the gate in only 15 minutes and the ability to double their market share in some recent years. So has Kelleher's leadership style, the factor most often credited with the successes (Reed & Maier, 1994). Kelleher runs one of the most consistently person-centered organizations in the country. He cares about his people. He makes it very clear that he will do all he can to increase their overall satisfaction with life. He insists that all associates be partners in the Southwest enterprise, a role that his people seem to adopt with vigor, and even glee.

In an effort to learn more about Kelleher's leadership strategies, I investigated the Southwest management system by studying its effects on the person who is the object of all the fuss—the typical employee. In Cleveland, Ohio, I interviewed baggage handlers who are part of the Southwest Airlines family. The first thing I discovered is that this is a group of people who are delighted to talk about the company, their feelings about their jobs, and their CEO.

Dan Ross is a ramp agent with Southwest. His job has several responsibilities, including baggage handling, deicing, guiding planes from access runways to the gate, and towing planes away from a gate. Dan trained to be a fine artist at the Chicago Institute of Art, returned home to the Cleveland area when he graduated, and showed his work in galleries in Ohio and elsewhere. Dan has held a variety of jobs to make ends meet as he makes a name for himself in the art world. For a couple of years, he says, he had wanted to "get on at Southwest." Why? "Because everybody told me they're so great to work for."

> What I like best is that I can be myself. You don't have to hide anything here. Like, my art is just accepted. In fact, they encourage it. I suggested that I paint a mural for this terminal—or somewhere else—and everything's all set now. I'm going to do that. Lots of people here have degrees and even if they don't, they're smart people. For example, safety isn't an issue here. Nobody ever talks about safety. It's like nobody ever talks about oxygen, but it's a priority. Southwest hasn't had a major accident. I believe it's because of all the people at this airline. We get the job done. We work together.

As he talks about the teamwork, he says that in the midst of a busy day, it's never a surprise when a pilot leaves the plane to come help the ramp agents unload baggage. People pitch in when it's time to get the jobs done and when it's time to celebrate. Dan says it's also not uncommon—"just for the heck of it"—for supervisors to buy everyone pizza and ribs. "Everybody notices what you do and gives you genuine compliments. Everybody listens to all your ideas. And we laugh, man. Everybody *laughs* all the time."

When Herb Kelleher came to Cleveland, Dan came in to the airport, even though it was his day off.

> Herb is our outstanding spokesman. He's phenomenal. I can't say enough about his contribution. We don't have a hidden agenda here. We want to do more of it and we want to do it cheaper. Herb keeps us aware of the competition. For example, when American Airlines does something new somewhere else, Herb sends us a note, a videotape, or we get the word through *Love Lines,* our publication. We try to brainstorm it to see if we can come up with something better. When we do, we let people know. It's never a surprise to see your idea start being used.

Dan reports that his paintings are beginning to sell. I asked this 28-year-old new father if that means he'll be leaving Southwest sometime soon. "No," he said thoughtfully, "my work doesn't really pull me away from Southwest because they make room for it here—like with the mural, and when I have to switch shifts because of a show or something. Actually, I'm thinking of trying to move up. That's really what I'd like to do. It may sound like a cliché, but this company really does care about you. They really do."

Mark Figgins, in his early 30s and a father of three children, is another ramp agent who has been with the company for about 2 years. "They make you feel like you're really making a contribution. It's hard to describe, it happens from the beginning, from the training. There's just an atmosphere and attitude that lets you know you really count."

Mark talks about a program called "A Day in the Field" in which associates can decide to go somewhere else in the company to observe how another job is done in case they might be interested in that kind of work. "You're always encouraged to go for anything else in the company that interests you."

Mark drives 92 miles round trip each day to the Cleveland airport. He says he's had a couple of opportunities only 5 to 10 miles from his home

> but, it wouldn't be worth the switch. They're very fair with their pay. I've had several raises. And I've also worked other places. Before this job, I always dreaded going to work. But people here just don't mind coming to work. To me, that's worth the drive every day.

> The day Herb Kelleher came last year, I came in to talk with him. He's just like you'd expect him to be—laid-back, joking. He never forgets a name. He let's us know *we* make the difference at Southwest. It's because of us that this airline is breaking all records.

Certainly, these ramp agents echo what observers are saying about Southwest Airlines and its CEO. Herb Kelleher is dramatic in his approach to management; he uses colorful language, dresses in costumes, shows up with surprises. He has used these tactics to get his associates' attention. Whether he gets the knowledge through intuition or through management study, Kelleher knows that the typical person who comes to work can be creative and dedicated and can produce outstanding work if you just make him or her a partner in design, management, and profit. He believes that if you give employees attention, and let them know you care, they will perform for the company and will enjoy happier lives. The ramp agents I spoke with are living evidence of the remarkable effectiveness of this person-centered approach.

The Employee's Need for Self-Expression and Attention: FedEx, Mary Kay, Quad/Graphics

At Federal Express, CEO Fred Smith's personal style and management philosophy have been far more low-key than Herb Kelleher's and others' (Denton, 1992; Trunick, 1989). But his approach to employee recognition has not been low-key and that has been one of the most important strategies responsible for the success of FedEx. It has earned him the respect of the national business community as well as his employees. Within the *People, Service, Profits* philosophy of this company—known worldwide for delivering what it says it will deliver exactly when it says it will do it—it may be surprising to learn that it is the FedEx people who come before the service. But that is not an accident. As Smith has said, "I think a lot of companies talk about how their employees are their most important asset, but where you can really tell whether it is very important or not is how much time their senior management spends on the issues" (Denton, 1992, p. 10). Smith reports that he spends a full 25% of his time on personnel issues. Much of what he thinks about has to do with employee recognition programs—including a multiplicity of award programs and an outstanding program of responsiveness to employees that requires management to respond to an employee concern within 14 days. At FedEx, individual employees know they matter. They know they will get attention for what they do well and for the complaints they want to share. As a result, one has confidence that one's overnight letter is going to arrive on time. The employees at FedEx have made that such a virtual certainty that at this point people have come to simply take it for granted.

Although FedEx is considered a mainstream organization, there have been some who have looked askance at the Mary Kay Cosmetics organization, suspecting that the company is some kind of aberrant phenomenon, hardly worth emulating (Farnham, 1993). Yet no one would dispute the fact that Mary Kay Ash, the company's founder, has made a tremendous amount of money over the years (current fortune in excess of $320 million) and so have many of the people who work for the organization (6,500 associates have the use of complimentary upscale cars worth over $90 million). The reason for the Mary Kay success has been simple and almost completely due to the motivation that results from the recognition that Ash gives her employees. At each step of an associate's advancement, she is celebrated. "That feting is the key to the company's success. Emotional compensation matters almost as much as cash. To women who have made their pile, it probably matters more" (Farnham, 1993, p. 71). Mary Kay Cosmetics revenues have amounted to billions since the company was founded 35 years ago. Its management strategies are founded almost entirely on principles of rugged individualism. The message is clear: *You can do this. You can be extraordinary if you work hard, believe in the product and company, and help us figure out what we need to do better. When you succeed, we'll give you diamonds, cars, and cash. But we're also going to give you parties, videotapes of your personal successes, roses, home town publicity, personal recognition from Mary Kay Ash herself, and anything else you and we can think of to let you know how great you are and how much you've accomplished.* What could be a more historically American message? Despite the suspicion her work sometimes engenders, Ash has created a very profitable company and she has done so by working within the country's culture and by mastering the leadership art of giving personal attention to each person who works along with her.

Harry Quadracci is the successful founder and president of one of *Forbes* magazines's 100 Best Companies to work for in America, Quad/Graphics (Berman, 1995). He also has a simple approach toward the psychological needs of people. He believes in the value of attention: Everybody deserves it, everybody gets it—starting with himself. To make a symbolic point, Quadracci has been known to walk a high wire at work and to arrive at the Christmas party on an elephant—all this in the name of getting the message across that people are free to express themselves without worrying about artificial conventions and limitations. Although these theatrics may seem superficial to some, they clearly are not experienced that way by his workers, who have developed themselves personally at the same time they were developing Quad/Graphics into a force in its field. Quadracci says,

> We hire people who have no education and little direction. They are the kind of people who look at their shoes when they apply for a job. They join the firm not for its high wages—starting salaries on the floor are only about $7.50 an hour—but because we offer them a chance to make something out of themselves. (Berman, 1995, p. 46)

The Quad/Graphics philosophy welds individualism to classic TQM empowerment. The result is teamwork that encourages people to do their best on behalf of the team, the company, and themselves as individuals.

Summing Up

Some person-centered companies concentrate on giving individuals attention through emotional and material rewards as well as opportunities to express themselves in their work.

Creativity Development:
3M, Nickelodeon, Nike

In his own way, the CEO of 3M, Desi DeSimone, is every bit as creative as Smith, Ash, and Quadracci in knowing how to motivate people and to participate in the profitability that results when their talents are turned loose (Collins & Porras, 1994; Loeb, 1995). In fact, 3M has consistently appeared on annual lists of the top most-admired companies. But unlike others who often make those lists, 25% of 3M's profits have consistently resulted from new products that have been in the product line for less than 4 years. This particular bit of 3M wizardry results from DeSimone's attitude toward his employees and their potentials. This is a company that plans for innovative success and does so by recognizing the psychological needs of the people who are expected to create those innovations. At 3M, DeSimone has long insisted that technicians be free to spend at least 15% (and sometimes 50%) of their regular work time on any research project they wish, including those that are inspired by personal interests and hobbies. (Recall, that's how Post-it Notes were conceived.) *But despite the emphasis on individualism, this is a related, not rugged, individualism.* A strong part of the company culture emphasizes sharing—of time and ideas. Anyone is free to e-mail anyone else at 3M to get some innovative expertise. Individual and team successes get lots of personal attention at many 3M celebrations throughout the year. This legendary balance between teamwork and individual creativity results in a management group that has been at 3M, on the average, well over 20 years.

In just 15 years, Nickelodeon's Gerry Laybourne has turned a pint-size outfit into an organization that posted an estimated $330 million in revenues in 1994 (Stewart, 1995). She has done it by creating dozens of innovative management strategies designed exclusively for one thing—unleashing the individual creativity of Nickelodeon's employees. At her insistence, project offices are round, oval, or perhaps oblong. If employees have creative ideas while wandering in the intentionally crooked halls, there are chalkboard walls on which to write. People are encouraged to play with a puttylike substance during meetings. Laybourne's innovations on behalf of creativity arise from a strong sense of respect for individuals as people, not just as creators. "I'm one of those sick executives who abolished the corner office to create a more egalitarian space," she has said (Stewart, 1995, p. 70).

At Nike, Phil Knight has specialized in strategies that, as some observers say, "balance a team of individualists with the constraints of business" (Yang, Oneal, Hoots, & Neff, 1994, p. 88). In other words, like Jim Mullen, Knight is an iconoclast who has provided leadership by encouraging his people to treasure their uniqueness and to use that uniqueness to move against the tide. Although Knight's reclusiveness has led to less reliable knowledge about his philosophy than might be desirable, there is fundamental agreement that standard business practices have been despised and discarded at Nike and that the company rewards individual creativity and innovative maneuvering on the part of management. The legendary 2-hour lunchtime exercise break at Nike has produced—by many accounts—the most muscular employee group in the country and a company culture that seems as determined to change the popular culture as it is determined to beat competitors while making billions. It is no secret that Phil Knight's intention has always been to use Nike as a tool to help craft a popular culture that provokes risk taking on behalf of physical fitness and individualism. Although Nike has had its fiscal ups and downs in recent years as it rapidly grew into an international powerhouse, what has not changed is Knight's attitudes toward management. He talks about the source of Nike's power in terms of the Nike management culture: "The team on the run. Everyone up to speed. Everyone on the same team" (Katz, 1994, p. 317). In many ways, Nike has been the epitome of related individualism in the corporate world. Teamwork is critical; individual initiative and creativity are mandatory.

Summing Up

Some person-centered companies specialize in creating
expectations and opportunities for personal creativity.

Taking the Experts Seriously:
Wal-Mart, Allen Machine Products

In a 1994 episode of a popular emergency room television drama
series, an administrator tells a depressed physician that he's not supposed to get good feelings from his work; "if you want to like your
job, go work for Wal-Mart," he says. People who heard that line from
the perspective of those who are aware of current changes in corporate America knew exactly what was being cited—the David Glass
approach to leadership. At Wal-Mart, CEO David Glass has never
been blocked from his management goals by his unprepossessing
style (Saporito, 1993). Despite the ability of his persona to blend into
the woodwork, Glass's reputation among his employees is perpetu-
ally high. That's because he has insisted that when it comes to knowing how to run the stores and the company, he and Wal-Mart management need to make their highest priority job listening to the
experts, their employees. Wal-Mart employees like to be listened to,
and they like working for this company. On the annual lists of most
admired companies, it is never a surprise to see Wal-Mart in the top
10 and to find David Glass at the top of the list of most admired CEOs.
     When Glass visits a store—as he often does—he typically asks,

> How are sales? He wants to know. What's the competition doing? How
> is apparel selling? Who's the biggest competitor in menswear? Depart-
> ment 19 isn't doing well; got any ideas? Should we be doing something
> different? Where did you work before you came to Wal-Mart? Are you
> challenged enough by the work? (Saporito, 1993, p. 80)

Glass is invariably described as a down-to-earth kind of person who
truly understands that great wisdom resides in the people who clerk,
stock, sell, clean, and manage the typical Wal-Mart store, whether you
find it in Auburn, Arkansas; Cedar Rapids, Iowa; or outside Wash-

ington, D.C. Glass sincerely appreciates people, and by all measures, people appreciate Wal-Mart—both the employees who work hard there and the customers who spend upward of $50 billion there each year.

At the opposite extreme from Wal-Mart in terms of size is Allen Machine Products. For Peter Allen, owner-operator of this relatively small, but high-quality, custom-metalworking shop, the route to recognizing employee expertise was through a series of personal growth experiences (Schreiber, 1995). Over the course of the past 5 years, Allen and his managers have taken many psychology-based courses whose sole purpose was individual growth. He and his management staff thought it important to get back to personal basics and in doing so managed to triple profits, which reached $5 million in 1994. Allen did that while Long Island, the company's home, experienced one of its worst recessions and lost around 100,000 jobs. Allen credits their success, in large part, to expertise. He recognizes the limits of his knowledge and the location of the real expertise. "We're really in this together," he says. "The people out on the machines know a lot more about those machines than I do, so if I don't share with their knowledge and I just come in here as a boss, it doesn't work. This is a shared operation, just as it's a shared level with our customers" (Schreiber, 1995, p. 43). A related individualism seems to be the only management philosophy in operation at this small but growing U.S. company.

Summing Up

A relentless emphasis on the worker-as-expert creates person-centered cultures in some companies. There, management habitually listens to the typical employee.

Ethics and Values: Levi Strauss

Although other person-centered leaders focus on empowerment and creativity, a growing number of corporate chiefs are finding it more and more comfortable to give play to their desires to bring the values and morals of their employees to center stage. Among these, Levi Strauss Chief Executive Robert Haas stands out (Impoco, 1993; Mitchell & Oneal, 1994). Management aspirations for the company highlight the role of recognition. Levi's strives to "provide greater recognition—both financial and psychic—for individuals and teams that contribute to our success . . . those who create and innovate and those who continually support day-to-day business requirements" (Mitchell & Oneal, 1994, p. 47).

This aspiration represents a very clear statement of person-centered values. In fact, it could serve as a mission statement at most person-centered companies. Yet Levi Strauss is moving even further into uncharted leadership territory. Because of Haas's leadership, Levi's intends to consciously return morality to the workforce—that is, it intends to make morality fashionable again within the U.S. company, just as it so often was in past centuries. Here is a CEO who has seen the damage wrought by asking people to leave their personal selves and values at home when they come to work. He wants his employees to feel whole again. A couple of years ago, Levi's cited "pervasive violations of basic human rights" as it began to phase out contracts with Chinese manufacturers. Although Haas believed this was the "right thing to do," he continually reaffirms that he believes good ethics are good business. In this case, Levi's was concerned that their "jeans are often equated with the rugged individualism and free spirit of America's Old West. . . . Dubious business practices at home or abroad, could damage its image—and perhaps its commercial success" (Impoco, 1993, p. 50).

Although record profits at Levi's were posted several years in a row, 1994 sales were disappointing. Haas, a former peace corps worker, does not intend to lose Levi's competitive edge. He has come to believe that his company and the country are now willing to understand that "responsible commercial success" is the only way to achieve corporate goals. For example, a marketing campaign that followed a single young man in 501 jeans down a street was a bust in U.S. Hispanic communities, where people wondered if the poor fellow had no friends. The individualism taken for granted in that advertising campaign was viewed with confusion in the more communal Hispanic culture. Levi's current attention to issues of diversity made it possible for them to pick up on the gaffe. They produced a more family-and-friends-oriented campaign for Hispanic markets. Results improved. Haas maintains that social responsivity is not just a feel-good tactic—it's always smart business. Within the company, successes with diversity and empowerment have been impressive. According to federal labor reports, the company's percentage of women in management (54%) significantly exceeds the average for U.S. corporations. When listening to the low-key, well-reasoned ethical approach of Robert Haas, the power of the U.S. personal-public separation ideology becomes even more clear and more impressive —and of even greater concern. The Levi's philosophy quite consciously intends to get American business back on an ethical track again.

Summing Up

It is not uncommon for person-centered leaders to dedicate the company to the creation of robust ethical points of view that the company can use in efforts to be responsive to employees as well as customers.

The Human Spirit:
Herman Miller, Rosenbluth Travel

Some contemporary leaders, like CEO Kerm Campbell at Herman Miller, realize that an individual-by-individual approach to management inevitably leads us to a redefinition of the role of the corporation in society. Campbell is a visionary who does not limit himself to constructing visions for his company (Day, 1994). He cares just as much about the future of U.S. culture. Campbell believes that companies can no longer be concerned only with revenue development. "We've got to help people build lives as well as careers," he says (Day, 1994, p. 38). As he took the reins a few years ago from Max DePree at his highly successful Michigan furniture manufacturing company, Campbell helped design an innovative annual report that contained 39 informal essays he had written on what it means to be human in today's corporation and in today's world. In *On Risk*, Campbell

wrote, "Only by risking something do people and corporations progress . . . only by taking risks do people *live*." Like his predecessor,
Campbell is unashamed to comment publicly on his views about
right living. He thinks the corporation and its leaders have an obligation to do so because the job of the corporation concerns the development of the human spirit every bit as much as it is about the development of the company's profits.

This is a very person-centered and results-oriented company
whose leadership spends a primary amount of time developing individuals as well as developing teams. Campbell says the leader's
most fundamental objective is "to release human potential and liber-
ate the spirits of the people in the organization we work for" (Day,
1994, p. 36). Now that Campbell stands watch, Herman Miller has
two primary objectives: a substantially increased share of the international market and substantially decreased time for getting the
product to market. Rather than putting the customer first to accomplish these, Campbell says,

> We start with the employee, because I believe that you have to get it
> right inside before you can do it right outside. My focus is on liberating
> the human spirit within the company, so we can furnish environments
> to our customers that will allow them to reach their full potential. (p. 39)

As the Herman Miller philosophy illustrates, a firm commitment to
individual growth finds the company balancing its focus on customer, product, and revenue with an equally important commitment
to the employee.

Rosenbluth International Travel is another company committed to
quality of life as much as it is committed to the quality of the bottom
line (Holzman, 1993; Rosenbluth & Peters, 1992). Owner-operator
Hal Rosenbluth has written,

> Companies have profound and far-reaching effects on the lives of the
> people who work for them, so it becomes the obligation of companies
> to make the effects positive. All too often companies bring stress, fear,
> and frustration to their people—feelings they bring home with them
> each night. This creates problems at home which people bring back to
> work in the morning. The cycle is both terrible and typical, but not what
> most companies would want as their legacy. It's certainly not what our

company wants: especially when there are so many things we can all do to enrich the lives of our people. (Rosenbluth & Peters, 1992, p. 10)

As at Herman Miller, the customer comes second at Rosenbluth International because the employee comes first. Mr. Rosenbluth presents the logic of this approach:

> The highest achievable level of service comes from the heart. So, the company that reaches its people's hearts will provide the very best service. . . . Only when people know what it feels like to be first in someone else's eyes can they sincerely share that feeling with others. (pp. 24-25)

So, at this highly successful international travel company, the individual comes first. The core of Rosenbluth's management strategies involves management workshops where people engage in personal growth activities designed to develop their potentials and self-understanding. These experiences are called "Live the Spirit" seminars, a title that conveys the Rosenbluth attempt to encourage people to bring their spirits, their complete selves, to the workplace. As is the case in most person-centered companies, the strategies used to develop individuals and company profits at Rosenbluth are as unique as the company itself, limited only by the creative capacities of the employees who design them.

Summing Up

Some person-centered companies emphasize personal development and encourage associates to bring their spirits and hearts to work along with their brains.

Companies in Person-Centered Transformation

The list of quality companies run by top-notch CEOs who believe in person-by-person management is already impressive, but still growing. Although many of these corporate chiefs do not necessarily use the label *person centered* when thinking about their management styles, they nonetheless can articulate the need to give special attention to each employee, and they understand the relationship of that strategy to success and to social responsibility. As revealed by the illustrations above, many of these companies were begun or were jump-started within the past 20 years by leaders who have come into their philosophical prime during this important moment in U.S. management history. In many of these companies, this person-by-person way of doing business is the only way business has ever been done.

Yet there are many companies wanting to move from unsuccessful and outmoded forms of management toward newer ways of thinking. Among these are the companies that have tried TQM and failed. There are good models of person-centered achievement for this kind of company also. For example, L. L. Bean, the catalog sales company, provides a solid case study of transformation ("At L. L. Bean," 1994). Since its inception in 1912, L. L. Bean has been known for outstanding customer service. Stories of employees driving miles to deliver goods have made the rounds for years. But as the century headed toward its close, the company found itself locked into an infrastructure that limited real communication across departments. Bean started to watch the competition get ahead. The leadership turned to TQM but had the foresight to realize that focusing on process improvement—as others have done—wasn't going to get the job done. Instead, they moved into an employee-centered initiative. New rewards—psychic as well as financial—were instituted. The internal customer became the most important customer. After several years' experience with the new management practices, Bean has begun to experience increased profits in several areas.

Olin Pool Products general manager Doug Cahill reports on another transformation success story (Stewart, 1994). Formerly, the company blamed poor performance in sales on bad weather rather than bad management, and customer dissatisfaction on bad employees. At that time, he says he'd

> talk to every person who touched that order, looking for the person to kick. I'd talk to four people—and all four people did their job. After three trips of not being able to kick somebody, I said, "This is crazy. It isn't the people." (Stewart, 1994, p. 48)

One observer has written, "Like a cartoon character who races off a cliff and out into thin air, Olin Pool Products was in trouble without knowing it. . . . TQM helped, but not enough" (p. 48). Cahill's response to his dilemma was to design an organization that gave attention to its people and then empowered them. Cahill says he designed "an organization so flat you could stick it under a door" (p. 48). At times, Cahill reports, he would knee-jerk back to the old controlling ways when something went wrong. But then he'd swing back toward letting people know that only the customer needed to be satisfied—not management. Eventually, the creativity of his people forced him toward a more balanced approach to his own person-by-person management philosophy. Olin survived a plant fire; the company got back on a solid financial footing.

Summing Up

Although many person-centered companies have been started by entrepreneurs who were interested in this kind of leadership from the early days of company development, other companies are choosing to undertake person-centered management revitalization. They are borrowing some of the quality improvement and participatory management strategies but are primarily focusing on person-by-person transformation.

Summary

Reports such as the ones in this chapter have been flourishing in the popular press as well as in textbooks these days. Picking out the person-centered companies becomes a relatively easy matter because the language is different. *These leaders don't just talk about empowerment; they talk about the company's responsibility to develop the human potentials of its people—all of its people.* These executives don't confine themselves to discussions of team functioning; they also talk about the individuals who make the teams win. *Above all, person-centered leaders aren't embarrassed to talk about the heart, spirit, values, ethics, and emotion.* They reference these important human capacities just about as often as they talk about their ideas and production, marketing, and export capacities.

People who truly pay attention to employees inevitably talk about people things as well as company things. But so often in these reports —especially in popular press accounts—the specific steps these leaders took to get where they are have been glossed over or at other times misunderstood. This problem is compounded by the fact that in many important ways, good person-by-person leadership is idiosyncratic to each situation and each leader; it's individualistic. What, then, are the commonalities? What can be done to move a company into person-centered management?

References

At L. L. Bean, quality starts with people. (1994, January). *Personnel Journal,* pp. 60-61.

Berman, P. (1995, February 27). Harry's a great storyteller. *Forbes,* pp. 42-47.

Collins, J., & Porras, J. (1994). *Built to last.* New York: Harper Business.

Day, C. R. (1994, November 7). Kerm Campbell: We need to change the meaning of management. *Industry Week,* pp. 36-40.

Denton, D. K. (1992, Summer). Keeping employees: The Federal Express approach. *SAM Advanced Management Journal,* pp. 10-13.

Farnham, A. (1993, September 20). Mary Kay's lessons in leadership. *Fortune,* pp. 68-77.

Flying straight with Southwest Airlines Chairman Herb Kelleher. (1994, October 10). *Brandweek,* pp. 36-40.

Hartley, R. F. (1994). *Management mistakes and successes* (4th ed.). New York: John Wiley.

Holzman, D. (1993, August). When workers run the show. *Working Woman,* pp. 38-41, 72-74.

Impoco, J. (1993, August 2). Working for Mr. Clean Jeans: Levi's leader Robert Haas cares about morals as well as money. *U.S. News & World Report,* pp. 49-50.

Katz, D. (1994). *Just do it.* New York: Random House.

Labich, K. (1994). Is Herb Kelleher America's best CEO? *Fortune, 129*(9), 44-52.

Loeb, M. (1995, January 16). Ten commandments for managing creative people. *Fortune,* pp. 135-136.

Mitchell, R., & Oneal, M. (1994, August 1). Managing by values. *Business Week,* pp. 46-52.

Reed, S., & Maier, A. (1994, May 2). Cleared for takeoff. *People,* pp. 67-70.

Rosenbluth, H. F., & Peters, D. M. (1992). *The customer comes second.* New York: William Morrow.

Saporito, B. (1993, February 8). David Glass won't crack under fire. *Fortune,* pp. 75-80.

Schreiber, P. (1995, February 6). Touchy-feely approach gets results. *Newsday,* p. 43.

Stewart, T. A. (1994, November 28). How to transform your organization. *Fortune,* pp. 48-61.

Stewart, T. A. (1995, February 6). Creatively managing creativity. *Fortune,* pp. 69-78.

Trunick, P. (1989, December). Leadership and people distinguish Federal Express. *Training and Development,* pp. 19-22.

Yang, D. J., Oneal, M., Hoots, C., & Neff, R. (1994, April 18). Can Nike just do it? *Business Week,* pp. 86-90.

Thinking Creatively: Part II

1. What are the differences among the Mullen, Kamen, and Davis person-centered leadership approaches?

2. What are the similarities among these three person-centered approaches?

3. Which person-centered principle identified in the Mullen, Kamen, and Davis chapters could you most likely use with comfort? Which would be the least comfortable for you?

4. In considering Chapters 7 through 10, what list of 10 personal characteristics might best describe effective person-centered leaders?

5. To be remarkably effective, does a person-centered leader have to be charismatic or in some other way unusual?

6. Weaknesses are identified for each man in the Mullen, Kamen, and Davis chapters. What weaknesses of your own might co-workers find noteworthy these days? How can you best minimize their effects on an organization?

PART III

Making the Changes
That Make a Difference

11

The Possibilities
for Transformation

Person-centered leadership is not something that only the leadership gifted can accomplish. It surely also is not a style of leadership that only works for the few charismatics among us. As Kouzes and Posner (1987) pointed out after studying well over 1,000 organizational managers, leadership, in general,

> is not only an understandable but also a universal process. Leadership, we conclude, is not the private reserve of a few charismatic men and women. It is a process ordinary managers use when they're bringing forth the best from themselves and others. (p. xxi)

So it is with this uniquely American, person-centered style of leadership that relates individualist values to social values, transforming rugged individualism into a related individualism that makes it possible to effectively translate quality improvement methods into a U.S. organizational structure.

Summing Up

Person-centered leadership excellence can be achieved by anyone. You don't have to be charismatic to be a good leader.

A Word About Continuous Quality Improvement

Person-centered leadership is an approach that can be used to transform any set of Western management methods into a useful model for the organization. But these days, arguably the most important set of management methods getting a lot of attention are the continuous quality improvement models. Continuous improvement methods are particularly compatible with a person-centered approach because of the TQM focus on the worker as expert. This can put the worker at center stage—which, from a person-centered perspective, is right where he or she ought to be.

It is important to point out that person-centered leadership strategies are not a substitute for continuous improvement strategies any more than they can be a substitute for a company's unique goals and visions. Emphasis on shared information and vision spinning, teamwork, and statistical measurement are powerful TQM tools that have been shown to work quite effectively in many settings around the world—particularly within those cultures that have deemphasized individualism in favor of more relational ways. There is every reason to believe that they also can provide an effective and long-lasting addition to the U.S. corporate management toolbox. So, rather than as a substitute for such methods, person-centered leadership is best seen as a method of leadership that provides the kick-start and fuel for continuous improvement in organizations residing within national cultures that are individualist in orientation and likely to retain that individualist spirit.

Summing Up

In this country, person-centered leadership can provide the fuel that gets management models such as TQM finally up and working.

Person-Centered Basics

There are three fundamental theoretical differences between person-centered leadership and other approaches. These need to be constantly in focus and continually communicated and refined within each unique organization.

RELATED INDIVIDUALISM

The first basic principle of person-centered theory is captured by the term *related individualism.* The individual is primary—not more important than the team, but never to be sacrificed for the team or the group goals. Everything that gets done is accomplished through person-by-person management, one individual at a time. Individuals get attention. They get recognition. This is not, however, a rugged individualism that asserts the *independence* of the individual; rather, this is a related individualism that recognizes that the ultimate strength of the organization lies in its teams, in the accomplishments of the whole. This is about individuals working together for personal satisfaction *and* for the common good (cf. Arnold & Plas, 1993).

Summing Up

In this culture, organizational strength is created by strong individualists who know how to work synergistically in teams.

AUTHENTICITY: PERSONAL-
PROFESSIONAL INTEGRATION

The second unique theoretical position holds that U.S. citizens need to reduce the separation that currently tends to exist between the personal self and the public self. Person-centered leadership is about authenticity. Now is the time for personal values and styles to start gaining more acceptance in work settings. Failure to do this has resulted in a loss of authentic emotion in the workplace. Individuals have believed they ought to leave their feelings at home when coming to work. This has been disastrous at times for American workplaces because it has resulted in the disconnection of personal feelings from the job—the disconnection of emotions from the company, coworkers, and the work. So, it has been difficult for people to develop loyalty, pride, and enthusiasm for their companies. It has also made it very difficult for people to enjoy what they do for a living. The job has become, for many, just a place to put in time to make it possible to do the things they love to do on the weekends. As more and more corporate heads are beginning to realize, when people bring their authentic selves to work, they do better work and develop stronger loyalties to the company and to work-related friendships. Only in authentic work atmospheres is it possible to make of work something that is enjoyed for its own sake rather than simply as a means to an end.

Summing Up

Authenticity at work leads to loyalty, pride, and enthusiasm for the company and its products.

ACCEPTANCE OF STRENGTHS AND WEAKNESSES

The third theoretical foundation of person-centered leadership involves acceptance of strengths and weaknesses. Within this paradigm, it becomes unnecessary to hide either weaknesses or strengths. As the spotlight shines authentically on each individual, everybody on the team can see firsthand what each is bringing to the mix—the positives and the negatives. No longer is the goal to hide personal weaknesses. The new—and certainly more rational—goal is to build an organization that can render the weaknesses harmless while building on the strengths.

Although Americans often point out that "nobody's perfect," each of us nonetheless has been brought up within a culture that has sent strong messages that we ought to continually strive for perfection. The subtle cultural subtext reads: *Sure, nobody's perfect, but if you try hard, you can become perfect enough.* Of course, there is nothing inherently wrong in striving to become the Aristotelian ideal, the person who has become all that she or he can be. What is extremely counterproductive is the strict public denial of personal weaknesses that has accompanied this attitude toward personal growth. Human frailties are as much a fact of life as is human competence. Within the human species, weaknesses are as plentiful as greatness.

Within a person-centered management model, people stop pretending. When the system is aware of weakness, it can compensate for it. The contextual nature of personal weaknesses can be taken into account. When you know you do less well in situation A than B, and the company wants to work smart by recognizing it—without blame or prejudice—you get to spend some time in situation B with happier personal results and a better corporate product. In contrast, in non-person-centered organizations, when weaknesses are withheld from public knowledge, the corporation often gets blindsided by them. Within the person-centered model, this fact of human existence is recognized and the team and the company take advantage of the knowledge, without blame and to the betterment of all concerned.

Summing Up

Human frailties are as much a fact of life as is human competence. When you acknowledge weaknesses, you are in the best position to minimize their influence.

Transformation: A Beginning

The steps necessary to produce related individualism, authentic integration, and acceptance of weaknesses and strengths in the workplace are not at all complicated or difficult to understand. They also are not particularly difficult to put into practice once the most difficult part of the process—attitude change—has made it possible to get ourselves and those with whom we work to give ourselves permission to treat one another differently. Most people who hear this message in workshops that I give in this country and elsewhere immediately resonate to these ideas; the message feels *right*. The basic truth of these ideas and the need to move in these directions is accepted so readily because the principles feel natural to people who have been disillusioned within the workplace for quite some time.

But what does seem difficult for some is the implementation. They rush quickly to the belief that they ought to start treating their colleagues and employees differently starting tomorrow, but intuitively they realize that such is not likely to happen. People know these are the right ways to proceed, but they—quite literally—cannot imagine themselves actually doing such simple things at work as saying, "I'm sorry" or "I don't know how to do this" or "Let's have a really honest conversation for a change." The culture has for so long militated against such authenticity at work that even when we know this is the right way to treat people, we still can't quite bring ourselves to do it.

The roadblocks are quite clear; the solution for removing the roadblocks is very basic. One cannot begin a person-centered organizational transformation by learning new strategies for dealing with others. First, one has to learn new strategies for dealing with the most crucial individual involved in this change process—the individual who wants to become a person-centered leader or manager—*you.*

References

Arnold, W. W., & Plas, J. M. (1993). *The human touch: Today's most unusual program for productivity and profit.* New York: John Wiley.
Kouzes, J. M., & Posner, B. Z. (1987). *The leadership challenge.* San Francisco: Jossey-Bass.

12

Person-Centered Strategies

The Focus on You

It makes little sense to expect that you can see talent and potential in others and care authentically about their work and development if you cannot do these things for yourself. I have yet to meet a person-centered leader—whether a corporate president or a department head—who would deny that the first critical step that had to be taken was to think seriously about, and to work on, the self. Most of these early person-centered leaders have been trailblazers and are reasonably eager to point out that in the beginning, they "hadn't a clue." They muddled through this self-knowledge, self-improvement stage as best they could—often alone, sometimes with the help of spouses or coworkers. As Jim Mullen of Mullen Advertising once commented to me, "When I take my eye off myself, I'm likely to make my worst mistakes."

The first step in developing a successful person-centered management transformation does not involve changing some of the ways you relate to your associates. The first step has to involve changing some of the ways you are currently relating to yourself. Through my conversations with person-centered leaders and through the organizational research and corporate workshops I have conducted, I have identified a list of strategies that can be effective. By design, the group of strategies presented here is neither large nor complicated. People who have gone through this kind of transformation report that keeping their focus on two or three key strategies was all they could manage given the extraordinary demands on their attention by their organizations and families. They also believe that a small list is all that is really necessary if there is genuine commitment to learning better ways to lead and manage. The strategies most likely to create real transformation are related to personal integration and a growing ability to claim personal weaknesses as well as strengths. Genuine improvements can be relatively easy to obtain when working on openness and honesty, values, and creativity.

Becoming More Integrated:
Accepting Weaknesses and Strengths

Separating your personal self from your career self is no longer as required as it once was in U.S. work cultures. In fact, we now see how detrimental that separation has been for many individuals and organizations. But if the old rigid distinctions are to be broken down, we are left with the problem of what a new personal integration ought to look like. What of your personal self is appropriate and important to share with people at work, and what is best held private? Unfortunately, at this point, there are no quick answers or blueprints available.

As organizations find themselves desiring, developing, and recruiting more creative, spontaneous, and intuitive management teams, it is incumbent on those who want to be tomorrow's leaders to give more generously of their authentic selves. That much is clear. What is not clear is just exactly what that means. At Microsoft recently, the team that worked on *Windows 95* encountered delays and much stress while debugging the system prior to getting it to market. Each member of the team consistently came to work in whatever version of casual dress—usually *very* casual—that was personally comfortable. They responded to a supervisor's request for greater speed by deciding it would do them more good to take the day off to go skiing—which they did. Because of their willingness to bring their personal selves to this gargantuan project, they got the product they wanted. But although that team made a set of unique authenticity strategies work for them, it doesn't make sense that a model of authenticity such as that one could work in all other environments.

Invariably, as I present the idea of workplace authenticity to those in U.S. work settings, I run into resistance. It is not, however, a resistance based on a fundamental disagreement with the *need* to become more authentic at work; it's a resistance based on the fear that some may require deeper revelations of the personal self than is comfortable for an individual. This fear is based almost completely on the worry that the corporate culture might begin to demand authenticities from self or others that could be difficult to handle. This worry is understandable, but it is quite the opposite of the point. The move toward more authenticity in the workplace reflects a reaction to dysfunctional cultural standards rather than a desire to force additional cultural standards on the working public. Authenticity must, by definition, always be a personal act, a personal decision. How else could it be authentic?

These days, the workplace does not so stringently dictate that certain parts of ourselves ought to be left behind when we enter the company parking lot. Rather, the individual is in charge of those decisions to a greater extent. The idea is to create more energy through authenticity—energy that will aid the development of a better product and a better workday. The goal is to contribute to coworkers rather than to diminish their dignity or to usurp their right to establish their own guidelines for how they share themselves at work.

In practice, all this actually tends to work and feel a lot better than it might when considered at a purely theoretical level as we are doing here. But there are no cookbook approaches for how to become more authentic at work. Each act has to be an individual matter if it is truly to be genuine. Given the current lack of guidelines, I've found the best approach involves identifying the realms in which more authenticity is desired rather than the specific behaviors that might be cultivated. As I have observed how person-centered leaders in a variety of corporations are going about the task of becoming authentic in their organizations, I've learned that people want more openness and honesty, more opportunity to express values, and greater opportunity for personal creativity.

Summing Up

Try acknowledging a weakness: A fundamental step toward developing a more integrated self is the recognition that weaknesses needn't be held so secret anymore—especially in today's more cooperative work environments.

AUTHENTICITY THROUGH HONESTY AND OPENNESS

Forty years ago, honesty and openness were less available in work settings than they are today. Now, people are much more likely to seek out organizations that encourage them to say what they think and feel about what's going on at work. For example, it was all but unheard of a few decades ago for a manager, executive, or salaried or hourly employee to share the fact of personal weaknesses that might affect their work. At the time, people said, for example, "If you let them know where your soft underbelly is, they're going to use it against you." To some extent, that may have been true in yesteryear's corporations, especially those that used internal competition as a primary motivation tool. But in the contemporary organization—where cooperation and teamwork are so highly valued—it's counterproductive to continue to play everything so close to the chest. The team needs to know where your interests and skills lie and, conversely, where the disinterest and weaknesses are.

I have found that sharing personal weaknesses in an honest and open way is one of the slowest components of person-centered leadership to get started in a company. On first consideration, it strikes many people as far too threatening. We worry that sharing our vulnerabilities may be a strategy that's going to blow up on us. As one department head once said to me, "Sounds fine. You, first." For me, that attitude reflects a universal attitude. This is one risk most of us want to see actually work well when taken before we try it ourselves. Inevitably, the solution for removing this roadblock to good teamwork lies in the president's or CEO's office. In the up-and-running person-centered organizations I've studied, it has invariably been the top leaders who have begun this kind of honest dialogue. One corporate president described in an earlier chapter puts an announcement of his latest goof-up on the company bulletin boards along with an apology. As they are beginning a new project, another leader asks just where his senior people expect that one of his clay feet is going to show up. A managing partner of a real estate firm I've worked with has made it known that the quality of his writing skills is not what he desires of someone in his position so his executive secretary has been specifically chosen for those skills. He doesn't hide that fact—it's important for this president to be up-front about how he is compensating for his experienced lack in an area of importance to the company.

One of the things that's so interesting about the attempt to hide personal weaknesses at work is that most of the time most people are very much aware of the boss's faults and foibles anyway. Discussing them is a favorite pastime in many organizations—especially the ones where people are not happy. The advantages for the boss of revealing personal weaknesses are numerous. For example, you rarely hear of a boss who didn't gain quite a few points and additional respect for revealing what everybody already knew. Especially in cases in which some may have begun to wonder if the boss is so insecure or limited as to be unable to see what everyone else sees. The danger of trying to keep your weaknesses hidden in a situation like that is akin to that for a manufacturer who doesn't know where the weaknesses of his product lie while customers all over the globe are acutely aware of the product's limitations.

Another great advantage that accrues to leaders who tell the personal truth about the downside of their talents is that their employees feel more comfortable in doing the same. Then, there is a great deal of very useful information available to the company interested in quality improvement. When Bill Arnold was at the helm, one of the departments at Centennial Medical Center ordered coffee mugs for all employees that said, "Honesty Without Fear." The message was clear: *Let's share with one another the positives and the negatives, knowing that we do that for the good of the team and that we'll protect one another for having done it.*

As far as the organization is concerned, the biggest advantage to sharing personal strengths, weaknesses, and opinions is probably the fact that the process yields so much useful information. This is an Information Age strategy of the most sophisticated sort. The more people are open about what they really think and what they're really doing, the more usable information that hits the system and the more people learn to trust the system—which breeds further useful revelations.

For the individual, the major advantage no doubt is the emotional positives that accompany authentic actions. In some areas of the organization literature (Fineman, 1993), the term *emotional labor* has come to represent an important concept. The term refers to the energy that is required to pretend one is feeling an emotion other than what is truly being felt. For example, an angry and hurt secretary, having been ignored during Secretary's Week, fakes an unusually pleasant and carefree pose whenever the boss is in the office. For most people —the secretary included—masking feelings requires a lot of energy. The expenditure of this kind of emotional labor results in lost work time, errors, venting with other people, and eventually strained relationships. In most cases, this is an unfortunate and unnecessary use of time and energy. Just after Secretary's Day, I once observed a neglected secretary, in a position like that just described, avoid this counterproductive emotional labor. She works for a supply department manager who has made it clear that he has faults and weaknesses and that when one of those gets in someone else's way, he wants to hear about it. In that particular case, he was appalled to realize he'd overlooked our national recognition day for secretaries. He had no particularly compelling excuse for having forgotten. What he did possess was genuine respect for this person's work and genuine remorse for his mess-up. What did she actually say to her boss? She stuck her head into his office, passed along a phone message, and said,

I've got to take you at your word, Boss. I've got to let you know that mine is the only secretary's desk in this building that didn't have flowers or something else special on it last week. It was secretary's week, you know. Did I maybe forget Bosses Day or something?

Subsequent to this event, the manager told me that this sort of exchange is not uncommon around the organization. He said he was deeply grateful for his secretary's candor, that he had made up for his neglect, and that the occasion served to strengthen rather than weaken his relationship with this executive assistant. Contrast that kind of authenticity on both their parts with the hours of wasted time in other companies because responses to this kind of situation were kept secret and left to fester.

This kind of authenticity is what person-centered organizations are getting so excited about these days. A problem like the one above can be worked through easily when it is revealed. If kept secret, it can take a large toll in terms of time, sapped energy, and even errors of all sorts. If you can't take the risk to start being more open, it hardly seems useful to ask your employees to start doing so. Making a personal commitment to be more open about your genuine thoughts, strengths, and weaknesses is all that it takes to get many people started. The rewards are huge.

Summing Up

Try just admitting the feeling when you're genuinely grateful or a little miffed: Authentically communicating thoughts and feelings at work feels better to most people and encourages the development of trust among colleagues.

VALUES

Values need just as much attention as openness and honesty. Many people say they have grown weary of living out a public-private personality split while on the job. For many of us, it has been draining to habitually try to pretend that we do not believe in certain things, do not hold dear certain ideas and institutions. Now, there is new encouragement and acceptance for being more open about your values. At Mullen Advertising, I was particularly intrigued to learn how the company's person-centered management code encourages people to bring their values to work. Those values are translated into the company ethic—not by mandate but through the individual. For example, when a new company presents itself, asking Mullen to work up a set of advertising strategies that would become part of the company's competitive bid agenda, Mullen's authenticity ethic is greatly in control of the Mullen response to that request. People at Mullen are not told they have to work on that potential new account; rather, the creative staff is polled to see if anyone has any energy for working on the development of the account. An account that might compromise personal values—for example, a product of dubious health benefits or products manufactured in countries that violate civil rights—just doesn't attract the energy of Mullen staff members. When no one shows energy for working on something, Mullen then doesn't offer a bid for that account. In a very real sense, the personal values of individuals have created the "community standards" in that company (cf. Mullen, 1995).

At DEKA, under the leadership of Dean Kamen, I found a core cadre of creative engineering types who value spending their time on the development of new medical apparatuses that have the potential to make a difference in the lives of those challenged by often ignored medical difficulties. Simply put, they want what they do to make a difference in people's lives—preferably for people with unique and neglected physical needs. Certainly, revenue counts at DEKA. But equally important are the "humanitarian" values brought to bear by the kind of person who is attracted to work at this person-centered research and development company. Examples like these provide models of organizational strategies that depend on personal authenticity. They also provide insights for what the individual might do to facilitate the use of personal values at work.

I recently sat in on a senior executive meeting at a midsize company whose CEO was interested in developing a more authentic management model. The meeting had been conceived as a retreat of sorts with morning sessions devoted to presentations and the afternoon scheduled for discussion. By 3:00 p.m., it had become obvious that the idea of getting personal values out into the open was clearly intimidating for most of the 14 people in the room. Silence reigned supreme. A couple of men began to wonder out loud if the system didn't work as well as it does in this country precisely because we keep our personal beliefs to ourselves when in public. "Why risk what works so damn well?" another muttered. Like so many, these senior VPs were worried that this "authenticity thing," as they called it, was going to encourage people to reveal political, religious, and cultural differences that they'd then have to fight over.

At that point, I asked the people in the group to consider for themselves the three things they'd most like their coworkers to say about them when they died. If they could be a fly on the wall at their own funerals, what would they most like to overhear colleagues saying about them? I then asked each person to share his or her list. One wanted simply to be known as an honest and just man. Another wanted to be known as a caring father and husband as well as a boss who cared. A third wanted people to say that they knew when she said something, she meant it—that people could trust her word to be her bond. Three VPs wanted to hear that the people who worked below them thought as positively about them as did their peers in the organization; they wanted to be known for being fair to all. One said he wanted to be remembered as a good-humored, fun-loving person who was liked and respected by all kinds of people. When the final person revealed his list, he said, quietly, "I want people here to say I was a loving family man who loved this company and gave it my best."

As this group listened to one another, they realized that the values they themselves wanted to bring to the work environment had little to do with their religious and political beliefs and everything to do with what they valued as mature and well-developed persons. Authentic conversation erupted and didn't stop that afternoon till well past 6 o'clock. One of the most important things the group uncovered was the fact that although their individual lists represented personal characteristics that were highly valued and very important to each of them, very few had ever used these words at work—words like *honesty, love, fairness, caring, frankness, goodwill.* They hadn't told their employees they valued these things, nor had they asked their work teams to keep their eyes on these values as they went about their daily jobs. Yet they realized they were unconsciously evaluating their employees—and themselves—on the basis of these traits all the time. Once this group was able to reveal the specific characteristics that really matter to them, they found they weren't at all inclined to argue about the differences. Rather, they found themselves wondering out loud why they'd never mentioned these values within their departments. In an outstanding, insightful moment toward the end of the conversation, one 20-year member of the company said, "I don't know why it never occurred to me that I could tell my people what I stand for. . . . I've always hoped my actions would reveal the things that matter to me, but why leave something that important to chance?"

Being authentic about values at work probably doesn't have to amount to much more than what I've just described. Giving yourself permission to stand for something at work doesn't necessarily lead to conflict. When we reveal that we value old architecture, sports camps for kids, and underground utilities—or honesty, good humor, and lives of balance—we move a lot closer to bringing our true selves into the work picture. The result is that we feel more included, have more fun, and release more energy.

Summing Up

Let the people who work near you know which values you admire: This can be inspirational as well as communicative. Don't hide such an important and authentic message.

CREATIVITY AND AUTHENTICITY

Largely because of the prevalence of continuous improvement programs in corporate organizations, the idea of developing personal creativity at work has gained legitimacy. When presented with the three authenticity areas that usually need attention—honesty and openness, values, and creativity—people I've worked with state in overwhelming numbers that the creativity area is the easiest to develop. It's almost as if people in U.S. corporations have just been waiting for senior management to ask them to get creative, to use their imaginations in the service of team and company goals. In fact, a focus on personal creativity almost has to go hand in hand with a commitment to the individual as expert. Any expert uses a fair amount of personal creativity when tackling most on-the-job problems. One of the main reasons employees in a company such as Dean Kamen's so often mention the "fun" they have is that they have so many opportunities for personally creative moments.

But whether you're interested in developing more creativity or more authenticity, the most important person to focus on first in person-centered leadership is you. The kinds of changes that need to be made can happen fairly quickly once you've given yourself permission to be the kind of person at work that you like to be when you're off the job. The kind of authenticity this creates will be very compelling for most people who work alongside you. It creates more energy for everybody's use. The resulting work environment is more relaxed, and invariably, it is more productive.

For information about useful psychology books that present ideas for personal transformation, see the annotated list that appears at the end of Chapter 13.

Summing Up

Give yourself permission to try something innovative each week: Expressing yourself through creativity in your organization creates feelings of well-being almost instantly for many people.

Summary

Before you can make changes that affect others, it's critical to make person-centered changes within yourself. The kind of integration between personal and public selves that you'd like for your employees has to be attempted in your own life if you want to be successful at providing these opportunities for others. Begin by taking another look at your weaknesses and strengths. Many corporate leaders are finding it easier than they had previously thought to give a little more public attention to personal weaknesses, modeling for associates a new freedom to be human and to be genuine while at work. Giving yourself permission to be more open about your values and to develop your creative potentials will get life back into your job. It will also help create the kind of person-centered relationships that make it possible for the people in your department or organization to take advantage of the growth opportunities inherent in person-centered leadership.

References

Fineman, S. (Ed.). (1993). *Emotion in organizations.* Newbury Park, CA: Sage.
Mullen, J. X. (1995). *The simple art of greatness.* New York: Viking.

13

Person-Centered Strategies

The Focus on Associates

_____

The following discussion of strategies for person-centered leadership transformation may contain a level of specificity that is unnecessary for some readers. Although that risk is present, it has been my experience that when making suggestions to leaders for associate and system change, the overwhelming majority of people with whom I consult asks for suggestions that are very specific. They have maintained that precise suggestions tend to be the ones that are most easily used and most helpful. Thus, the following discussion is designed to anticipate specific reader questions and needs. Those who prefer a more general rather than precise approach to transformation issues may wish to concentrate on the introductory remarks within each topic area below.

Following an introductory section on the need for action, each stage and strategy that is discussed is accompanied by a Strategy Box of specifics, which outlines actions, suggests hints for success based on the experiences of selected companies, and offers cautions about the typical areas where difficulties can be encountered.

The Need for Action

Creating meaningful person-centered leadership changes within yourself generally amounts to changing personal attitudes. But helping to create meaningful changes in the system and within associates usually requires a focus on behaviors in addition to attitudes. It is very important that you act.

Actions need to be (a) authentic, (b) a departure from what has been typical for you, and (c) consistent. We have already discussed the reasons that authenticity is so important. But now we need to take a moment to think about the second and third characteristics of transformative action. For at least two reasons, during the beginning stages of management transformation, it is important that your person-centered actions be somewhat different than is typical for you. First, whether your person-centered management skills succeed depends greatly on whether you've been successful in working on your own openness, authenticity, and creativity. If the first phase of transformation—with its emphasis on you—has been successful, you will already be using behaviors with your associates that are relatively new for you. The second reason for departure from normalcy is that you need to get the attention of busy coworkers. Nothing does that quite so quickly as a change in behavior in the boss's office.

Consistency is also critical. Once you have set your course on person-centered transformation, you likely will be regarded with distrust or cynicism if you knee-jerk back into old, more distancing or blaming ways of operating. No matter what new set of strategies is being implemented in the business world today, initial concerns usually include the question: "Is this just another management method that's going to last only 6 months before the next one gets brought in?"

As I begin studying a person-centered management system, I immediately pursue this issue of consistency. One of the first questions I ask of those in the system is this: "How do you know this leadership system is for real; how do you know it's not just another flavor of the month?" I vividly recall the reply to that question of a senior vice president in Centennial Medical Center some years ago. He quickly responded:

Because Bill Arnold doesn't knee-jerk. Even when things go wrong, he reacts exactly the same way, not blaming people but encouraging them to get creative. No matter what the crisis is, he continues to put caring about the associates ahead of everything else.

My experience with a variety of person-centered companies has shown that it is the rare individual who can remain consistent from the very beginning of a transformative management attempt. But the successful individuals are the ones who self-correct by (a) recognizing they reverted to old habits, (b) communicating that they wish they had handled the situation a little differently, and (c) taking steps to get things back within the person-centered model. In a very real way, this kind of self-correction after inconsistency adds to the trust because it communicates the message: "Mistakes happen. But I'm serious about managing person by person and we're going to stay the course."

How to Begin

The best way to begin a person-centered transformation is through the immediate involvement of others—associates at all levels of the organization. A planning group of a manageable and representative number of people should be given the charge to (a) investigate person-centered management and (b) devise a plan for creating a person-centered management model that is uniquely suited to this particular company. A specified period of planning time ought to be identified. The company president[1] becomes a member of this team, but the *leadership* of the team is best rotated among the individuals who are serving. In addition to participant functions, however, the initiating leader ought to adopt two additional and unique functions —encourager and information provider. At several points in the process, each member of the team ought to meet with other associates in the company to share planning information and get feedback.

It is often very useful during this planning stage to involve a variety of consultants in Planning Team discussions. I recommend inviting at least two people—with somewhat different points of view—

who study the kind of organization you are trying to develop or who assist in organizational transformation through consultation. One of the most effective things that can be done at this point is to follow these discussions with Planning Team visits from associates in another organization that has moved successfully through the beginning stages of person-centered management. Bringing in people who serve in maintenance, secretarial, and department head roles often can be more effective than bringing in top leadership people who have gone through the process. In one of the most effective consulting approaches I've witnessed, an automobile-related company with which I've worked brought in three very articulate people from a company in a nearby state that had moved in the direction of person-centered management—two department heads and the CEO's administrative assistant. The conversation among the participants was, at times, electrifying. The number of viable quality ideas that were generated that day was way above average—for *both* companies that were represented in that room.

The strategy of involving people at all levels of a person-centered organization as consultants in the transformative process of another company is a new one that is so promising that I recommend it strongly to all those involved in person-centered planning efforts. It is perhaps not surprising that such people are relatively easy to identify (most consultants can provide suggestions, as can many people who work within your organization), and the cost of bringing them is not an expenditure that's likely to break the bank. But the biggest advantage of this approach is that it sets a person-centered tone. The Planning Team acknowledges from the outset that company experts are located across a variety of roles and functions. It gets people used to listening to the unique and very valuable insights of people who are essential to a company's successful operations. When word travels that some of the experts consulted included maintenance workers, delivery people, and secretaries from another company, associates quickly consider that this new management approach may indeed be something that they genuinely could get interested in and endorse.

Strategies: Planning Team

Actions

1. Name a representative and manageable number of associates from all levels to a Planning Team charged with learning about the possibilities for transformation and creating a person-centered model unique to your company.

2. Invite input from at least two leadership consultants or researchers with differing perspectives.

3. Invite input from consultants from other companies—associates at various levels within that person-centered organization.

4. Let Planning Team members know that your role is the same as theirs with additional responsibility for anticipating needs for information and encouragement.

5. Rotate leadership of the team.

Hints

1. Keep duplicated copies of relevant person-centered management articles in and just outside your office. Offer a copy of something relevant to each person with whom you meet.

2. *Each day,* contact someone not on the Planning Team to find out if they've heard about the planning process and what initial reactions they might have.

3. As part of your remarks to introduce the planning process and as part of your "encouragement" remarks throughout the process, share results of your self-development processes, those new attitudes that result from consideration of issues identified in the previous chapter.

4. Remember that this should be *fun*. This process conceivably can be one of the most enjoyable and rewarding you will encounter during your career.

Cautions

1. It is perfectly all right—in fact, advisable—for you to make decisions in a nondemocratic way about who is to be on the Planning Team.

You know what you're after and need to involve people in the planning who can truly help you achieve that. As long as the group is representative of roles in the company, a nondemocratic choice process is best. Don't make the mistake one company did of having each area elect its representative to this team. (Many of the people chosen could not easily appreciate the need for person-centered management, and inevitably, they sabotaged the process.)

2. You're probably going to want to establish direction for the Planning Team when they seem to want to go in a direction you consider unimportant, ineffective, or inefficient. Resist the urge. Remind yourself that you handpicked these people because of their expertise, wisdom, and creative thinking and that now you've got to "do the person-centered thing" and go ahead and trust them. While you're biting the bullet, however, it never hurts to let them know that you're doing it. That kind of openness helps develop the authenticity you're after.

3. Do *not* put other priorities before Planning Team meetings. As soon as person-centered leadership stops being your priority for that hour, it stops being a priority for the others for a week. As you are tempted to miss or reschedule a Planning Team meeting because "something important" has come up, consider the one-hour to one-week multiple-interest-loss ratio and the inevitable effects of that on the transformation process.

Next Steps

Next steps always need to be dictated by the Planning Team. Some companies have kickoff meetings or dinners. Others use formal and informal get-togethers within departments and program areas. But whatever your team has decided, the next stages will include communication and implementation. Usually, however, if Planning Team activities have been as successful as they need to be, personnel across the organization already are aware of the transformation agenda and have had opportunities for input. The implementation of a person-centered mode of leadership will have already begun. The basic components of such a model will vary from organization to organization, but most or all of the following components of person-centered leadership probably will be represented in some way. More comprehensive discussions of these strategies can be found in previous chapters, especially Chapters 4, 5, and 7 through 10; in Arnold and Plas (1993); and in various other sources that have been cited throughout the book.

The Golden Gripes

It is hard to imagine a successful person-centered transformation effort that does not make internal complaints one of the company's highest priorities. Elsewhere (Arnold & Plas, 1993), I have referred to complaints as *golden gripes* because they represent pure gold to the leader who is dedicating the company to person-centered management.

Recall the kinds of complaints you yourself have had recently about the company and other organizations with which you're involved. If you are like most people, you'll realize that only a very small percentage of your complaints these days are trivial. Surely, some of them are personal, several may be focused on details, but nonetheless they are not trivial. Your current gripe list may contain a few picayune points (e.g., Why doesn't mail arrive in your offices until 2:30 p.m.? After all, the postal center two floors below gets it at 9:30 a.m.). It may contain a few personal points (e.g., Why doesn't the company lunchroom stock low-fat snacks in addition to chips and donuts?). But the fact that these gripes emerge from personal desires or concern about relatively minor issues does not mean these are not big problems—for you and for the company. For example, a host of departmental communication problems may be represented by the late mail delivery, and the lack of low-fat lunchroom snacks may send a message that the company is unconcerned about employee health and/or personal needs.

Each person who works with you probably has a similar set of gripes about how things get done in the company. When a person-centered leader listens and responds to these complaints, energy is released for use in more productive arenas. Loyalty and caring for the company and its leaders inevitably develop. Responding to associate complaints has been proven so often to be critical that I have come to believe it is the single most important thing that a person-centered leader can do.

We're all familiar with a variety of strategies currently in widespread use that have been designed for dealing with employee concerns —mechanisms such as open-door policies, complaint boxes, and internal e-mail bulletin boards. We're all too familiar with organizations that have such mechanisms but are nonetheless uninterested in taking complaints seriously—especially certain kinds of complaints. For example, an organization with which I'm familiar keeps a box outside the executive offices that is labeled, "Suggestions: Positive Suggestions Only." Needless to say, the box stands empty most of the time.

A leader who wants to move in a person-centered direction is well advised to begin a serious attitude adjustment with regard to complaints. All gripes are golden. They let you know that someone still has some energy to invest in the company. A person who offers a complaint is offering you a chance to establish a relationship. This is how person-by-person management most often begins—with an employee concern. In fact, the complaints that seem more "selfish" or personal often may present the biggest opportunities.

Recently, an industrial food service company I've observed began a quality improvement initiative that was to rely on person-by-person management. One Friday afternoon just before closing for the weekend, a counter worker uttered her typical Friday afternoon gripe, "I don't know why they won't let me take some of this leftover cooked food to my neighbors instead of telling me to just throw it out! It just makes me sick to garbage good hamburgers like this." For the first time, a passing supervisor, now charged with the responsibility to hear such complaints rather than ignore them, countered with, "Let me tell you why we can't, because maybe we can figure some ways around all the concerns the company has." I'm told the counter worker was so surprised at getting a response that she dropped her spatula. She also was surprised to realize she hadn't considered issues such as liability if food spoilage occurred before the food was transported and served and how to justify giving it to her rather than making it available to everyone in the company. When I last heard about that situation, three people had put themselves in charge of figuring out how to use the leftovers rather than throw them out—and that particular counter worker had become the unit's most energetic and loyal associate. One of her coworkers told me she's actually begun to sing in the lunchroom much of the time.

Stories such as these are not uncommon these days as companies move toward quality improvement and person-centered management models. That being the case, why then can't all companies move successfully in this direction? Why do some companies fail at this kind of thing? I believe the reason for the failures is that people have been viewing these instances exclusively as an opportunity for quality improvement, a chance "to do the sensible thing." The focus, then, is on policy and process improvement rather than on the specific needs of a specific individual. When these instances are viewed as associate complaints within a company culture that values complaints, a different effect occurs. People begin to develop *relationships*. Management person by person creates the kind of relationships that create a strong organization.

Strategies: Golden Gripes

Actions

1. Encourage associates to help you and themselves change attitudes toward the value of complaints. Only when you become convinced of their value will you be able to use complaints wisely.

2. Establish an open-door policy that is meaningful.

3. "Walk the talk" by making regular visits to all areas of the company. Stop to listen. Don't just use this time as an opportunity to communicate what you want your people to hear.

4. Establish a Listening Forum each month, a time that is set aside to meet with all employees who want to come and air concerns. Have someone accompany you who can record what is said. Be sure to get back to each associate—in writing—letting him or her know what

action has been taken in response to the concern, that is, what the impediments to action are and who is working on a response to the problem.

5. *Every day,* stop an associate somewhere—for example, in a parking garage or at an on-site automatic teller machine—and ask, "If you could eliminate one complaint you've got about our company, what would it be?"

6. Regularly communicate to all executives, management personnel, and associates your desire to make responsiveness to complaints a top priority for the company.

Hints

1. You probably can't pull off an effective open-door policy without the assistance of your administrative assistant or secretary. Put that individual in charge of figuring out how it can actually work.

2. Put informal visits to various areas of the company in your schedule on a regular basis. Don't assume you can make these visits whenever you have "extra time." This activity needs to be a priority rather than something that is accomplished after other priorities are fulfilled.

3. Assign to an individual geographically close to you the responsibility of following up on complaints that are shared with you. This is critical. Do not expect yourself to do this by yourself but arrange for such follow-up to proceed.

4. If you're not good at hearing the emotional content of messages, take some steps to learn that skill just as you would take steps to learn any other skill you need. Remind yourself that this is the Information Age and a leader can no longer afford to ignore emotional information. If you can't attend a private course or workshop, bring in a consultant who can provide some training for a small group of company leaders committed to learning how to listen—perhaps the Planning Team?

Cautions

1. Resist the temptation to try to solve the problems that people come through your open door to share with you. Most of these concerns won't be within your areas of responsibility. Don't put yourself in the position of alienating supervisors by "fixing" problems in their areas of responsibility. All you have to do is (a) listen, (b) respect the individual by taking the complaint seriously, (c) refer the inquiry to the appropriate place, (d) follow up on it within a specified period of time.

2. Repeatedly communicate to executives, middle managers, and supervisors that a complaint from someone in their area will *not* be taken by you as an indictment of their abilities or policies. Even after a person-centered leadership program has been up and running for several years, this message must be conveyed with genuineness on a regular basis to keep levels of trust at their highest.

3. Be aware that by the time the complaint gets to you—especially in the first 3 years of the transformation process—people will likely be carrying some emotion into your office along with their complaints. Take the steps necessary to make sure this fact of life does not unduly concern you or get you off track (see Hint 4 above).

4. Especially in the beginning, be sure not to allow the more cautious people in your organization to convince you that these policies will only increase complaining and that middle management will get resentful because "they'll be the ones who will have to clean up the problems that all your complaint encouragement is going to cause." As middle managers begin to use this strategy themselves, the reality will emerge that fewer complaints will be forthcoming rather than more.

5. Remember that with each complaint you hear, your ultimate agenda is to build a relationship, person by person. Even when you and your organization cannot solve a problem you'd genuinely like to solve for an associate, if you communicate your disappointment at being unable to act, the relationship will be strengthened.

6. When you are momentarily overcome by a problem you are hearing— should you feel deeply saddened, overwhelmed, confused, distrustful, choked up, or even betrayed by what you are hearing—do not berate yourself or abort the process or program just because you clutched. Be consistent. Stick with the program. You might try excusing yourself from continued conversation at the moment by scheduling another appointment for some time in the very near future. Take a little time to recover and relax.

7. In the beginning—and especially if you are normally used to spending time on large financial or strategic decisions—don't give in to the feelings of "foolishness" you might experience as you suddenly realize you've just spent the past 30 minutes listening to a complaint that has to do with whether or not the rest rooms ought to be painted a peppy purple or a bouncy blue. Remember, you are not primarily investing time in the issue under discussion; you're investing it in the

individual, in the relationship between the two of you. There are only a few things in your organization that are as critical as the relationship between a leader and an associate. Good relationships take and deserve your time.

Encouraging Risks

These days, risk taking is a valued component of many quality improvement and other management paradigms as well as person-centered models; but to some, it's somewhat surprising to learn that encouraging risk taking is such a fundamental part of a person-centered approach to leadership. How does encouraging your people to take good risks add to the development of the kind of excellent in-house relationships that we've been discussing?

When you encourage people to take risks, you encourage them to be authentic. Within every good risk lies an element of prediction. To be a good predictor, a person has to gather the right kind of information. But he or she also has to trust instincts and take calculated chances on behalf of things that are valued. Thus, most good risks are often associated with authenticity.

Without risk taking, there is no creativity. Many people report that expressing themselves through a creative thought or act is one of the most exhilarating things that they feel in their work lives. Most people seem to thrive on this kind of self-expression. Truly, the creative act is something that profits both the individual and the company.

In fact, any effort at person-centered transformation is, in itself, a creative risk. This is true primarily because person-centered leadership is committed to developing authenticity in the workplace. Especially in the beginning, it usually feels risky to move toward genuineness, to begin to share the truth rather than to withhold information about weaknesses and mistakes. When you, the leader, encourage risk taking, you send a strong message that you trust your associates. Person-centered leadership is built on a message of trust.

Strategies: Encouraging Risks

Actions

1. Let it be known that the methods that have been used in the past are not sacred, that you're always looking for better ways to do things and better things to do.

2. In your regular written communications, let people know about the innovative ideas and projects that associates in your department or company are developing. Share this information informally and verbally as well.

3. Schedule a meeting every now and then that is devoted only to brainstorming new goals and methods. Get into the habit of questioning everything during these meetings.

4. Build in mechanisms for dealing with failures. For example, schedule a few minutes during regular staff meetings to talk about the failures, the innovative ideas that didn't work out. In this way, you begin to establish the value that it is worse not to risk than to risk and fail. You also create a learning environment in which people are encouraged to share mistakes and benefit from discussions of how to make lemonade out of lemons.

Hints

1. Develop mechanisms that will assist people in bringing their creative ideas quickly into development so that your organization can learn to respond quickly to mistakes. Make rapid pilot testing a norm.

2. When you have a manager of a department or area who seems slow to take advantage of the risk-taking culture you're developing, invite him or her to work with you on something that requires creative development in another area of the organization. Many people often need to feel success with this kind of thing before they're willing to commit to the concept.

3. Part of the risk taking you will be concerned with is devoted to developing more authenticity at work. When you model that kind of sharing, others are much more inclined to give it a try.

Cautions

1. Only a leader who trusts his or her people as well as human nature in general can authentically—and thus effectively—encourage risk taking. If you notice yourself being overly concerned that people are going to waste time, money, and other resources on creative ideas, you probably need to take steps to create an attitude adjustment on your part. Invite a consultant. Have some serious talks with senior people who *do* find it easy to trust and encourage. Spend time in those departments that are making this strategy work. If you are not genuinely supportive of creative risk taking, you likely will be capable of unconscious sabotage.

2. Initial attempts to create a company culture that reveres risk taking will be met by resistance from those who are prone to caution and anxiety as well as those who have not had much experience with the dividends associated with this kind of management. Expect this. Be persistent. Eventually, many will move beyond this stage as success stories emerge within the company and attention is given to the risk-taking strategy.

3. You must expect failure. Not all creative ideas are good ideas; some are ahead of their times. Part of the price you have to pay for the rewards that are achieved by risk taking includes some of the negative outcomes that can accompany failed efforts. If you make everyone aware that mistakes are undesirable but inevitable and provide mechanisms for rapid recovery, your organization will be able to learn even more from the mistakes than it does from the successes.

Developing Teamwork
and Related Individualism

Developing the kind of teamwork that people get enthusiastic about is crucial but very tricky. As we have discussed in previous chapters, ours is not a culture that has made great progress in learning how to develop teamwork while supporting the cultural primacy of the individual. It is precisely this situation that has caused so many of the recent quality improvement failures. But despite the lack of well-developed theory and practice related to individual-within-team functioning, enough progress has been made that there is light at the end of the tunnel. Better theory and increasingly more solid strategies for developing good teamwork are becoming available.

RELATED INDIVIDUALISM

As we saw in Chapter 5, a growing number of corporate leaders are taking on the task of developing cultural perspectives that can guide the company as opportunities emerge that demand cultural transformation. The need for teamwork is one such area. A leader interested in person-centered transformation will want to encourage effective teamwork throughout the organization. Therefore, such a leader will be required to develop within the company the cultural attitudes that can guide teamwork development. In many corporations, without attention to this kind of cultural development, teamwork strategies will be vulnerable and perhaps even predisposed to failure. Although strategies for rapid development of culture within a rapidly developing technological and social climate currently are not well known or well defined, they are nonetheless crucial. Experimentation will be necessary. The person-centered leader intent on transformation will need to be up to the task of deliberate work on attitude change.

The leader needs to understand and feel comfortable with an attitude-change agenda. He or she will be filling an educator role as associates in the company are introduced to the ideas that are represented by the term *related individualism*. It is important that the leader clearly and directly let people know that the individual worker is at the center of this leadership model, and because of that fact, new techniques for giving attention to the individual-within-the-team will have to be worked out. Each person in the company ought to be challenged to contribute to this creation of culture.

Strategies: Creating a Culture of Related Individualism

Actions

1. *Before* moving into a teamwork mode, take time to expose people to the issues involved in introducing teamwork within a rugged individualist culture.

2. Suggest that the Planning Team develop a strategy for creating a related individualist company culture.

3. Strategies for making people aware of the issues might include cross-department meetings of small groups of people (12-15) who share with a Planning Team member their concerns about moving toward a teamwork model. Many of the identified concerns will involve individualist issues. For example, associates are likely to worry about issues of recognition and reward.

4. After considering the feedback, the Planning Team may want to ask similar small groups to brainstorm possibilities for protecting individual recognition and reward while working within a teamwork model.

Hints

1. Just getting the issues out in the open will contribute greatly to culture development. It will be immediately apparent that management respects the issues that are intuitively important to employees. In fact, the leadership will be in position to name concerns that many associates may have felt but were unable to articulate.

2. Remember that the creative thinking of the associates may well be your best response to the problem of attitude change. Rely on associates to come up with novel ways to change the company culture in the desired direction of related individualism. This is an area where relatively little has been written or tried, so this is an area where associates can provide much-needed leadership.

Cautions

1. It is important that you embrace your role as culture change agent with acceptance and enthusiasm. Although this is relatively un-

charted territory for a leader, it is crucial for person-centered management transformation because teamwork strategies are vulnerable to failure if successful attitude change has not occurred.

2. Do not assume that quick progress on the part of the discussion groups will be maintained without further intervention. You may have to reconvene these small group culture-change meetings throughout the first couple of years of the transformation process.

TEAMWORK

After the first round or two of small group attitude-change discussions have occurred, you ought to be in position to begin moving in earnest toward establishing teams. It is often wise to begin this process as a pilot test by establishing a few teams that show promise of success and might be used as a model for the rest of the organization.

Strategies: Team Development

Actions

1. Build teams around functions or projects and make sure that a variety of skills and points of view are represented.
2. The team task should dictate the number of people to be involved, but in the beginning of person-centered transformation, it's always better to err on the side of too few rather than too many team members. Too many people—especially as the organization is developing its teamwork style—often results in lack of action. If there are too few, others can always be brought on board to respond to an identified need.
3. During the initial team meeting, members should be encouraged to express any reservations they may have about team membership.
4. A clear distinction between process and production functions ought to be made in the initial meeting. *Production* function assignments have to do with who is going to do what to accomplish the group's

goal. *Process* function assignments have to do with who will do what to get the team up and functioning smoothly as a unit.

5. Among the process issues that need to be considered from the beginning are leadership (Should it be rotated or fixed?) and meeting format (reports? brainstorming? task assignment? education?).

6. It is important that a variety of roles be clearly identified for the team. These roles will be process as well as task roles and their identification will depend primarily on the kind of work that the team is to do.

7. Strategies for providing reward and recognition to all roles and individuals should be identified during the initial meetings. Team members should come to agreement on possibilities and expectations for individual recognition.

Hints

1. It will probably serve your goals well if the first teams that are established are charged with creating something new rather than problem solving. It is generally harder for a problem-solving team to be successful than it is for other kinds of teams because it is starting from a position of system failure; that is, the organization has already experienced failure and discomfort in the area of concern. If this were a relatively easy problem to fix, it likely would have been fixed before this point. Therefore, although problem-solving teams can be of enormous value to the company, it is best to launch a teamwork model that maximizes chances of success by establishing a team that is not charged with solving an organizational problem. A good choice for an initial team would be a design team or an information-gathering team such as product development investigation.

2. The contrast between successful sports teams and unsuccessful corporate teams is a good one to discuss during initial meetings (see Chapter 4). Through a serious consideration of successful sports teams, your people can see the need to identify roles clearly and to reward the roles that tend not to be center stage. Bringing local athletes in to talk about individual versus team needs can be very useful because articulate athletes usually have much that is relevant to say about good teamwork and because, for many people, this kind of "real-world" consultant adds interest to early team meetings that participants might otherwise have been dreading.

3. Make sure that after the first few meetings, the team has identified a very clear picture of just exactly what their goals are—process as well as product goals. It can be very helpful if one of the goals directly identified refers to the team's desire to enjoy themselves while working within a teamwork model. High on the goal list of each team ought to be the desire to meet individual needs by providing opportunities for creative thinking, recognition, and some general fun and camaraderie.

Cautions

1. Let us suppose that the first stage of team development in your company involves establishing four teams with varying task goals. Do you expect that all four teams will be successful in meeting the goals they have been given as well as the goals they have generated internally? The issue of success rate is one that the Planning Team ought to consider seriously. How will success be judged? Given your criteria, can you claim success if only two teams produce exemplary products? Having a clear set of expectations will serve you well in the long run as teams experience varying degrees of success. (In my view, only one team—the Planning Team—should not be permitted the luxury of failure. During the initial stages of transformation, all other team failures become opportunities for learning.)

2. When teams first meet and begin discussing Action 7 above, some individuals no doubt will state that they do not desire individual recognition; they are willing to give it to others, but they themselves do not require it. This generous attitude is not uncommon, but it tends to represent a land mine for the process. Many people are used to denying needs for individual recognition and have not fully investigated the personal power of those needs. Others fear that if a move is made to reward individuals, it may represent a hidden agenda that has to do with blaming individuals as the process gets under way. Whatever the motivations, it is wise to accept these attitudes and feelings but to make strong attempts to educate people to the need to shift the focus in this culture from individual to group and back again. It is important that uninvestigated personal attitudes toward recognition do not show up late in the process at a time when group goals can be undermined.

3. Once one or two teams have struggled toward success and others toward failure, it is time to capitalize on what they have learned. A member of a failed team and a member of a successful team might form a consultant team for newly developing task teams. The important point is to make sure the organization is in a position to profit from its own experience with teams by having formal mechanisms in place that can contribute to a learning agenda.

4. Continually remind yourself and others that putting together a successful teamwork model is a grand achievement in and of itself, a goal that many other organizations have attempted unsuccessfully. Your organization will be trailblazing in many important ways. The downside of trailblazing often is experienced as frustration, slow progress, and occasional lack of direction. If you expect the negative feelings associated with trailblazing, you'll be likely to persist long enough to experience the remarkable rewards.

Strategy: Person-by-Person Management

Responding positively to complaints, encouraging risk taking, and developing teamwork based on related individualism are person-centered leadership strategies whose success ultimately depends on your ability to do something even more fundamental—focus on one individual at a time. Within this model, you are not concerned primarily with objectives or problem solving, or even systems and processes. Neither are you primarily concerned with the workforce in general. Rather, your primary attention is always on a single individual. Even more specifically, your focus is always on the relationship between you and an associate. Some find the idea of person-by-person management a bit daunting, especially in large organizations. They worry about the impossibility of creating so many good relationships. But the focus is not so much on developing large numbers of relationships as it is on (a) developing genuineness in relationship and (b) making sure that the invitation to relationship is open to all individuals in the company.

Strategies: Managing Person by Person

Actions

1. All interactions with associates should be seen as opportunities for person-centered leadership. All interactions require two phases: listening to what the associate needs to say and sharing information about the company as well as your own thoughts and feelings.

2. If you are not a good listener, this is the time to develop that skill. Think of the listening process as panning for gold. You're looking for things that the associate might share that could offer opportunities for you to assist, learn, support, and develop.

3. Nonverbal communication sometimes conveys more than words. If you're not particularly good at reading body language, this may be a good time to investigate the possibilities. There are a number of interesting books on this subject and no doubt a number of interpersonally skilled people in your personal network who could share some good perspectives. If you are not excited about this prospect, remind yourself that we've entered the Information Age and often certain kinds of information are ignored at our own peril.

4. One of the key actions required by person-centered leaders is concentration. Throughout the day, concentrate exclusively on the single individual with whom you are speaking rather than on the many other things that are making demands on your attention. Actually, it is not as difficult as you might expect to get into this habit. Many people have reported that after just a few weeks of practice, it seems to have become not only a habit but also a preference.

Hints

1. To remember to concentrate on the individual with whom you're involved at that moment and to remember that you are now committed to developing individual relationships with people all over the organization, carry a private symbol that will remind you of these new leadership goals. Many leaders have tried this strategy and found it successful. Some have shifted a watch from one wrist to the other, where its unusual position constantly attracts their attention and thus reminds them of their leadership mission. One CEO I know balances

a picture of his family precariously on a bookcase that is always within his sight when he's in his office. It unnerves him so much—because it always appears as if it will fall, and indeed it often does—that he often glances toward it. It works as a perfect symbol for him that he needs to keep his focus on the individual in front of him. Another CEO I know began wearing completely different ties than he previously had been attracted to, and because people often remarked on them, he often was reminded of his transformation agenda. Adding a ring to a finger that has been ringless also works. I know two leaders who mentally choose a color—for example, red—so that whenever they see the color, it becomes the symbol that calls attention back to the leadership agenda. Of course, when you habituate to the symbol you have chosen, you will need to choose another.

2. Countless times, you will be tempted to cut a conversation short or avoid having one because your attention is being pulled away from an individual toward problems, decisions, and "fires" that need to be put out. Commit for a single week to the idea that you will not allow distractions from your person-by-person transformation agenda—no matter what. At the end of that week, assess what you've gained and what you've lost from sticking to your plan. For most people, the gains will be so big that commitment to a second week will be much less difficult to make.

3. Check in periodically with other members of the Planning Team to compare notes about progress and share new ideas. Misery loves company, but so does success.

Cautions

1. Remember that many of your interpersonal interactions will reveal complaints and that gripes are golden. It's important to avoid promising that you personally will respond to a problem that an associate might reveal—which is an unrealistic commitment. Rather, your obligation and goal is to listen, to genuinely care, and to get the information to an appropriate person so that the system is stimulated to produce a response.

2. Be consistent. It is not desirable—even though it is a very "human" thing—to successfully respond person by person for several days and then to lose patience or react to stress or crisis by becoming abrupt and distanced from the people with whom you work. Make special efforts to stay the course. You needn't be perfect at this, of course, but it needs to be an issue of which you're constantly aware.

3. Expect that you will occasionally feel boredom, frustration, impatience, and stress. This sort of management certainly isn't any easier than other ways of leading an organization. It results in better products and a better company, provides a greater number of satisfied moments, and results in opportunities for personal growth. But it's not easy.

Summary

Throughout this book, especially in Part II, you have encountered numerous strategies that real leaders are using to develop person-centered organizations. One of the goals of person-centered leadership is creative personal development. This yields unique individuals, unique organizations, and management strategies that are custom-made. Some of the strategies that will be most successful for your organization and situation will have to be developed by you and your associates—and often these result from crisis or failure. It is very useful to remember that when all the planning and consulting is over and done, the experiences of your own organization eventually will produce the most reliable set of person-centered management methods. Fundamentally, the most important thing that you personally can do at all stages of the process is to develop greater respect for your own leadership abilities and for the skills and abilities of your associates. Therein lies the greatest expertise—with them and for you. (Consult the Background Reading List at the end of this chapter for psychology books on motivation, cognition, systems, and other topics that can provide useful background information for your transformation process.)

Closing Comments

These are challenging and very exciting times. The world 25 years from now will be remarkably different than it is today. For each of us, the move into the next century will be accompanied by information overload, risk, stress, and opportunity. The demands of our lives and our organizations can only be met successfully and with zest if we return to the basics—and those basics include an increased respect for the power inherent in the individual and the individual relationship.

It is our relationships that will guide us safely and successfully into the new era. The days of the rugged individualist in this country are almost gone. Yet the essence of the individualist spirit shows no signs of passing. It is the rugged person, the one who has expected himself or herself to do it all and to do it alone who is passing from center stage in our culture. Tomorrow will belong to the new individualists, the people who reach for a personal ideal, who will develop and use themselves to the very best of their abilities within a new cultural mind-set that includes the realization that most good things—that have been and will be—emerge from the efforts of a group of growing individuals.

Teamwork is here to stay because now there is so much to know and so much to do. A single person can no longer be the rugged individualist who takes it all on and succeeds. Those who learn how to master teamwork—making it fun and making it pay off—will be in charge of our organizational tomorrow. Person-centered leaders surely will be among that group.

Note

1. Occasionally, the term *president* will be used in this chapter to represent other titles associated with ranking leadership roles such as CEO, regional manager, or department head. Transformation can be successfully instituted by people in a variety of ranking leadership positions within a company. When the label *president* is used, the reader should relate it to the organizational role that is most relevant for him or her.

Reference

Arnold, W. W., & Plas, J. M. (1993). *The human touch: Today's most unusual program for productivity and profit*. New York: John Wiley.

Psychology Background Reading List

The following books span a range of areas within the field of psychology, including perspectives on emotion, motivation, stress, cognitive psychology, and humanistic psychology. These are not so-called self-help books but tend to be scholarly—often empirical—in approach. It is not expected that the reader will find each one equally useful or readable; the list is meant to provide suggestions for a variety of interests and reading tastes.

Anderson, J. R. (1995). *Cognitive psychology and its implications*. New York: Freeman.

A scholarly look at the role of cognitions in human development.

Beck, J. S. (1995). *Cognitive therapy*. New York: Guilford.

Written for therapists, the book provides a look at how the cognitive therapies are using "self-talk" when working on personal change.

Breggin, P. R. (1994). *Beyond conflict*. New York: Oxford University Press.

A psychiatrist takes a humanistic and nonconfrontational approach to conflict resolution.

Charlesworth, E. A., & Nathan, R. C. (1985). *Stress management*. New York: Ballantine.

Provides a readable and comprehensive approach to the issues confronting those who need to better manage stress.

Cherniss, C. (1995). *Beyond burnout*. New York: Routledge.

Emphasizes the influence of work environments on stress levels.

Csikszentmihalyi, M. (1989). *Flow: Steps toward enhancing the quality of life*. New York: HarperCollins.

Talks about the development of states of intense concentration and absorption in what one is doing.

Deci, E. L. (1995). *Why we do what we do: The dynamics of personal autonomy*. New York: Grosset/Putnam.

Helps the reader to begin thinking about the possibilities inherent in adopting a personal autonomy point of view.

Freeman, A., & DeWolf, R. (1989). *Woulda, coulda, shoulda: Overcoming regrets, mistakes and missed opportunities*. New York: HarperCollins.

Aaron Beck's preface echoes the judgments of many who think this book can be a useful tool in the war against self-defeating beliefs.

Fromm, E. (1989). *The art of being.* New York: Continuum.

Each of Fromm's well-known works may be of interest to the person who is beginning to think seriously about his or her life and its meaning.

Gallagher, W. (1993). *The power of place: How our surroundings shape our thoughts, emotions, and actions.* New York: HarperCollins.

A good source to stimulate thinking about the effects of one's work settings on one's emotions and behavior.

Gardner, H. (1989). *To open minds.* New York: Basic Books.

A cognitive scientist writes about creativity.

Goldberger, N. R., & Veroff, J. (Eds.). (1995). *The culture and psychology.* New York: New York University Press.

Contains a nice section on culture and diversity.

Hillman, J. (1960). *Emotion.* Evanston, IL: Northwestern University Press.

In this classic book, a psychologist and existentialist begins to think about emotion and meaning.

Hillman, J. (1989). *A blue fire.* New York: Harper Perennial.

Here, Hillman thinks about creativity, love, work, and money.

Howard, A., et al. (1994). *Diagnosis for organizational change: Methods and models.* New York: Guilford/Society for Individual and Organizational Psychology.

Helps the reader design diagnostic strategies for organizations in distress.

Izard, C. E., Kagan, J., & Zajonc, R. B. (1984). *Emotion, cognition, and behavior.* New York: Cambridge University Press.

A well-known work that attempts to bring together research and theory on feeling, thinking, and behaving.

Jung, C. (1957). *The undiscovered self.* New York: Little, Brown.

In this small book, Jung writes about the "plight of the individual in modern society."

Kast, V. (1993). *Through emotions to maturity.* New York: Fromm International.

A popular German psychologist investigates basic fears and anxieties through a look at fairy tales.

Korman, A. K., et al. (1994). *Human dilemmas in work organizations.* New York: Guilford/Society for Individual and Organizational Psychology.

A psychologist turned management professor at City University of New York takes a look at interpersonal dynamics in work organizations.

Peck, M. S. (1979). *The road less travelled.* New York: Simon & Schuster.

This best-selling book by a former practicing psychiatrist often makes sense to managers who are beginning to take their lives and dreams more seriously.

Peterson, C., Maier, S. F., & Seligman, M. E. (1993). *Learned helplessness: A theory for the age of personal control.* New York: Oxford University Press.

Well-known theoreticians and researchers describe what happens when individuals live with uncontrollable events.

Polster, E. (1987). *Every person's life is worth a novel.* New York: Norton.

A psychotherapist talks about the dignity of every individual and the value of writing about an individual life.

Rogers, C. R. (1961). *On becoming a person.* Boston: Houghton Mifflin.

This is the landmark book that began the person-centered tradition in psychology.

Rogers, C. R. (1977). *Carl Rogers on personal power, inner strength and its revolutionary impact.* New York: Delacorte.

Rogers writes about individualism issues from a person-centered perspective.

Tavris, C. (1984). *Anger: The misunderstood emotion.* New York: Simon & Schuster.

This widely read book offers speculations about the nature of anger, especially within adult relationships.

Vaillent, G. (1993). *The wisdom of the ego.* Cambridge, MA: Harvard University Press.

A psychiatrist finds the mind's defensive trickery to be functional and creativity based.

Thinking Creatively: Part III

---

1. What is your attitude toward the need to change *yourself* before attempting to influence your associates? When compared with other parts, is this likely to be an easier part of the process?

2. Which strategy in Chapter 12 is best suited for you as you think about moving toward personal transformation?

3. What actions do you think are best taken when trying to influence associates after a person-centered transformation is under way?

4. In the Strategy Boxes, Chapter 13 identifies a number of cautions. What three cautions do you think ought to be added to those lists?

5. For you personally, what is likely to be the most difficult part of leading a person-centered transformation process?

6. What would be the most difficult part of the change process for you if someone else were leading it and you were—at least initially—a follower?

7. In the organization with which you're currently most familiar, what transformation strategies would be likely to prove the most difficult to incorporate? What would be the easiest?

8. What are the best strategies for shifting focus continually from team to individual and back again? What strategies could you add to the list of team-building strategies found in Chapter 13?

APPENDIX

Methodological Approach to the Study of Organizations

Organizational study results found in Chapters 7, 8, and 9 and in portions of other chapters have emerged from my investigations. These results are representative of the findings, but they do not—in any of the cases presented—constitute the full body of information resulting from study of these organizations.

Both a theoretical and an inductive approach was used for all studies that are partially reported here. Support for taking a theoretical perspective came from my previous work on person-centered leadership and from literature cited in this book that offers support for the effectiveness of components of a person-centered management model. Because person-centered approaches only recently have gained widespread interest and implementation, it was reasoned that variables of importance may not yet be known. Thus, a supporting inductive approach to the issues yields insights and data that can be used for the formation of better theory to guide future studies. A primarily qualitative rather than quantitative approach uses multiple sources of data within a three-phase methodology (cf. Plas & Lewis, in press).

Overview of the Model

DATA SOURCES

The following are the sources of the data reported here:

1. My on-site observations, including multiple meetings with the company leaders across multiple and sequential days
   (Return visits often follow the development of further hypotheses that resulted from an initial extended stay with the company.)

2. Written materials produced by the company, including personnel policies, human resources reports, and financial reports
3. Written descriptions of the company and its management policies found in such sources as business magazines and newspapers (e.g., the *Wall Street Journal* and *New York Times*)
4. Materials related to the company that are produced by independent organizations such as reports from quality improvement networks and organizations
5. Personal and public documents shared with me by company personnel
6. Communications to me from the leader and other company personnel
7. Any existing written descriptions of leadership focus and style that have been produced by the leader or other personnel

NATURALISTIC APPROACH

As Lincoln and Guba (1985) have pointed out:

Naturalistic inquiry is always carried out, logically enough, in a natural setting, since context is so heavily implicated in meaning. . . . The human instrument builds upon his or her *tacit* knowledge as much as, if not more than, upon propositional knowledge, and uses methods that are appropriate to humanly implemented inquiry: interviews, observations, document analysis, unobtrusive clues, and the like. (p. 187)

The three-phase methodological (triangulation) approach used in the studies discussed in this book was based primarily on the Lincoln and Guba model in which inquiry cycles and recycles through four methodological stages involving sampling, inductive analyses, theory development, and development of next steps based on what has been learned to that point (cf. Argyris, 1990; Jick, 1979; Kirk & Miller, 1986; Morgan, 1983). Very careful attention is given to subject experience and the sense and meaning subjects make of that experience.

Phase 1. Phase 1 begins with an initial, and often lengthy, telephone conversation with the leader followed by a phone conversation with the president's[1] administrative assistant. These conversations are critical to the process. Initial questions are designed to elicit information about the president's validity and reliability as a person-centered leader. For example, the question, "What's the biggest mistake you've made during the past month?" yields initial data about the leader's level of authenticity and willingness to admit mistakes.

Company materials are sent and studied at this point. A tentative schedule for the researcher's time at the company is constructed. The schedule includes lengthy conversations with the leader, observational access to the leader's daily schedule, conversations with people at all levels of the organization (sampling), and unscheduled time that the researcher uses for informal interviews that emerge from random visits throughout the company.

Phase 2. In Phase 2 of these investigations, I use an aspect of Gummeson's (1991) qualitative model called *preunderstanding*. In this method, the researcher is aware of the theoretical approach and the data that are to be collected, but he or she moves systematically through an organization in more of a participant observation mode, not giving attention to the research plans or variables. The researcher "walks through" the organization, open to discovering approaches to the investigation that might be suggested by the natural context.

This methodological approach typically is put in practice as the researcher arrives at company headquarters prior to the time that formal interviews have been scheduled. One or more walk-throughs of randomly chosen areas of the company occur at this initial point. Informal conversations with associates working in walk-through areas provide preliminary information on which the researcher can base further methodological strategies and interview questions.

Phase 3. In Phase 3, relying more heavily on the Lincoln and Guba methods rather than the Gummeson adaptations, formal subject interviews are conducted in selected samples of an organization's population. Interviews with the company president occur each day. On more than one occasion, the researcher accompanies the president throughout most of a typical day. Each afternoon, new decisions are made about additional people who need to be interviewed and additional events that need to be scheduled for observation. Interviews with spouses and families typically occur in the home environment.

Comments About the Method

The methodology briefly described here permits the researcher access to the personal as well as professional self of the leader as well as thorough access to the company. Sampling strategies provide access to associates at all levels of the organization—including those who clean the toilets, repair the xerox machines, and sit in the vice-presidential offices. Associates and family members are interviewed both formally and informally. In addition to lengthy interviews with the president, this methodology requires that the leader be observed in typical situations so the researcher can record what the president actually does. Because person-centered theory is concerned with weaknesses as well as strengths and authenticity, many questions and much of the observation are geared toward eliciting these kinds of data.

Ethical considerations in these investigations include an explicit understanding with each leader that the investigator is searching for weaknesses as well as strengths. This issue is rarely troublesome, because these person-centered leaders are used to being more open about weaknesses than other kinds of leaders might be. Another aspect of the initial agreement is that the researcher agrees to permit each president review of the results of the study. The explicit understanding is that the leader agrees to share thoughts openly and to make the company available for study in exchange for the right to ask that results not be published if he or she believes they might do harm to self or company. The researcher's commitment is to provide that right, but the leader understands that the researcher cannot change the content of observations, alter data, or change the interpretation of results based on the leader's desire to censor. In other words, having read the results, if the leader requests substantial change, the agreement is that the work will not be published. In this way, the researcher honors the president's right to protect self and company as he or she sees fit, and the leader honors the researcher's need to present data and interpretations that are unbiased by the leader's concerns. Therefore, the researcher does not change data or perspective. The report is published as written, or it is not published at all. This arrangement provides maximum integrity and security for both the researcher and the leader who is the object of study. Without this kind of mutual arrangement, it might not be in the best interests of the leader to permit the study, nor could the integrity of the research process be protected.

Note

1. The term *president* is used here to represent all titles associated with corporate leaders, such as CEO and chairman.

References

Argyris, C. (1990). *Overcoming organizational defenses.* Boston: Allyn & Bacon.

Gummeson, E. (1991). *Qualitative methods in management research.* Newbury Park, CA: Sage.

Jick, T. D. (1979). Mixing qualitative and quantitative methods: Triangulation in action. *Administrative Science Quarterly, 24,* 602-611.

Kirk, J., & Miller, M. L. (1986). *Reliability and validity in qualitative research.* Beverly Hills, CA: Sage.

Lincoln, Y. S., & Guba, E. (1985). *Naturalistic inquiry.* Beverly Hills, CA: Sage.

Morgan, G. (1983). *Beyond method: Strategies for social research.* Beverly Hills, CA: Sage.

Plas, J. M., & Lewis, S. (in press). Environmental factors and sense of community in a planned town. *American Journal of Community Psychology* [Special issue on methods of ecological assessment].

Index

Alger, H., 32, 48
Allen, P., 181
Allen Machine Products, 181
Argyris, C., 27
Arnold, W. W., 49, 99
Ash, M. K., 176-177
Associates:
    and employee complaints, 217-222
    and person-by-person management,
        11-12, 230-233
    and related individualism, 224-227,
        234
    and risk taking, 222-224
    and teamwork, 224-225, 227-230, 234
    and transformation necessity,
        212-213
    planning team for, 213-217
    See also Person-centered leadership
Authenticity, 25-28, 196, 198, 202-205,
    208-209
Autry, J., 22, 63

Bass, B., 60
Bellah, R., 32-33, 47-49, 101
Bennis, W., 21, 22, 23-24, 36, 63, 75-76,
    109
Benson, T., 65
Berkley, J., 57
Boorstin, D., 34, 92, 96

Campbell, K., 183-184
Caring, 3, 22, 23, 27, 28, 38, 47, 150, 207,
    213, 217
Carnegie, D., 23
Champy, J., 57, 58, 77
Cherniss, C., 26-27
Continuous quality improvement, 6-8,
    194-195. See also Participatory
    management; Person-centered
    leadership; Total quality
    management (TQM)
Corporations, traditional:

245

About the Author

Jeanne M. Plas is a member of the Psychology and Human Development faculty at Vanderbilt University, where she has been associated with clinical and community psychology training for 20 years. Her research and theoretical writing have received national and international recognition and praise. Two of her best-selling leadership and management books, *Working Up a Storm* and *The Human Touch,* have been translated into Chinese and Portuguese, and English editions of her work have been distributed in more than a dozen countries. Dr. Plas has been a consultant to such diverse organizations as General Motors, Newfoundland Light and Power, the California Financial and Banking Network, Dow Jones & Co, and the U.S. Army. Currently, her research, writing, and consulting activities are connected to the development of participatory management and leadership strategies that fit within corporations and countries that value individualism as much as teamwork.